FOUR THOUSAND YEARS OF EDUCATION IN BHARATVARSHA

FOUR THOUSAND YEARS OF EDUCATION IN BHARATVARSHA

(VOLUME - II)
British India, Democratic India
1765 AD - 2002 AD

Amalesh Kumar Mishra

Published, 2019

Published by

Gyan Publishing House
5, Ansari Road
Daryaganj, New Delhi-110002
Phone: 011-47034999, 9811692060
www.gyanbooks.com
E-mail: books@gyanbooks.com

Printed at: G. Print Process, Delhi.

Cataloging in Publication Data—DK
Courtesy: D.K. Agencies (P) Ltd. <docinfo@dkagencies.com>

Mishra, Amalesh Kumar, author.
Four thousand years of education in Bharatvarsha / Amalesh Kumar Mishra.
2 volumes cm
Includes index.
Contents: volume 1. Pre-historic period to 600 BC, 320 AD - 1765 AD — volume 2. British India, Democratic India, 1765 AD - 2002 AD.
ISBN 9788121219570 (set : paperback)
ISBN 9788121219587 (vol.1 : paperback)
ISBN 9788121219594 (vol. 2 : paperback)

1. Education—India—History.   I. Title.

LCC LA1151.M57 2019 | DDC 370.954   23

Contents

Part - VII

1765 A.D. - 1813 A.D.

Historical Perspective

This part, part-VII of this book, deals with the history of education of India from the death of Aurangzeb, to the third Maratha war (1818). It was an eventful period that witnessed the end of Mughal rule. The rise and fall of the Maratha empire and the foundation of the British empire in India. This period paved the way for India's transition from Mediaeval to Modern Age. It is said to be the period of Indian Renaissance. In this period, the Indian first learnt the English language.

R. C. Majumder has observed, which may be regarded as the most important single factor that brought about those far reaching changes in indian life, thought and education as well as social and religious concepts in the course of one hundred years in the 19th Century, such as were not noticed during the previous thousand years. [Preface Vol-8, HCIP]

The chaotic political situation of this period invited two foreign invasions, one of Nadir Shah (1733-39) and the other of Ahmed Shah Abadalli (1764) which were in nature and effect equal to sultan Mamud (1000-1027) Chengish Khan (1221) and Taimur Long (1398-1399).

But before a planned system of education was introduced in India by the British, we can note some comments of the renowned Britishers of the time.

In his book the History and prospects of British education in India, F. U. Thomas wrote, "The English found in India, a widespread system of elementary education and higher education of which the former was mainly practical, the latter mainly literary, philosophical and religious." [P-148].

William Jones considered Sanskrit language to be "of wonderful structure, more perfect than Greek, more copious than the Latin and more exquisitely refined than either." [Calcutta Review 1885, P-264].

From Calcutta Review in 1872 we can know that Nadia in 1782 was the Oxford of the province [Vol-IV, P-97].

Grant Duff in his book History of Marathas (Vol-II, P-532) writes about the Peshwas that they greatly encouraged education. They paid donations and rewards to Brahmins "Whose proficiency in Science and Mythology, entitled them to distinction and rewards were conferred in proportion to the acquirements, moral conduct and sanctity."

In Munro's Minute on Native Education, dated 10 March, 1826, it is written that in the Madras Presidency schools were supported partly by the endowment of native princes but chiefly by the voluntary contributions of the people.

Bernier describes Benaras in the 17th Centurty, "The Athens of India."

We are to care the point that before the advent of British, there was no system of education organised by the state or central political power. There was no Education Ministry and no education policy. We simply know that Mahammedan rulers were keen on Quranic education and financed selectively. But in India, before the advent of Islam and Christian, better to say, foreign rule of Turks, Pathans, Mughals and Britishers, there existed an indigenous system of education and it continued somehow or other even to the time of the Britishers.

Education was patronised all over India, by local rulers, members of the aristocracy, benevolent persons by donations and endowments. The old universities or contres of learning of even international repute had disappeared in course of time under the bigotry of foreign forces who had might enough to destroy a mind of education and culture. But the flow continued as we have noted in the comments of some notable Britishers before they began to build up their own structure of education in this country.

The celebrated lady ruler Rani Bhavani of Natore, Raja Krishna Chandra of Nadia were great patrons of education in their own jurisdictions. Raja of Darbhanga was a patron of it in Mithila.

The institutions for higher learning in Sanskrit, known as Chatuspathi or Tol existed in Bengal, Bihar, Kasi, Tirhut, Utkala, and South Indian States.

Nadia of Bengal was the abode of Astronomers whose Panjikas or alamanacs still regulate the festivals. Raja Joy Sing II established observatories also.

Forbes in his Oriental Memoirs remarked - We contemplate the Hindoo colleges and Brahmanical Seminaries, at Beneras and different parts of Hindusthan, with pleasure, they are useful institutions, and however limited in their benefit to particular castes and description of people, they are the nurses of literature, medicine and sciences as far as deemed necessary among the Hindoos. [Vol-II, P-233-234].

Persian education then was in a flourishing condition being patronised by muslim rulers. For many years it was an official language. Consequently Hindus too inclined to learn it. Some of the Hindus were well learnt in the language. Raja Navakrishna of Sovabazar was the Persian tutor of Warren Hastings in 1750. Poet Bharat Chandra had a good knowledge of this language. Azimabad of Patna was a famous centre of persian language and students both Hindus and Muslims of Bengal and Bihar attended as students. In the mid 18th century some scholars and well versed persian came to India from Iran and settled in Patna and in other parts of Bihar. It is learnt from the Europeans that elementary schools were well spread. There were schools in all the town and principal villages. Malcolm in his memoirs of centre India (Vol-II, P-157) writes "Though there is not one public place of instruction endowed or supported by any state in this country. Yet private schools, both in town and villages are very numerous." He also refers that every village having above one hundred houses had a school master who taught the children of the Banias or shop keepers and those of such cultivators as choose. "There were schools in towns and many villages but reading was confined to Brahmins, Banias and such of the agricultural classes as have to do with accounts." This was the observation of Elphinstone of the territories acquired by the British from the Peshwas. Forbes in his memories also mentions that in all towns numerous schools were there for general boys, but those were generally in the open air. There were maktabs attached to Mosques.

Generally in the institutions of primary education, teachers were appointed and students were admitted irrespective of caste and creed. In Bengal, some of the so called depressed classes worked as teachers in such schools and at some places there were muslim teachers for Hindu boys.

The general features of elementary education were similar in different parts of India, with some differences in details. In the village schools, the students were taught to write in four successive stages of instruction, on the ground, palm leaf, plantain leaf and paper. They learnt the rules of arithmatic and accounts and some of the rudiments of physical and natural science.

[The References are from foot-notes in Vol-8 of HCIP, P-765-766 of an article by K. K. Dutta, Vice Chancellor of Magadh university P-751-754, Vol-8].

In this part (Part-VII) of our discussion we have taken up the period from 1765-1813. Within this time-scale different Trading companies of Europe had settled in India. The most prominent of those was East India company. There were French, Dutch and Portugees with the same interest of trading. Their economic exploitation made India poorer. The companies had their own fight for supremacy in India.

The period which is being discussed in this part (VII) of this book witnsessed two major instances. the one in 1765 and the other in 1813.

The East India Company, though a trading concern, yet decided the fate of India at least for 350 years directly and otherwise since its registration as a company in 1600 A.D. It undertook no educational activities for nearly hundred years of its existence and a trading company is not expected to undertake any initiative for furtherance of education in a country where it is allowed to trade only. More so because the country had its own indigenous system of education which continued from an era when the British state did not even evolve. Its attention was drawn to education matters by the charter Act of 1813 (England). This required the company to maintain priests (for Christian affairs) and schools for the education of the children of the European servants working in India. The company was a trading concern composed of merchants and for the sake of trade European servants were necessary. At the time of charter Act of 1793, Wilberforce moved in the House of Commons (Lower House of the British Parliament) that it was the duty of the British Govt. to send Chaplains and school teachers through out British India. His idea was to foster Christianity. He was so requested by Charls Grant.

By the middle of the 18th the circumstances changed. Aurangzeb had died (1707) and the Mughal empire shattered. Though eleven of his successors continued as emperor till 1858, but the Mughals had no practical control over India. Again the East India Company of the Britishers had by this time, emerged successful in the trading competition with its other European competetors, such as Dutch, Portugeese and French. Taking the advantage of the weakness of the Mughals, the East India Company managed the grant of Diwani in 1765, on 12 August from the Mughal emperor Shah Alam II who reigned from 1759 to 1806. He was the dejure emperor and never a defacto one. The consideration money which the emperor Shah Alam II was given by the East India Company was the promise to pay Rs. 26 lakhs per anum. By the grant thus received, the company got the power and license to collect revenue from Bengal, Bihar and Orissa and to judge and decide Civil matters of those three states.

In the meantime in 1757 on 23 June in the battle of Palasy (23 miles or 37 km from Murshidabad, Bengal), 50 thousands artilary and 18 thousands cavalry of Nawab of Bengal fought against 800 European Plus 2200 hundred Indian a total strength of 3000 soldiers of the company.

The Nawab (Siraj-u-daula) was defeated and was brought to headquarter Murshidbad on 2nd July 1757 and was killed.

It was only then that the company was called upon to encourage education among its subjects. But as the Board of Directors of the company was unwilling, the company refused to recognise any obligation on its part for the education of the Indians.

Many things contributed to the awakening of conscience of the people of England to what had been in India, and to the consequential enactment of Parliament of the Regulating Act of 1773 (The East India Company Act, 1773). The object of this Act was aimed at better management of the company in India and in England.

Since the accession of the Company to the Dewani, stories of various abuses and iniquities on the part of the Company's servant in this country and of 'colosal fortunes' acquired by many of them, often by unscrupulous means, unhealthy influence exercised by many, war in Mysore with Haider Ali, the famine of 1770 in Bengal, the report of the Select and Secret committee of House of Commons appointed in 1771, payment of ever increasing divident to the share holders of the company and a tribute to the British Exchequer of an annual sum of Rs. 40000.00 and ultimately financial embarrasment of the company and asking of its loan to British government and all these led the British Parliament to enact this in 1773.

It appears that slavery became wide spread in India in the 18th century. The governors of the provinces seized the wives and children of those cultivators who could not pay the revenue, made them into slaves and sold them in auction.

The price of slaves mentioned by Buchanan (Journey from Madras to Mysore, Canara and Malabar) was - an adult Slave - Rs. 15 to Rs. 20, A lad of 16 years - Rs. 12 to Rs. 15, A girl of 8 to 10 years Rs. 5 to Rs. 15. The slaves were mainly employed in farm lands. the allowance usually given was a piece of coarse cloth and about 15 maunds of grain.

Slaves were also used to be exported abroad normally from Bengal in the 17th Century and were also included among the exports of Dutch and English traders at Surat, Madras and Masulipatanam.

By a Proclamation in 1789, the traffic in Slaves was abolished in India.

After the grant of Diwanee to East India Company in 1765, the following major famines were 1769-70 Bengal and Bihar and 1788 - Bengal. In 200 years of Mughal and East India Company rule - 29 major famines occured in India from 1595 to 1799. Each famine in the past resulted in appaling mortality, starvation, salvery and even canibalism.

As has been mentioned, that the Charter Act of 1698 though insisted on maintaining priest in schools, the company did not adhere to it.

In 1765 when the company managed the Diwanee of Bengal, Bihar and Orissa, it was called upon to encourage education. Again the company refused the obligation on its part for the education of Indians.

Conflict and Confusion

We must mention here of the conflict and confusion arose on this issue which led to the enactment of 1813.

The conflict was on two issues (1) the Directors of the Company was unwilling to accept the responsibility of education of the Indians. (2) The Christian missioneries desired to go to India to convert the Indians to christanity and wanted setting up education centres as tools to their purpose. But the company did not like it as they thought that this conversion factor of the missioneries might give rise opposition among the Indians which might mar their trade.

Among those confusion and conflict, Warren Hasting the Governor of Bengal, who entertained a general admiration for the laws and literature of India, founded the Calcutta Madrasa in 1781. Jonathan Duncan dstablished the Benaras Sanskrit Colleges in 1792. Asiatic Society of Bengal was founded in 1784.

Since the company needed judicial officers well versed in Sanskrit, Arabic and Persian, this policy of encouragement to classical learning was based on political expediency and administrative requirement.

Among some of the civil servants of the company, Sir William Jones, H. T. Colebrooke and Nathanial Halhed developed a general interest and appretiation of India's cultural heritage.

It may be accepted that Charls Grant who was a religious reformer and was associated with the company's administration in Calcutta and London for nearly forty years, started the movement of education for Indians in 1792. He wrote a pamphlet and circulated among the members of Parliament and other influencial persons.

Charls Grant was an Evangelist. William Wilberforce, Mecaulay and Henry Thronton were his supporters. The common character of all three was, they had no respect on Indian education. Grant said - "India is a fabric of Error. The Hindu erred because they were ignorant." Mecaulay commented, "A single shelf of good European Library, was worth the whole native literature of India and Arabia." [H. Sharp : Selections from Educational Records 1781-1839 - P-109].

Fort William College in Calcutta was established in 1800. It was a prudent attempt of Lord Welesly who proposed such an institution on 9th July 1800. His object was not to spread education among the Indians, but to educate the English men who were in service and who would be in service. The Institute started on 18 Aug 1800. Subjects to be taught were. Arabic, Persian, Sanskrit, Urdu, Bengali, Telegu, Tamil, Marathi and Kannara, Mahamedan and Hindu Law, Ethics, Civil Jurisprudence, English Law and in many other subjects.

But this did not serve the purpose of education of India. What was the real picture of indigenous Indian education was revealed to the Britishers, when the reports came of the enquires in Madras, Bombay and Calcutta Presidencies.

In Madras, an enquiry into indigenous education was ordered by Sir Thomas Munro in 1822 and the information obtained referred to all the Districts of the Madras Presidency excepting Kanaras. In Bombay Presidency a similar enquiry was ordered by Mountstuart Elephinstone in 1823 and statistics were obtained of most of the Province. In 1829 Similar statistics were obtained through the judicial department. In 1823 the statistics were obtained through collectors. In Bengal, a special enquiry was conducted in 1835-38, under the orders of Lord William Bentinck by William Adams - a missionary. Adam submitted three reports of which the first is a digest of the earlier reports, the second is a thorough enquiry of five district of Bengal and Bihar out of total 19 districts, the other report was a thorough enquiry of one thana of Rajsahi.

It may be assumed that reports taken together will give a full picture of the indigenous education system of the country. But such an assumption is not very sound from the statistical point of view but in the absence of any other data, we have to rely on what were obtained. But all these were post 1813 Charter Act.

Analysis of Charter Act of 1698

By analysing the charter act of 1698, we can at least comment that as conversion of Hindus to Islam was one of the policies of the Mulsim invaders, conversion of Hindus to Christanity was also a policy of the Britishers who invaded India as traders through East India Company.

It may be said that a company meant primarily for commercial concern, is not expected to take steps for the education of Indians. But as early as in 1614 steps were taken for recruitment of Indians for the propagation of Gospel among their countrymen. [Ref. : N. N. Law Promotion of Learning in India by early European Settlers].

When the charter of company was renewed in 1698, the famous missionary clause was inserted in it by British Parliament. The clause directed the company to maintain men (Ministers) of religion at their factories in India and to take a chaplain (Priest) in every ship of 500 tons or more. The ministers were required to learn Portuguese language which was commonly understaood by the infirior servants of the factories and also to learn the native languge where they shall reside.

The Charter also directed the company to maintain schools in all their garrisons and bigger factories.

It is clear that the British wanted the trading concern to preach Gospels among all the Hindu employees of the Company at least, if not among all.

This proselytisation activities cannot be treated as an act of spreading education in India. It may safely be realised that this missionary clause has laid the foundation of the education of proselytisation in one hand and education of the anglo Indian. children who lived in the orbit of the company on the other. The anglo-Indians were those whose fathers were not Indians but mothers were Indians, mostly Hindus as Islam had no interest in Christanity. Once Islam, Islam for life was the practice and theory. The anglo-Indians born of company's soldiers and from their Indian wives were neglected ones. The chaplians wanted them in christian fold. As a result, charity schools were established by collecting subscription. It was an English Model which indicated that the schools were meant primarily for poor and orphan children having sustenance from charity.

N. N. Law in his book - Promotion of learning in India by Early European settlers has given a detailed account of their working. [Ref. : A students' history of Education in India, by J. P. Naik - Syed Nurruddin, subsequent referrence of this book will be as J. P. Naik].

But conducting school with Portuguese as medium could not be continued. English became the medium of instruction. However, at Madras, Rev. W. Stevension was the first to establish such an Institution - St. Mary's Charity School in 1715. Rev. Richard Cobbee established such a school in Bombay in 1719. Chaplain Bellary found such a school in Calcutta some time between 1720-1731. In 1787, a Female Orphan Asylum was opened at Madras and named after Lady Campbell, the wife of the Governor, who took a leading part in collecting funds. In the same year a Male Asylum was started at Madras by Rev. Dr. Andrew Bell.

These schools were maintained by subscriptions and donations. The company did not give any regular financial grant. Yet the company, (may be for the sake of Christanity) (1) sanctioned recurring grants for maintenance, (2) permitted lotteries in their support, (3) gave non-recurring grants for building on provided sites, (4) allowed their officers to collect fund, (5) accepted the funds of the school as deposits at comparatively higher interest. [Ref. : J. P. Naik, P-35].

Education Policy of the Company : 1765-1813

By getting the grant of Diwani of Bengal, Bihar, Orissa from Emperor Shah Alam in 1765, the Company now became more a political power than a trading concern. It became the successor to Hindu and Muslim rulers who encouraged Higher learning in Sanskrit, Arabic, Persian and established institutions for the purpose. So the company could not neglect this trend. Moreover, they wanted to consolidate their power by attracting the support of higher classes. May be with these considerations Calcutta Madrasah and Benaras Sanskrit colleges were established in 1781 and 1792 respectively and was patronised with fund. Warren Hastings established the Calcutta Madrasah (1) to conciliate the Mahamedans of Calcutta (2) to qualify the sons of Muhamedan gentlemen for responsible and lucrative jobs (3) to produce competant officers for courts of justice. [A Howell, Education in India as referred to by J. P. Naik in his book.] Due to mismanagement of Fund and land and inefficient management, a European secretary was finally appointed for efficient management. With the same consideration (as was in the case of Calcutta Madrasah) Beneras Sanskrit College was established in 1791 by Jonathan Duncan, the resident of Benaras. As was the problem with Calcutta Madrasa, the Sanskrit College also suffered mismanagement and inefficiency. Consequently a European superintendent was appointed.

Then there arose two views which contradicted each other and when the Charter of company came up for renewal the difference became transparent.

One view was named as Orientatist view and the other was Missionary view. Orientalist view wanted that in the field of education, classical learning in Sanskrit, Arabic and Persian only should be encouraged. The company must maintain political neutrality and must not support, the enterprises of the missionaries. The missionary view wanted proselytisation through education. The first and foremost object of the missionaries was to convert people of India to christanity and in doing that schools were the best media.

The schools are very important as a means of communication with different section of people. It is to be noted that formerly the missionaries were least interested in establishing schools as they thought then that the priests has no business to found schools. But the practical experience compelled them to change their views. They realised that the schools were both cause and effect of proselytization.

As the company began to grow, it became more and more important for it to maintain religious neutrality - the policy which the missionaries discarded.

In 1793, when the time came for renewal of the charter of the company, protagonists of missionaries advocated motion in the House of Commons of the British Parliament, demanding the company should work for the advancement of knowledge and religions as well as moral improvement of the people of India.

The company opposed vehimenly this move. They had no option but to maintain religious neutrality. Their advocates in the Hosue of Commons observed that the Hindus has a good system of education a good system of faith and moral. So it would be madness to attempt their conversion.

The British Parliament negated the arguments of missionaries. It was a great set back for the missionaries, the company, on the other hand, was strengthened and began to put obstacles in the Path of missionaries.

Before we come to the next renewal of the Chrter in 1813, we have to have a glimpse of the missionary work in Madras and Bengal.

Danish Mission in Madras (1706-1792)

Ziegenbarg and Plustschau were the first two missionaries (Protestant) who first started their missionary works at Tranquaber - a Danish Station in South India within the East India Company territories in as early as 1706 just before the death of emperor Aurangzeb.

These two missionaries established a printing press in Tamil (1713). An institution for training of teachers was opened in 1716. Two charity schools one for Portuguese Pupil and the other for Tamil Pupil were founded in 1717.

Ziegenbarg died in 1719. His works were continued by Plustschau, Grundler, Kiernander and Schwartz. Near the Fort St. David, Kiernander founded two charity schools one for the Eurasians, other for Indians in 1742. Being invited by Clive he came to Calcutta and founded a charity school in 1758. Kiernader worked in Bengal for the rest of his life. More important was the work of Schwartz who is looked upon as the pioneer of education in Madras. At Trichinopally, Tanjore, Ramnad and Shivaganga he founded schools with the object of teaching English to Indians. He got the assistance of John Sulivan, the resident at Tanjore.

Thus, the missionaries were active in those early days and founded schools for teaching English to the converted Indians and others also. They introduced printing press also and began to print in Indian languages also. The company maintained a friendly and sympathetic attitude with this missionary activities.

Srirampur Missionaries (1758-1813)

The Danish missioneries in the South got the sympathy, protection and assistance from the East India Company. But the missioneries who worked in Bengal were not in the good book of the company. They had to struggle hard against a hostile attitude of the company. But they were fortunate to get Dutch support in Srirampur and Chinsura of present Hooghly district of West Bengal.

Dr. Carey, a representative of the Baptist Missionary Society, started his work in Calcutta in 1793. But finally he shifted to Malda (WB) as a superintendent of a indigo factory but spent his spare time in translating the Bible into Bengali.

In 1799, two other missioneries Ward and Marshman came to Calcutta. They persuaded Carey to join them and the three decided to settle at Srirampur - a Dutch settlment just 32 km. away from Calcutta. These three - Carey, Ward and Marshman are known as the famous Trio'. Marshman was a school teacher, Ward was a printer and Carey was a propagandist.

M. A. Sherring in his book - The history of protestant Missionary in India, observes, "In no country of the World, and in no period of history of Christanity, was there ever displayed such an amount of energy in the translation of sacred scriptures from their original into other tongues, as was exhibited by a handful of earnest men in Calcutta and Srirampur in the first ten years of the present century.".....Not content with their labour in thus direction, they also published a great multitude of tracts, the Srirampur press alone issuing them in twenty languages, and in addition books for schools and collges.

[Ref. : J. P. Naik and Nurullah's A student's history of education in India P-43].

This trio also conducted several schools in Srirampur, Calcutta and other places. The company prohibited the circulation of the book - Addresses to Hindus and Mahamedans, published by the Trio, as the book may offend the religious sentiments. The Trio were ordered to submit works intended for Circulation in the company's territories, to the inspection of its officers.

In a ward the relation between the Company and the missionaries was very much strained during the period 1793 (Renewal of the charter) to 1813 - the next renewal. In this period (1793-1813), the company did not oridinarily issue a permit to any missionary to work within the territories of the company.

In India the missioneries were powerless to fight against this policy. They and their friends, began an intensive agitation in England with the object of persuading the parliament to legislate giving necessary freedom and assistance to missioneries.

The foremost of this agitatators was Charles Grant who had a very poor and ignoble view about the Indians and their education [This poor fellow had no idea of the glory of ancient India particularly in the field of Education]. But he is respected as the father of modern education in India. To Charles Grant "Hinduism was a fabric of error and the Hindus erred because they were ignorant. Patriotism is absolutely unknown in Hindusthan". He published his panphlet in 1797. (Observation on the state of society among the Asiatic Subjects of Great Britain, known as Observations).

Grant to his personal satisfaction published his hatred for India and her sons. According to him, the causes of miserable condition of Indian people were two : ignorance and proper religion. So to improve India - they are to be given education and should be converted to Christanity. Grant suggested the Western light and knowledge should be communicated to the Indian people through the medium of English language. He also wrote, it would be extremely easy for the Government to establish, at a moderate expense, in various parts of the provinces, places of gratuitous instruction in reading and writing English, multitudes, specially of the young, would flock to them and easy books used in teaching, might at the same time convey obvious truths on different subjects. To him there was nothing wanting to the success of the plan, but the hearty patronage of the government. If they wish it to succeed, it can and must succeed. The introduction of English in the Administration, judicial p;rocedings and other business of the government, where in the Persian is now used, and the establishment of free schools, for instruction in this language, would ensure its diffusion over the country, the interest of Natives would induce them to acquire it.

On the question what should be the subjects of study, Grant suggested in addition to English - special emphasis should be laid on the teaching of natural sciences in order to break down the superstitious belief prevalent among the people and on the teaching of the use of mechanical inventions in order to bring about agricultural and industrial development of the country. However, the most precious subject of instruction was the Christian religion.

He felt that it was in the best interest of England herself, the Hindoos and Muslims of India should be educated. Such education would secure the gratitude of the Indian people and would ultimately lead to greater extension of the British Commerce in India.

As was suggested by Grant, English should be the official language in administration, judiciary and commerce, was accepted by Lord Bentinck by some forty years later. That conversion to christanity alone could regenerate Indian Society, proved wrong. Similarly the conversion of Hindoos to Christanity to make India a Christian land was proved utterly wrong. The Islam also tried it for seven hundred years to Islamise India.

[Charls Grant began his career in Bengal in 1768 and remained a dominant figure in the East India Company till his death in 1823].

His suggestion of English as the medium of instruction was accepted by Macanlay who too had very poor idea of the Indians. But he correctly foresaw the eagerness of the Indian people to learn the English language.

The prestige of Grant as one who had known India at first hand, [He started his career in Bengal in 1768] as an influential director of the Company, and a member of the Parliament lent weight to his 'Observations' and paved the way for the education clauses of the charter act of 1813.

In this connection observations of Lord Minto who was the Govenor General of India at that period (1806-1813), should be adhered to. Like Grant and others, he did not make any obnoxious remarks but expressed his deep concern on the issue of education in India at that period of time. He observed - "It is a common remark that science and literature are in a progressive state of decay among the natives of India. From every enquiry which I have been enabled to make on this interesting subject, that remark appears to me but too well founded. The number of the learned is not only diminished but the circle of learning, even among those who still devote themselves to it, appears to be considerably contracted. the abstract science is abandoned, polite literature neglected and no branch of learning cultivated but what is connected with the peculiar religious doctrines of the people. The immediate consequence of this state of things is the disuse and even actual loss, of many valuable books and it is to be apprehended that, unless

Government interfere with a fostering hand, the revival of letters may shortly become hopeless from a want of books, or of persons capable of explaining them.

It is seriously to be lamented that a nation particularly distinguished for the love and successful cultivation of letters in other parts of the empire, should have failed to extend its fostering care to the literature of the Hindoos, and to aid in opening to the learned in Europe the repositories of that literature, dated 6 March, 1811.

[Ref. : Report of the select committee of House of commons on the Affairs of the East India Company (1832).

Thus, before the Charter Act of 1813, the missionary view and the view of the Orientalists entered into violent controversy.

The Charter Act of 1813

The Charter Act of 1813, is a turning point in the history of education in India which is known as modern education, so to say, British education in India. The missionary view came to a successful conclusion. The Company was made to share the expenses on education to the extent of one lakh each year.

The most important issues were : (1) should missionaries be allowed to work for proselytization and education in the territories of the company in India. (2) Should the company accept the financial responsibility and if so, what would be its nature and scope.

On the first issue it was resolved that missionaries were to be allowed to enter India and to reside there. They may preach, found church and discharge all political duties.

On the second issue the opposition was strong. At that period of time even in England, the Govt did not take complete financial responsibility for education. So the company cannot be compelled to take such a burden in such a big country. So it was resolved that a sum of not less than one lakh of rupees in each year should be set apart for revival and improvement of literature, encourage to the learned natives on India and for the introduction and promotion of a knowledge of science among the inhabitants of the British territories in India.

[*Source* : H. Sharp's selection from Educational records]

This clause implied that the company might fulfill its responsibilities as mentioned in the clause, even by creating its own agency, independent of the missionaries.

Part - VIII

1813 - 1835 A.D.

Historical Perspective

That the English education was introduced by the British rulers with the sole object of turning out clerks, is only part of the total truth. The enlightened Hindoos were no less interested in English education. Raja Rammohan's letter dt. December 1823 to Lord Amharst is a clear indicator. The enlightened Hindoos wanted liberal education and participation in administration. To participate in Administration, once the Hindoos learnt and cultured Persian and Arabic also. A school was established in Calcutta (Bhawanipur) in 1800 and another in 1814 at Chinsura (Hooghly dist, WB) by its Magistrate Mr. Forbes.

Two notable institutions which did Yeoman's work in this direction were (1) Hindu college and (2) Calcutta Book Society, both in 1817. The object of the Book Society was to make good books available. The Society undertook to prepare such text books and to print and publish them. Vidyasagar also did the same work for Vernacular (Bengali) education in the mid period of this century. He too, like Rammohan, was in favour of liberal english education and introduced English as a subject of study in Sanskrit college. Though Rammohan was against the idea, yet Sanskrit College was established in 1824 in Calcutta - which was completely modernised by Pandit Iswar Chandra Vidyasagar.

There were Indians in Calcutta (Bengal), Bombay and Madras who found a knowledge of english very useful for the purposes of trade as well as for obtaining employment under the company or in private agency houses.

The new modes of revenue assessment in 1823-33, required the employment of large number of Indians for survey and assessment. So turning out clerks who should be employed at a cheap rate, was of course, necessary. But that was not the only reason. The decision to introduce english education was the result of a mixture of administrative, economic, political and religious may be cultural also, motives. It did not emanate from enlightened groups in England only. In India too, Missioneries, officers of the Company as well as a group articualte urban Indians also were working for it.

But the missionaries were more zealous as because they thought English Education was the first step towards conversion to Christanity.

Even Macaulay, though not directly a missionery, wrote to his father, "It is my firm belief that if our plans of education are followed up, there will not be a single idolater among the respected classes of Bengal thirty years hence. And this will be effected without efforts to proselytize, without the smallest interference with religious liberty, mainly by natural operation of knowledge and reflection". David Hare also expressed similar views. [Ref. P-36, Vol-10, HCIP]

This practically happened in Hindu college of 1817, turned Presidency College in 1855. Under the influence of Derozio who joined Hindu college as a lecturer in 1826 and served for 3 years when he was dispensed with his services. He died at the age of twenty three.

Between 1813 and 1835, the East India Company did not develop any education policy in India. The general policy of the company was to encourage traditional learning in India by giving pecuniary aid and not to interfere with the education or to suggest alternative methods, for fear that this might contraven the policy of the religious neutrality. The task of spreading english education was left mainly to Christian missioneries whose chief target was proselytizing through the means of English education.

The General Committee of Public Instruction was set up in 1823 - at Calcutta (17 July 1823) and was put in charges of the existing government Instutitons and of the one lakh grant with some arrears to be paid by the Company as per the provisions of the Charter Act of 1813.

To be informed of the position and performance of the then indigennous education system, an enquiry into indigenous education was ordered by Sir Thomas Munro in Madras in 1822. In Bombay a similar enquiry was ordered by Mountstuart Elphinstone in 1823. In Bengal a spcial enquiry was conducted by William Adam, under the order of Lord William Bentinck. William Adam was a missionary and said to have devoted himself to the cause of Indian education. The enquiries of Madras and Bombay were not satisfactory relating to accuracy and throughness. They included neither all the schools nor all the pupils in existence.

Adam's enquiry was thorough and almost flawless. He took time also necessary for such enquiry. But Bengal, where Adam conducted his enquiry, had been a subject to general anarchy for a long time and where the system of indigenous education was in a state of decay and Adam also pointed to that.'

The Enquiry of Madras

We shall touch the issue in a nutshell.

The Board of Revenue was directed by the Govt. on 2nd July 1822, to ascertain the number of Schools and state of education in the province. The reports were collected through collector and submitted in February 21st, 1823.

The Board of Revenue noted that, if the total population was taken into account only 1 out of 67 boys and girls of the age group 5-6 to 10-12 years attended schools. But as the girls did not attend, the record will be 1 out of 34. This record excluded the number of pupils taught at home. In the town/city of Madras 26903 pupils were taught at home.

2. The Board of Revenue summed up that, the state of education was low as compared with that of England but higher than most European countries.

In this context, Report of the collector of Bellary may be peeped at. The collector reports that, 1. Education of the Hindu Youths begins at the age of five. The master and the scholars of the school to which the boy is to be sent, are invited to the house of parents. The whole are seated in a circle round an image of Ganesh and the child to be initiated is placed exactly opposite to it. The school master sitting by his side, after having burnt incense and presented offerings, causes the child to repeat a prayer to Ganesa, entreating wisdom. He then guides the child to write with its finger in rice the mystic name of the deity and is dismissed with a present from the parents according to their ability. The child next morning begins the great work of his education [Here we smell something of the ancient system of Hindoo education.]

2. Generally due to poverty or other reasons, the pupils discontinued after 4-5 years of schooling. Some continued till the age of 14-15 years.

3. The schools begin at 6 0'clock. The first child that enters has the name of Saraswati, written upon the palm of his hand as a sign of honour. The discipline and punishments are severe.

4. When all the students are assembled, they are divided according to their attainments, into several classes. The lower ones are partly under the care of monitors, while the higher ones, under the teacher. The number of classes are generally four.

5. After a thorough knowledge of letters, pupils next learns to write the compounds and symbol of vowels.

6. The economy with which the children are taught to write in the native schools is certainly admirable. The monitor system is also very much praise worthy. The chief defects of the native schools are - nature of books and want of competent teachers.

The Enquiries in Bombay (1823-25)

When the report was published it had R. V. Parulekar's editorial note where he observed, these reports do not cover the whole of the province as it then existed ...... But from such data as is available, the following general conclusions may be drawn about the then condition of indigenous education in the Province of Bombay.

(1) There was no exclusive house as school. Most of them were held in temples, private dwelling or sheds or houses of the teachers themselves.

(2) The average number of pupils per school worked out at 15 and varied from 2 to 150.

(3) The majority of teachers were Brahmins who were attached to the profession more by the respectability which tradition gave to it rather than consideration of actual gains in cash or kind. The school master of the time, however, could claim certain privilage from the community which compensated, for smallness of his earning. He was entirely a man of the people. He was always remembered in the heart and at the hearths of the people.

(4) The educational attainments of teacher were far from satisfactory.

(5) The pupils came from all Hindu castes, except Harijans. About 30 percent of the students were Brahmins.

(6) There were several indigenous schools which were attended by Muslims and those were in charge of Muslim teachers. These schools taught Persian and in some cases, Hindusthani. In several cases Muslim pupils attended Hindu schools.

(7) For higher education, there were 16 schools in Ahmednagar and 164 in Poona city.

The enquiry in Bombay 1829

This enquiry was different from those of 1823-25 because the information was now collected not through collectors but through Judges of the District. It showed the existence of 1705 schools with 35153 pupils for a population of 4681735 (roughly 47 lakhs)

Enquiries in Bengal

In Bengal the enquiries were conducted by William Adam who was a non-official, zealous missionary without any antipathy to India. The data collected were not through Revenue or Judicial Departments as was in the cases of Madras and Bombay. The enquiries were conducted with a longer time i.e. from 1935-1938.

Adam's First Report

Indigenous Elementary schools are meant those schools in which instructions in the element of knowledge is communicated, which have been originated and are supported by Natives themselves, in contra distinction from those that are supported by religious or philanthropic societies. The number of such schools in Bengal is supposed to be one lakh in Bengal and Bihar and assuming the population of the two as 40 crores, there would be a village school for every 400 persons.

There was difference of opinion as to the correctness of the report. If institutions mean one of permanent nature the report may seem incorrect. But if institutions mean a place where instruction is given and includes centres of domestic instruction, Adam's report was correct.

Adam's Second Report

Now Adam made a thorough and comprehensive enquiry of a thana. It was Natore in Rajsahi district. Of the total population (195296) of the thana 129640 were Muslims and 65656 were Hindus. the number of villages was 485. Adam found only 27 elementary schools with 292 pupils.

> 10 Bengali schools with 167 pupils,
> 4 Persian schools with 23 pupils,
> 11 Arabic schools with 42 pupils,
> 2 Bengali + Persian schools with 30 pupils,
> Total 27 schools with 262 pupils.

The number of students under domestic instructions was nearly nine times the number of pupils in public schools. The age of admission was 8 years, school leaving age was 14, teacher's average earning was Rs. 5-8 per month.

There was no indigenous college by Muslims. Hindus had 38 Sanskrit colleges with a role strength of 397. Age of admission was 11, average age after completing the course was 27 years. Of the 397 students, 136 belonged in the village nearby the college. The rest 261 belonged to distant villages and received food, lodging and education free.

Female education was almost non-existent. In Natore only 6127 had some education that meant literacy was 3.1 percent to the whole popualtion. It may be inferred that only 6 percent of the male had some sort of learning excluding the female population which may be taken as half of the total population.

Adam's Third Report

This third report had two parts. In the first part he gives the statistics collected from five districts : Murshidabad, Birbhum, Burdwan, South Bihar and Tirhut. In the second part of his report, he gives proposals for the reform of indigenous schools.

It must be admitted that the statistics submitted by him are the most reliable of the reports and statistic gathered at that period of time. The statistics were on - (1) Number of schools in each district and how many of those in Bengali, in Hindi, in Sanskrit, in Arabic, in English and for girls. The no of Bengali schools in total was 2567 of which only 6 for girls. The number of schools : in Murshidabad 113, in Birbhum 544, in Burdwan 931, in South Bihar 605 and in Tirhut 374. He gives statistics on the number of pupils which in total was 30915. This too was recorded districtwise.

District	Schools	Scholar
Murshidabad	113	1396
Birbhum	544	7350
Burdwan	931	15814
South Bihar	605	5036
Tirhut	374	1319
Total	2567	30915

These statistics exclude domestic schools. He submits statistics thanawise. All these figures show that the ratio of pupils to total population was 1 to 73. If only male population alone is considered, since female education was most neglected, the ratio will come to 1 to 36, as was observed by Munro in Madras Report (see Supra).

We have given here little bit of the total statistics collected by Adam. J. P. Naik and Nurullah in their book - A student's History of Education in India (2009 Edn) has shown that there were four types of indigenous schools in the beginning of the 19th Century.

Indigenous Institution Schools of Learning Elementary Schools Pathsalas of Hindus Madrasahs of Muslim Persian Schools Schools teaching through the Indian languages.

Schools of Learning

Schools of learning received pecuniary assistance from rulers, chieftains and opulent or religious citizens. There were teachers who served gratis and even provided food and lodging to pupils. The schools had no special building of their own, where these existed, they were built by the teachers themselves or at the expense of friends and patrons, or by subscription received from the people.

The Hindu schools were conducted almost exclusively by Brahmins. In the persian or Arabic schools, though the teachers were Muslims but Hindu teacher was not rare.

Elementary Schools : The indigenous elementary schools were the main agencies for spread of education, whereas, the schools of learning produced Maulavis and Pandits. The instruction given in these elementary schools was of practical type and mostly limited to 3 R's. There had no religious bias attached to those.

The chief merits of these elementary schools were their adaptability to local environment and the vitality and popularity they had earned under a variety of economic conditions or political ups and downs. Their defects were exclusion of girls (not always) and Harijans. The teachers were not well versed or well trained.

As to the question - whether a national system of education could be built on the basis of this indigenous system, we can answer with all certainty that the indigenous system had potentiality enough. Even in England and other educationally advanced countries, education was spread by gradual correction, expansion and improvement of the defects of the existing system. William Adam who took so much care to study the existing system also proposed a plan of working step by step that a national system of education could be built up on the basis of the existing indigenous system.

India's contribution to England

We talk of England's contribution to Indian Education. But do we know India's contribution to England's Education system ? The chief method by which England achieved expansion of Primary education at very low cost between 1801 and 1845, was Monitorial system'. And with all humility Indians can proudly say that this Monitorial system was India's contribution to England's Educational System. The Indian indigenous system of teaching with the help of monitors was a general feature everywhere. Dr. Bell advocated the adoption of this system in England in his book - An Experiment in Education made at the Male asylum at Madras. [Ref. : Enquiry Reports and Statistics are taken from J. P. Naik and Nurullah's referred to book P-1 to 32].

But in India, England did not accept this as there was Macaulay whose object was to "form a class of persons, Indian in blood and colour, but English in tastes, in opinions and in morals and in intellect."

However, the General Committee of Public Instruction, set up by the government in 1823, which was responsible for formation of policy and allocation of funds, was evenly divided and both sides appealed to the Governor General Lord William Bentinck (1833-1835). Bentinck asked Macaulay in his dual capacity as Law member and President General Committee of Public Instruction, to give his views.

The result was Macaulay's Minute dated 2nd Feb. 1835 which clinched the issue in favour of English education.

Anglicist like Trevelyan and Scottish Presbytarian Alexander Duff, who shared Macaulay's contempt for Indian learning were in favour of Macaulay. There were Oriental Scholars like H. H. Wilson and H. T. Princep who supported the study of Indian classical language.

Barely a month later, on 7th March, 1835, the Governor General Bentinck issued a memorandum which decisively asserted that "the great object of the British Government ought to be the promotion of European litereature and science among the natives of India, and that all the funds appropriated for the purpose of education would be best employed in English Education alone." [Ref. : H. Sharp - Selection of Educational Records 1781-1839. P.P. 130-132 quoted in C.H.I. P-44, Vol-8].

It should be noted that before Macaulay reached India, Bentinck had already formulated his plan. Macaulay came to India in 1934 and Bentinck was Governor General from 1833-35 and was succeeded by Sir Charles Metcaff (1835-36).

Back ground

Between 1813 and 1823 the East India Company did not develop any educational policy in India. The money sanctioned in 1813 remained unspent. The General Committee of Public instruction at Calcutta was formed on 17 July, 1823 and was put incharge of the existing government institutions and of the one lakh rupee with arrears.

The general policy of the East India Company was to encourage traditional learning in India by giving pecuniary aid and not to interfere with education or to suggest alternative method, for fear that this might contraven the policy of religious neutrality. The foundation of the Sanskrit College at Calcutta in 1823/24 by Lord Amharst represents the continuation of the same traditional policy. Rammohan was against this Sanskrit Institute.

The Despatch of the Court of Directors, 18 Feb, 1824, embodied the general policy of education to be followed in India. It was the first Directoral Despatch which shows contempt for traditional learning and stressed very clearly the superiority of Western education and insists on spending money on useful learning and not the useless fables of Hindu mythology or tenets of Quran.

The Directoral encouragement of the diffusion of useful knowledge continued through the Bentinck Resolution, 7th March, 1835.

Independently of the official attitude there was growing up in Calcutta and its neighbourhood a disposition to learn English through out the entire period. Rammohan's letter to Lord Amharst through Bishop Heber is oft referred to. But even the conservative Radhakanta Dev propagated the cause of English and was one of the more active governors of Hindu College [Calcutta Review XLV, 1867, P-318].

The study of Parliamentary Papers, Court Despatches and the accounts of travellers, indicates that long before the official Resolution of 7th March 1835, Indians were themselves sensible to the great advantage of learning English.

The funds placed in the disposal of the General Committee of Public instruction were limited and the question turned on how the money was to be spent - should Western Knowledge be diffused through English or the classical knowledge ? The question of making English a compulsory subject in the Arabic college at Calcutta "finally put the match to the train of major controversy of 1834."

As stated earlier, Bentinck had already formulated his plan before Macaulay reached India. He reached in India when the British power was established more firmly than at any former time. He had formulated his plans and was waiting for ripe time.

For a long time it has been generally held that it was Macaulay's minute (2 Feb, 1835) which proved decisive. His mentality was clear from his letter written to his father (mentioned Supra) and his purpose of 'to form a class of persons, Indian in blood and colour, but English in tastes, in opinions, and in morals and intellect' might have contributed to hold the idea that Macaulay played the decisive role. But the ground had already been prepared long before Macaulay arrived. The historical process had been in operation for a long time. Further more, the public employment of Indians in places where the number of Europeans could be curtailed on grounds of economy gave stimulons to education. The chairman of the Court of Directors, William Astell, in his letter to Bentinck, reflected the anxiety of the Court to afford every reasonable facility for the education of the natives. Astell's letter to Bentinck 4th Oct. 1830, Bentinck's letter to Metcalfe 16 Sept. 1829, his letter to Mancy 1st June 1834 are eloquent to understand Bentinck's stand.

Macaulay was a mixture of the Benthamite theory of legislation and Evangelical vehemence of sentiment. His Minute on Education was brilliant. His main thesis was that all the learning of East was nothing beside the metaphysics of Locke and the physics of Newton, and that it was only the torch of Western learning that could illuminate the Indian mind sub-merged in superstition and ignorance. So Macaulay strongly recommended that the object of education policy in India should be the spread of Western Learning through the midium of the English language. He also suggested that the existing institutions of Oriental learning should be used for the promotion of English education.

Lord Bentinck immediately accepted Macaulay's arguments and suggestions. His Resolution of 7th March, 1835, passed the following orders: (Summary1813 - 1835 A.D.).

1. His Lordship in Council is of opinion that the great object of British Government ought to be the promotion of European literature and science among the natives of India, and that all the funds appropriated for the purpose of education would be best employed on English Education alone.

2. But it is not the intention of his Lordship in Council to abolish any College or School of native learning, while the native population shall appear to be inclined to avail themselves of the advantages which it affords, and His Lordship in Council directs that all the existing professors and students at all institutions under the superintendence of the committee shall continue to receive their stipends .....

3. It has come to the knowledge of the Governor General in Council that a large sum has been expended by the Committee on the printing of Oriental works. His Lordship in Council directs that no portion of the funds shall hereafter be so employed.

4. His Lordship in council directs that all the funds which these reforms will leave at the disposal of the Committee be henceforth employed in imparting to the native population a knowledge of English literature and science through the medium of the English language, and His Lordship in council requests the committee to submit to Government with all expedition a plan for accomplishment of the purpose.

[Ref. : Selection from Educational Records Vol-I, P-130-131 also quoted in Naik's book].

After considering the personal view of Lord Bentinck on this issue as we have discussed, we cannot support the views of somebody that Macaulay was the 'torch-bearer in the path of Progress'. We may condemn his poor thinking and knowledge of India and his main intention of making Indians slave to Europeans, specially the British and his contempt for natives, but we may comment that he was responsible for the quick decision taken by Lord Bentinck.

Criticism of the Policy

A few points may be placed as the criticism of the New Policy of Education.

1. It has been stated that the new policy created a group sharply separated from their fellow.A new caste was added to the caste ridden country. A very small number of men were educated in English. They occupied the higher administrative posts and this created a cleavage between them and the masses.

2. English educated ones developed a dual mentality, their liberal ideas found no friend in the family, particularly the women folk who clung to the old customs, practices and ideas. The educated few could discuss with their friends in clubs but fell in the old groove as they returned home. This existenence was a sort of Jekyll and Hyde which was not conducive to mental peace.

    This was one of the main reasons why Western education did not produce all the benefits that could be reasonably expected.

3. It is objected that this new policy gave an undue favour to English against Vernacular as the medium of instruction.

As a matter of fact the decision merely meant that English and not Sanskrit or Arabic should be the midium of highest education. It had no reference to Vernacular which would remain the medium of a national education embracing every village of the country. This was clearly laid down in the report of the committee drawn up in the same year in which the above resolution on English education was passed. [Ref. : O'Malley as quoted by R. C. Majumder and K. K. Dutta in the article in Vol-10 be HCIP] A point to note in this connection is that vernaculars were not sufficiently developed to be used as the vehicle of instruction in higher branches of literature and science.

Reaction : The Orientalists did not accept the new policy lying down. As a protest two of them retired from the committee of public instruction. A petition signed by ten thousand Hindu inhabitants of Calcutta and Zillas, was sent to the court of Directors protesting against the Resolution of Lord Bentinck of 1835.

The Asiatic Society sent a memorial to the Local Government. Royal Asiatic Society also pressed hard.

Auckland became the Governor General (1836-1842) . He did not reverse Bentinck's decision but modified it and restored to a certain extent the altogether neglected Oriental learning which met the approbation of the Court of Directors in their despatch of 20th January 1841, though they did not express any decisive opinion on the midium of instruction.

Lord Auckland's Order

Lord Auckland (1836-1842) passed the order (Summary)

1. Guaranteed the continuation of the existing institutions of Oriental learning and the payment of the adequate grant for entertainment of the 'most eminent professors' and adequate scholarship to the students.

2. Encouraged the preparation and publication of useful books of instruction in Oriental language provided that the expenditure was kept within the limits of funds sanctioned for Oriental education.

3. Also directed that the first duty of the Oriental Colleges was to impart instruction in Oriental learning and that they may conduct English classes, if necessary, after the duty had been properly discharged.

This part (Part VIII) of this book covers the period upto 1835. Yet Auckland's view of 1839 and its approbation on 20th January 1841, are referred only to complete the Despatch issue of 1835.

We may conclude this part simply by observing that if 1813 was the first importabnt landmark in the East India Company's educational policy, 1835 certainly was the second.

Bengal

Medical and English classes were added both to Calcutta Madrasah (1781) and Sanskrit College (1824) between 1826 and 1828. Hindu College (1817) gained decided superiority over all other institutions in affording tuition in the English language and literature, ancient and modern history. This instittion was attended mostly by the sons of most respectable classes of the native society - who paid for their education. In the report of 1827-28 the studies described were Natural and Experimental Philosophy, Chemistry, Mathematics, Algebra. Elements of General History (written by Tytler), Modern Europe (by Russell), Milton and Shakespear.

Other early colleges were Serampur College (1818), General Assembly's Institution of the Church of Scotland founded by Duff (1830), Hooghly Mahasin College (1838) founded from the endowment of Mahasin, the institution of Free Church in Scotland (1843) and the Patna College (1863). In addition to the government colleges at Ducca, Behrampur and Krishnanagar, there were also Doveton, La Martiniere. St. Pauls and Bhowanipur College of the London Missionary Society.

Part - IX

1835 - 1854 A.D

Historical Perspective

Lord Auckland though saved the classicists from complete annihilation (as proposed by Macaulay), he gave a far greater impetus to the spread of English education.

A suggestion was being put forward from several quarters that modern Indian languages should be used as the media of instruction at least in the secondary schools. (By the time from Macaulay, 1835, the modern Indian languages that developed at this time). It was pointed out that the limited syllabus could easily be taught through the Indian languages if good class books were prepared and arrangements were made to train the teachers. It was also argued that such steps would give encouragement to literature of Indian languages. It was pointed out that Bombay used the Indian laugnages as medium of instruction in most of its schools of this type.

But by these arguments, Lord Auckland could not be moved. In 1842, the General Committee of Public Instruction was replaced by Council of Education.

In 1844, when Lord Hardinge was the Governor General, the Government announced the policy that educated Indians would be employed in Govt. Services. This was an encouragement. The Education Council made a proposal in 1845, for the establishment of a university at Calcutta, but that was not agreed to by the Court of Directors on the ground that it was premature. The President of the Council was Charles Hay Cameron.

In Bengal, the number of schools under the control of council of education rose from 28 in 1843 to 151 in 1855 (123 schools in 12 yrs). Annual expenditure increased from Rs. 4,12,284 to Rs. 5,94,428 schools increased almost (six times in the mean time).

There was some progress of English Education in the Presidencies of Bombay and Madras but those were less in comparison with Bengal.

The Presidency of Bombay

The province of Bombay was formed in 1818 as and when the rule of Peshwa in Maharashtra came to an end.

The Poona Sanskrit college was founded in 1821 after the model of Benaras Sanskrit College. Its maintenance was the main educational activity of the government till 1823 when a vigorous policy on education was prescribed for the whole country. The Governor of this Presidency - Elphinstone conducted an enquiry on the State of Education in the Presidency (see Supra). It must be mentioned that an organisation named The Bombay Native Education Society was working hard on the object of spreading education. On the recommendation of Mountstuart Elphinstone - the Governor of the Presidency, this socity was accepted as the main agency for spreading education. A grant was sanctioned to the Society by the Court of Directors.

This was a great official encouregement and the Society rendered very useful service from 1823-1840.

The Society upto 1840

(1) Conducted four English Schools at Bombay, Thane, Panvel and Poona. The Headmasters were Europeans.

(2) Conducted 115 Primary Schools in mofussil. The syllabus was Reading, Writing, Arithmatic, History of England and India, Geography, Astronomy, Algebra, Natural Philosophy. Geometry and Trigonometry. The number of classes varied from six to ten. The medium of Instruction was mother tongue. These schools may be treated as secondary schools.

Besides the institutions conducted by the Socity, the government itself conducted two colleges - Poona Sanskrit College and Elphinstone Institution.

In April 1840, the Government of Bombay decided to constitute Board of Education as an agency to look after the institutions. It was a body of seven members, three of whom were to be nominated from the Society. This Board continued to function till 1855 and the Society practically was wounded up.

In 1842, this Board

(1) Divided the Province into three educational Divisions and placed a European Inspector with an Indian Assistant Inspector.

(2) It undertook to establish one primary school in a village of 2000 people provided.

(a) a school house free of rent is available.

(b) the pupils agreed to pay a monthly fee of one anna (one sixteenth of Rupees) per month.

About the medium of Instruction : The Bombay Native Education Society which worked so hard through out a long time (1823-1840) for spread of education was of opinion that Western Knowledge could never be spread to the people through English medium. In its report (1825-26) it stated that the new ideas of Western literature could be easily spread through the mother tongue of each scholar.

But the Board of Education followed English as the medium of instruction.

A comperative study of Bengal and Bombay taken from its report for 1845.

	Bengal	*Bombay*
1. Population	37000000	10500000
2. Expenditure on educaiton	Rs. 477593	Rs. 168226
3. No. of pupils reading in Govt. school	5570	10616
4. No. of pupils reading in English school	3953	761

[Ref. : The book of Naik and Nurullah P-80-84]

It is already noted that Elphinstone was deeply interested in education of the masses and his view was to spread English or Western knowledge through the vernaculars. The Court of Directors accepted his views. In October 1845, the Grant Medical College was formally opened and the first regular session began in 1846, June. An engineering institution was in existence in Bombay in 1824. The Poona College of Science (grew out of that Engineering school) was founded in 1854.

The American Missionary Society established the first native Girls school in Bombay Presidency in 1824. Two years later there developed girls school and of these one was Boarding School. In 1831 two native schools in Ahmadnagar were established. Other female schools were established at Thane, Bassein and Nasik.

The Presidency of Madras

We have followed the enquiries made by Munro in 1822 regarding the State of indigenous education in Madras Presidency. Munro found that the condition of education was at low ebb on account of (a) absence of government encouragement and (b) the poverty of the people.

In his Minute in 1826 (10 March) Munro proposed of an attempt to educate the masses by improving the indigenous schools. To him the first need was better types of teachers. He proposed to establish two schools - one for the Hindus other for the Muslims in each collectorate and one in each Tahasil or Taluk of the province. The total cost estimated for this was 50 thousand rupees per year.

Munro's proposal was sanctioned by the Court of Directors in 1828, after a year of Munro's demise. The experiment on Munro's proposal was tried for a time and in Setpember 1830, the Court of Directors advised that the Govt. of Madras would do well to concentrate on the spread of English education rather than on mass education.

On the whole, the state of education in Madras Presidency through government initiative and management, was meagre summarily it may be stated that -

(1) The indigenous schools were not encouraged.

(2) Policy and policy making authorities changed frequently

(3) The District and Tahasil schools established by Munro were discontinued in 1830

(4) Establishment of an English college at Madras and of provincial English schools at some important places in the interior.

(5) A High School then called 'the University' was established in Madras,

(6) In 1833 a collegiate department was organised in that 'the University'.

(7) The sanctioned amount of Rs. 50 thousand per year for Madras Province, was not fully utilised.

The only relieving factor of the situaiton was the Missionary activities in large scale, Englisgh education was more extensively imparted. The Indian Education commission 1882, States that, in 1854 about 30 thousand boys were being educated in schools conducted by Missionary Societies and about 3000 were obtaining at least the elements of a liberal educaiton in English.

In Madras the foundation of collges began much later. The Christian College was established in 1837. In 1841 the Central School was converted to a High School (in 1853 a college department was added to it), later it developed as Presidency College. The Jesuits established St. Joseph's college. Medical Classes were started at the Madras Medical School (which turned to a college in 1851). Colleges were established in Trichinopally, Tanjore. By 1902, Madras had 15 first grade and 39 second grade colleges. The education of the girls was begun by Missioneries. In October 1821, it was resolved to form native girls school in Madras. But it took time to give effect.

The first attempt to train teachers in India was made by Dr. Andrew Bell at the end of 18th Century and his system, known as Madras system, was adopted in Europe and America.

Punjab Province

The province of Punjab was constituted in 1849. The only official institution that existed in Punjab prior to 1854 was a school at Amritsar which had Hindu, Persian, Arabic, Sanskrit and Gurumukhee departments.

Uttar Pradesh

Uttar Pradest (United Province / North-Western Province) is indebted to Mr. James Thomason lieutenant governor of North-West Province, for its intiation and expansion of education.

The oldest college of U.P. was the Sanskrit College (1781) at Benaras. It was to cultivate Law, Literature and Religion of Hindus. The college at Agra was established in 1823 and at Delhi an Oriental Collge in 1825. Egnlish was introduced in Delhi College in 1828. The Allahabad School was opened in 1834. Out of a high school founded in 1836 arose the Bareilly college in 1850. Canning College was founded at Luckhnow in 1864.

By a government resolution in April 1840, the Control of the educational institution in North-West province was transferred from the government of Bengal to the Local government with the funds belonging to those institutions. At that time there were three colleges and nine Anglo-Vernacular schools maintained by Government.

Mr. James Thomason, took up the idea of Adam's Vernacular education, brought in closer to the reality of Agricultural life and made the whole basis of general educaiton in the Province. It was in 1843. Thomason made people realise that elementary knowledge of reading, writing and arithmatic and agricultural accounts was indispensible for the preservation of their legitimate rights. His conception embraced the whole population, sepcially the peasantry. As compared with Bengal there was less encouragement for the study of English.

The Local Government decided to introduce education through the medium of Vernaculars and thus there began the multiplication and improvement of village schools, of supervision, advice and distribution of elementary books. As an experimental measure Tahasildari schools were established in eight districts.

He introduced a levy for the support of Primary schools. As early as in 1851, Thomason began to levy a tax for Primary educaiton.

He introduced the system of Halkabandi' (circles of schools) in 1854. Under this system, several villages conveniently situated, for the purpose are grouped together and in a central situation a school is established which is not to be more than 2 miles / (3 km.) distant from the centre forming the circle.

He made the Central Government and Court of Directors accept the principle that the indigenous schools should be developed and improved as a means of spreading educaiton among the people.

His another contribution was the organisation of a Regular Educaiton Department, the plan of inspection of schools and suggestion for improvement.

Official Policies 1833-1853

All these we are discussing only to assess the position of education of India before the famous Wood's Despatch 1854, which is still the spinal chord of the education system of this country.

We have so long discussed very briefly the status and development of education after 1835 to 1853 in India. Now we can make a review, the whole issue under the general heading :

Official policies during the period 1835-1853

The Policies of Education of the Britishers (Christians) in India under East India Company (1600) from Bentinck's Resolution 7th March 1835 to Wood's Despatch 19 July 1854, covering a period of twenty years may be summarised on three points.

(1) The Objectives of Education and medium of Instruction

(2) Attitude towards indigenous system and institution of education.

(3) To discharge the duty of the ruler.

1. Objectives : This issue can be placed from two angels - cultural and political. On the cultural angle, there were three distinct views. (a) there were those who had an admiration and appreciation of the worthiness of

the ancient literature of the Hindus and of the Muslims, wanted that the British Christians should study those and those ancient literatures were to be preserved. In this group were men like Duncan, Hastings, Minto, Prinsep Wilson and such other orientalists.

(b) The second view was held by extremists like Grant, Macaulay - who held that a single shelf of a good European library was worth the whole native literature of India and Arabia. Grant wanted that Western light and knowledge should take the place of Eastern Culture and religion. Macaulay wanted to create a class of persons who would be Indian in blood and colour, but English in tastes, in opinions, in morals and in intellect. He also proudly wrote to his father that if the policy inunciated by him was followed, idolatory in India will be abolished within thirty years. This group had an utter contempt of Indian religion and that which was Oriental.

(c) the third view was of synthesis. It held that Indians would loss if restricted mainly to Oriental studies. The annihitation of Oriental Culture was impossible and also it was impossible to substitute it completely by Western one. So the only practical and realistic approach was to bring about a synthesis-preserving what was good in Oriental system and introducing what was good in Western system. Raja Rammohan Roy and after him Pandit Iswar Chandra Vidyasagar of the Indians, colonel Jervis of the Europeans were of this view. Jervis maintained that "If the people are to have a literature, it must be their own. The staff may be in great degree, European, but it must freely be interwoven with homespun materials and the fashion must be Asiatic.

We noted that the golden mean was not enforced. Prior to 1833, Oriental view had a footing, but after Macaulay and Bentinck, the substitution of Indian Culture by Western one gained the ground.

Coming to the political and administrative angle, we mark that there were some who wanted to win over the opinion of the Indian upper classes by giving them English Education and offering government jobs. They took it for granted that education and culture will filtrate downward i.e. to masses of whom they had no concern. So they emphasised English Education for such people, no indigenous system, no mass education.

When the company's territorial extension started, it was no more a trading concern only. It became a political power. It became very much careful to maintain religious neutrality. Again, along with the territorial extension they needed more people in jobs. Exclusive employment of the English men was neither practicable nor financially feasible. This created a demand of educated Indians. The sub-ordinate services were Indianised thereby reducing the cost of administration.

Again, it was pointed out that the education of the subjects should be looked over by the Political authorities, meaning that to educate Indians was a duty of the Britishers under East India Company.

So the policies were -

(1) To spread Western Knowledge

(2) To secure properly trained servants for administration and other minor works, to reduce expenditure of the company

(3) To discharge the duty of the ruler by providing education to the people.

The Britishers wanted that the medium of instruction would be English and English only. The Institutions founded by the government initiative followed English medium. The institutions of Christian machinery also followed the suit. But there were others who relied on vernacular as the medium, was the best.

The Company wanted to educate the upper class of society and thereby to pacify those classes of society which had been adversely affected by the change of Govt. It was argued that their culture would naturally descend to lower classes. But the filtration theory did not work.

But the theory worked otherwise. The educational institutions conducted by the government or Missionaries remained a minority and they gave higher education to a very small number of the total population. But it is from the rank of these educated persons that a bulk of persons came out who did not care for government jobs but devoted themselves to the spread of education mostly through vernacular medium. It is to this patriotic positive minded men to whom the nation owes. They originated the idea of Private schools and colleges that spread all over the country. Private Indian enterprise soon became the principal agency for spreading primary, secondary and collegiate eduaiton. Modern literature in Indian languages were built up by these people who may be named 'Nation Builders'.

2. Attitude of the company to indigenous Institutions.

The Downward Filtration theory did not work as was expected.

Munro's attempt to improve the indigenous schools by founding Tahasil and collectorate schools was discarded. Munro was the governor of Madras.

Then came Elphinstone who was the governor of Bombay (1819-1827). He proposed that the company should try to spread education among the masses by encouraging indigenous institutions. He encouraged Bombay Native Education Society which worked as an agency for spreading education. Elphinstone had a plan on this. The important aspects of his plan were (a) mass education through mother language and for this purpose improveement and extension of indigenous institution. (b) English should not be the sole medium of Instruction.

When his minutes were placed before the Governor's Council, Warden, a member of the Council vehimently opposed. He wanted that the government should not shoulder any responsibility of education.

Elphinstone's proposals were not carried. But the Council accepted Bombay Native Educaiton Society as the agent of educaiton of the province of Bombay and hence no committee of public Instruction was appointed in Bombay.

In Bengal Adam's observations and suggestions have already been discussed. He also talked of the harmfulness of Downward Filtration Theory and proposed to improve and extend the indigenous system. But his eloquent defence was of no avail. Lord Auckland kept Adam in cold storage. We have recorded what he actually did.

The only man who could carry his plan was Lieutenant Governor Thomson of United province or North Western Province. His plan was accepted both by Central Govt. and Court of Directors. The plan or proposal was - the indigenous schools should be improved and developed as the means of spreading education among the people.

He was the first officer in India who collected education levy. His system of Haklabandi (discussed Supra) was also a memorable one. His third idea was to establish a regular Education Department.

The condition of female education (1835 - 1857)

By the end of the 18th century a woman's position in the society was almost that of an appendage to the male. The social system denied women education. This denial was reinforced by the spread of a superstitution among the majority of the Hindu families that education for a woman was likely to result in her widowhood. Women were denied the freedom of an outdoor life. The only justification for her existenace was that She was previlaged to cater the needs of husband and his family. There was early marriage of women. There was multi-marriage of men. Number of widows under 15 years of age was many.

The process of progressive deterioration of Hindu women in India was to a large extent due to Muslim rule in India. The Muslims married Hindu girls and Hindu Society did not like Muslim association as they considered Muslims as Mlechchas.

During the 1st half of the 19th Century, some members of the aristocratic society guided simply by consideration of management of estates, and the christian Missioneries prompted by their zeal of propagation of christanity through conversion, took interest in female educaiton. The company remained indifferent to it.

A picture of the abjectly low position to which women had been degraded in the early part of the 19th century may also be had from the writings of two pioneers who were most interested in the ameleoration of the condition of women in society. They were Raja Rammohan Roy (1772-1833) and the other was Pandit Iswar Chandra Vidyasagar (1820-1891).

From Adam's Report (1835-38) it is learnt that women education was the least important issue of the society and the rulers.

Adam found only 4 literate women against 21907 men in a total population of 496574. This is regarding Bengal.

Things appear to be no better in Bombay where Elphinstone made an enquiry in 1823. No girl pupil was attending the indigenous schools.

Munro's enquiry in Madras in 1822, revealed that "the women of the Rajabundah and among some other tribes of Hindus, were generally taught. The return of the indigenous schools showed as many as 5480 girls in a total enrolement of 184110.

In Punjab there were special schools for girls in charge of women teachers.

For the rest of India, nothing is known. On the whole, therefore, it may be concluded that excepting an extremely small number of women who received some education in the family or in the school, almost the whole female population of the country was deprived of education.

It appears that it was in August 1818, the movement for the abolition of 'Sati' system (the wife has to sacrifice herself in the funaral pyre of the husband) was taken up by right earnest. Rammohan Roy took a leading Part. A petition was submitted to the Governor, signed by a large number of the most respected inhabitants of Calcutta. After a few years the issue was reopened at the instance of the Judges of Nizamat Adalat. Lord Amherst declined to intervene though he considered 'Sati' as a 'detestable superstition.'

Lord Bentinck passed a Regulation dated 4 December, 1829, prohibiting the practice of 'Sati'. It was declared 'illegal' and punishable by the Criminal Courts.

The company avoided the issue of education of women simply by saying that the prejudice against the education of women which prevailed among the people was so deep rooted in their social and religious life that any attempt to educate women would create a very great commotion and the first attempt of the company should be restricted to the education of men who would themselves, at a later date, undertake the education of their women folk.

Bentinck courageously prohibited Sati system and after him Lord Dalhousi (1848-1856) decided that open patronage of government should be extended to the education of women. It relates to his order dated 11th April, 1850, a portion of which reads :

"It is the opinion of the Governor General in Council that no single change in the habit of the people is likely to lead to more important and beneficial consequences than the introduciton of education for their female children. The general practice is to allow them to grow up in absolute ignorance, but this custon is not required or even sanctioned by their religion and in fact a certain degree of education is now given to the female relatives of those who can afford the expenses of entertaining special instructures at their own houses.

The Governor General in Council requests that the Council of Education may be informed that it is hence forth to consider its functions as comprising the superintendence of native female education, and that wherever any disposition is shown by the natives to establish female schools, it will be its duty to give them all possible encouragement and further their plans in every way that is not inconsistant with the efficiency of the institution already under their management. It is also the wish of the Governor General in Council that intimation to the same effect should be given to the Chief Civil Officers of the Mofussil calling their attention to the growing disposition among the native to establish female schools and directing them to use all means at their disposal for encouraging those institutions and for making it generally knwon that the Government views them with very great approbation." [Selection from Educational Records Vol-II P-59-60].

This view was subsequently confirmed by Wood's Despatch 1854. Just a year back of this Declaration in April 1850, on 7th May 1849, Calcutta Female School was established by J. E. D. Bethun with the help of Iswar Chandra Vidyasagar who managed this institution after the sudden death of

Bethun. Bethun himself was a Law Member of the Governor General's Council and also the President of Council of Eduation. It was the first school of its kind. To commemorate Bethun's name, it was named Bethun school which subsequently was raised to the status of a college.

Vidyasagar was famous for his Learning and Donating. He was a reformer of all - Religious, Social, Educational practices and so on. His deep sympathy for the women folks was so realised by the Poet Madhusudan that he said, Vidyasagar has the heart and feeling of a Bengali mother. He was then the Principal of s and reorganised it in every way. He was given the charge of female education in the 4 districts of Bengal - Medinipur, Hooghly, Nadia and Burdwan as the special Inspector of Schools (at first as Asst. Inspector). He had set up 35 girls schools in 5 months (Nov. 1857-May 58). He even advanced money from his own pocket. The speed of Vidyasagar, probably irritated the then Director of Public Instruction W. Gordon Young. His relation embittered with Vidyasagar. Out of disgust and for the rarest sense of self-respect Vidyasagar resigned. But he continued his eduational efforts and reforms according to his own line of thinking which was practically inconcievable at that period of time and from a man of authority in Sanskrit. He made English a compulsory subject and had the partinence and knowledge to utter that Samkhya and Vedanta were false philosophies. He fought for widow remarriage and won it. He fought against child marriage and multimarriage of Hindu Males. But before he could attain any success, the upsurge of 1857 happened which made the Britishers cautious and afraid of interfering prevailing system.

The period from 1835 to 1855 was a period of controversies. The company was busy with commerce, conquest and consolidation. It thought it unnecessary to give attention to or to spend on educaiton.

As late as in 1855 (the time of Wood's Despatch), the total number of eduational institutions aided, managed and inspected by the company was as small as 1474 with 67569 pupils and total expenditure on education was not even one percent of the total revenue.

The only encouraging features were : large expansion of missionary enterprise with an ulterior motif of conversion and beginning of Indian Private enterprise in the modern system education.

[Ref. : Naik and Nurullah, Hironmoy Banerjee - Article in Cultural Heritage of India Vol-8, P-65-70. Aparna Basu - Article in CH-I, P-40-60, Article in Vol-10, HCIP by R. C. Majumder. K. K. Dutta, V. C. Magadh University and V. N. Dutta Reader in History Kurukshetra University].

The Brahma Samaj of Raja Rammohan has recorded a conspicuous service in this field. Some prominent members of the Samaj started journals from time to time for promotion of education and culture among women. But that not strictly within the period of this part of the Book. This part deals mainly from 1835 to 1855 i.e. from Macaulay - Bentinck to Wood and Dalhousi. Yet for the sake of mentioning it must be noted that only in Calcutta so many magazines were organised by so many stalwarts for the development of women folks in Bengal.

> Banibodhin 1863 Umesh Ch. Dutta,
>
> Abalabandhava 1869 Dwarakanath Ganguly,
>
> Mahila - Girish Ch. Sen,
>
> Antahapura, Sasipada Banerjee,
>
> Bharati - Dwijendrnath Thakur,
>
> Swarna Kumar Ghosal,
>
> Bharatamahila Suprabhat by a law graduate,
>
> Sisters - Kumudini and Basanti Mitra

Arya Samaj established a school for girls - Kanya Maha Vidyalaya at Jullandhar, Punjab. Gradually Secondary and Primary schools sprang up under the supervision of its branches in differents parts of India. The Prarthana Samaj and the Deccan Education Society also made important contributions to the cause of female education.

Sir Charles Wood's Despatch of 1854, remarked about female education in India in Para 83 of its report :

"The importance of female education in India cannot be overrated, and we have observed with pleasure the evidence which is now afforded to an increased desire on the part of many of the natives in India to give a good education to their daughters. By this means a far greater proportional impulse is imparted to the moral and educational tone of the people than by the education of men. We have already observed that schools for female are included among those to which grants-in-aid may be given, and we cannot refrain from expressing our Cordial Sympathy with the efforts which are being made in this direction."

[Ref. : P-66 of Vol-10 of HCIP]

But the policy of British Government in relation to female education in India was still one of caution.

Lord Canning's Government (1858 to 1862) declared that Govt. could not take such initiative in the matters of girls eduaiton as it has done in the case of eduation of the boys, but that such girls schools should be supported mainly by voluntary aid, and Govt. might encourage the existing schools by grant-in-aids. Nevertheless, some grants were made and in 1873 there were only 1640 girls schools of all kinds in British India. [Monier William - Modern India and the Indians P-325-326 as quoted in HCIP, P-67, Vol-10].

Between 1871 and 1882 there was an aggregate increase in female edcation in India. Large proportion of efforts was devoted to the primary education of girls as compared to their secondary or higher education. Except in Bengal, and to some degree in Madras, secondary education for girls was in the hands of Christian missioneries and 'native managers'.

When the doors of Calcutta University (1857) were opened to women as late as 18 years, two Bengali girls Chandramukhi and Kadambini Basu took advantage of this and passed B.A. Examination in 1882. They were the first women to do so in India. In 1884 Chandramukhi passed the M.A. Examination again the first women to do so in India. Kadambini went on to Medical College.

Iswar Chandra Vidyasagar hailed the occasion of Chandramukhi's passing the M.A. Exam as an event deserving special recognition.

After reviewing the situation about female education in India, the Education Commission of 1882 (Hunter Commission) remarked that it was still in 'an extremely' backward condition, and that it needs to be fostered in every legitimate way." The commission observed that, "female educaiton be treated as a legitimate charge alike on local, Municipal, and Provincial Funds and receive special encouragement (first of the twenty seven recommendations of the commisison).

Henceforth government grants for girls' schools began to be more liberally given and Govt. management more freely used than before. This helped the growth of number of schools and girl pupils.

After Wood's despatch in 1854, in roughly 50 years after and of Hunter's Commision (1882) after 20 years, in 1901-1902.

(1) 12 female college - 3 in Madras, 3 in Bengal, 6 in United province.

(2) The number of female college students - 177 Bengal - 55 Madras 35 Bombay 30 U.P. 49 Burma - 8 (at the end of the year)

(3) Secondary Schools for girls 461. Total no. of girls students both in boys and girls schools - 44695. Most of them were in Primary section, in secondawry section 9800.

(4) The number of Primary schools for girls was 5628.

(5) The average number of students per school was 35 in 1901-02.

(6) At the end of 1901-02, there were 390000 girls in the Primary and Secondary Schools.

[Ref. : Progress of Education in India 1897-98 to 1901-02, P-298-302 as quoted in HCIP Vol-10, Articles).

Still the percentage of girls in Public Institutions to girls of School going age was 2.2 in 1901-02.

Note : The period under review in this part (Part IX) of the book is from 1835 to 1854. The female educaiton issue is taken beyond that period upto 1901-02. It will be easy to comprehend the position upto the end of the 19th Century.

Part X

1854 - 1947 A.D. [Last Phase of British India]

Historical Perspective

By 1853, a stage had been reached when a comprehensive survey in the field of Education in India was needed. It was needed because a future prescription was to be prescribed.

This was exactly what the Education Despatch of 1854 did. The occasion was provided by the renewal of the Company's Charter in 1853.

Charles Wood was the President of the Board of Control. It was the famous Educational Despatch No. 49, dated 19th July, 1854, which was drafted by Sir Charles Wood, the President of the Board of Control, and forwarded to India through the Court of Directors and which imposed upon the Government the duty of - "creating a properly articultated system of Education, from the primary school to the University."

It was a long document of a hundred paragraphs and deals with several questions of great importance regarding Education in India.

The year 1854 is a red-letter year in the history of Education in India during the British period and even today it is the spinal chord of the education system in India. Even after 150 years of the said Despatch and even after 70 years of Transfer of Power (1947), the Despatch controls the education in India. No body can confidently demand that India has evolved a National system of Education of its own. There was no dearth of Educationist in India.

We could follow Vidyasagar, Sri Aurobinda or Rabindranath or any of the like. But we followed some foreign or so called six great educators - Montesari etc.

The reason of this failure to evolve a National system is not difficult to find out. In 1947 Power was transferred to those Indians who in Blood and colour were Indians but in tastes, in opinions, in morals and in intellect were English (Remember, what Mr. Macaulay said and wrote in 1835). One who imitates, can not invent. So a National system of Education based on Indian thought, Philosophy and Discipline did not evolve, has not evolved, though it had a glorious history of Education of her own.

In the Mediaeval period of Indian history, we have seen slaves turned Monarchs. They were slaves in status but Monarchs in mentality. But the opposite happened in the history of modern India that Monarchs in status turned slaves in mentality.

The Despatch of Wood

The object : The Despatch relates that to afford a good education to the natives of India limited by the available resources, was sacred duty of the Britishers. India may derive vast moral and material blessings from her connexion with England.

"We have, moreover, always looked upon the encouragement of education peculiarly important, because calculated not only to produce a higher degree of intellectual fitness, but to raise the moral character of those who pertake of the advantages, and so to supply you with servants to whose probity you may with increased confidence commit offices of trust." (as said in the Despatch).

It is worthy to note that the Despatch does not condemn the Orientalists as Macaulay did. [It is, I believe, no exaggeration to say that all the historical information which has been collected from all the books written in the Sanskrit language is less valuable than what may be found in the most paltry abridgments used at prepatory schools in England. In every branch of physical or moral philosophy the relative position of the two nations is nearly the same - Macaulay in his Minutes 2nd February 1835. Quoted from R. C. Majumder P-83, Vol-10 HCIP].

The Despatch of Wood appreciates the advantages that spring from a study of the classical languages of India. It also says, "the success of many Oriental scholars in their praiseworthy endeavour to engraft upon Hindoo Philosophy the gems of sounder moral and more advanced science .... and the good effect which has thus been produced upon the learned classes of India who pay hereditary veneration to those ancient languages." The Despatch reads, "We must emphatically declare that the education which we desire to see extended in India is that which has for its object the diffusion of the improved arts, science, philosophy and literature of Europe, in short of European knowledge."

Medium of Instruction

As to the medium of Instruction to be adopted or followed, it says that in the, beginning the medium of instruction needs to be English as because, the vernacular languages have not so developed yet as to express the European knowledge. So it says - "In any general system of education, English language should be taught where there is a demand for it, but such instruction should always be combined with a careful attention to the study of the vernacular language of the district, with such general instruction as can be conveyed through that language and while the English language continues to be made use of as by far the most perfect medium for the education of those persons who have acquired a sufficient knowledge of it to receive general instruction through it, the vernacular language must be employed to teach the far large classes who are ignorant of, or imperfectly acquianted with English."

"The masters and professors who by themselves knowing English have full access to the latest improvement of knowledge of every kind, may impart to their countrymen, through the medium of their mother tongue. The vernacular literature of India will be gradually enriched by translation of European books."

"We look, therefore, to the English language and vernacular languages of India together as the Media for the diffusion of European knowledge, and it is our desire to see them cultivated together in all schools in India of a sufficiently high class to maintain a school master possessing the requisite qualification."

So the target is to diffuse European ideas and knowledge to all the people of India. To fulfill the target any medium that may appear useful be adopted.

Since Vernaculars are not sufficiently developed, English language is to be adopted.

Teachers and Professors having requisite qualification earned through English will later cater the needs of the masses through vernacular language.

The vernacular languages will develop by translating European books.

Before the significant step was taken as per Despatch of 19th July, 1854, in 1845, the council of Education in Calcutta, under the Presidentship of Charles Hay Cameron, drew up a plan for a University in Calcutta, but could not be implemented as the authorities in England did not agree.

The subject of education received serious consideration of the company's Government on the eve of the renewal of the Charter (1853). But Lord Dalhousie - the Governor General (1848-56) during whose period Wood's Despatch came, desired to establish a complete class of vernacular schools, to extend throughout the whole of India, with a view to convey instructions to masses of the people. He also proposed to place the higher education of the people, specially in Calcutta, on a footing adequate to the wants of the community and worthy of the Government of the Company. With such encouragement from the Governor General, the local Governments of Bengal, Bombay and the Punjab extended encouragement to vernacular educaiton.

The Wood's Despatch (19 July 1854) imposed upon the Government in India the duty of "Creating a properly articulated system of education, from the Primary school to the University."

This Educational Despatch of 1854, described as the Magnacarta of English Education of India," formed a land mark in the history of education in modern India.

[**Note** : 'Magnacarta' in Latin is 'Great Charter' in English. It is a document guaranteeing English Political liberties, drafted at Runnymede, a medow by the Thames and signed by King John in 1215, when Iltutmis or Altamas was ruling in Delhi Sultanate in India. The king signed the document or carta or charter under pressure from the rebellious barrons. Resentful of the King's high taxes and aware of his waning power, the barrons were encouraged by the archbishop of Canterbury Stephen Langton, to demand a solemn grant of their rights. Among the provisions of the Charter or Carta, there were clauses providing for a free church, reforming Law and Justice and controlling the behaviour of royal officials. It was reissued with alterations in 1216, 1217 and 1225. Though it reflects the feudal order rathar than democracy, The Magna Carta is traditionally regarded as the foundation of British Constitutionalism.]

The secretary of state for India confirmed the principles contained in the Despatch of Wood, in the Despatch of the 7th April 1859. Wood's Despatch commended to the special attention of the Govt. of India the improvement and for wider extension of education both English and Vernacular.

Recommendations

It recommended the following measures for attainment of the objects.

1. The Constitution of a separate department of administration for education.

2. The institution of Universities at the Presidency town.

3. Establishment of institution for the training of teachers.

4. The maintainance of the existing Government colleges and High Schools and the increase of their number when necessary.

5. The establishment of new Middle schools.

6. Increased attention to Vernacular schools, indigenous or others for elementary education.

7. The introduction of a system of grant-in-aid. The attention of the Govt. was specially directed to the importance of placing the means of acquiring useful and practical knowledge within reach of the great mass of people.

8. The English language is to be the medium of instruction in the higher branches and the vernacular in the lower.

9. English is to be taught where there is a demand for it, but it is not to be substituted for the vernacular language of the country.

10. The grant-in-Aid system is to be based on the principle of perfect neutrality of religion.

11. A comprehensive system of scholarship is to be instituted so as to connect lower schools to higher, and higher schools with colleges.

12. Female education is to receive the frank and cordial support of Government.

System at Work

In accordance with the recommendation of Wood's Despatch steps were soon taken to form an Education Department in each of the territorial divisions of India as then constituted and before the end of 1856, the new system was fairly at work. The formation of the separate Department continued over a period of 12 years from 1854-55 to 1866-67.

A Director of Public Instruction was appointed in each province, with a staff of Inspectors and Deputy or Assistant Inspectors. This organisation of inspection and control continued substantially unchanged in the subsequent periods with such addition and alteration as were required by the formation of new territorial divisions or by amalgamation of old ones.

The Education Department in each province came directly under the Provincial Government. In this arrangement, the Education Department became more or less officialised in character. Prof. H. H. Dodwell (the Cambridge History of India) has commented, that the men incharge of these Departments being primarily administrators, education tended to become a matter of administration routines. Probably he was right. The anomaly has continued more or less till today [Ref. Vol-10, HCIP].

A bit details on few issues

(a) Net work of Graded schools was an important issue in the Despatch. The Anglo-Vernacular and Vernacular schools were brought to same class. Below the High and Middle Schools, came the indigenous elementary schools, which the Directors proposed to encourage by suitable grant-in-aid. In this connection, the Directors drew the attention of the Govt. to the plan of Thomason in the North-West Province. (see Supra). As a connecting link between these various grades of schools, the system of scholarship was introduced. The scholarship is to be given to promising pupils to enable them to continue their studies at a higher school or college.

(b) **Grant-in-aid :** The Despatch suggests certain general considerations in the light of which provincial Govts. was expected to frame rules. Schools which (i) impart a good secular education, any religious instruction which they may impart being simply ignored, (ii) possess good local management, (iii) agree to submit to inspection by Govt. Officers and to abide by such other conditions as may be prescribed, and (iv) levy a fee, however small, from the pupils.

(c) **Training of Teachers :** To secure properly qualified teachers for schools, the Despatch refers to the plan which had been adopted in Great Britain which the Despatch considered applicable to India.

(d) **Employment :** The Despatch says, we believe that numerous vacancies of different kinds which have constantly to be filled up, may afford a great stinulous to education, where the other qualifications of candidates for appointments under Govt. are equal, a person who has received a good education, should be preferred to one who has not. A man who can read and write be preferred to one who cannot if he be equally capable in other respects.

Universities : Within a few years after 1854, the political atmosphere was greatly ruffled by the outbreak of 1857. Yet, the universities on the lines of principles laid down in the Despatch of 1854 were established in this very time. The university of London was to serve as the model for the Universities of India.

The University of Calcutta was incorporated by an Act passed on the 24 January 1857. The University of Bombay by an Act passed on the 18 July 1857 and University of Madras by an Act passed on 5 Sept 1857.

The affairs of the Universities were to be managed by a Chancellor and a Senate consisting of the Vice-Chancellor and Fellows who were mainly Govt. Servants. To start with, the Calcutta University Senate had thirty eight (38) members of whom six were Indians. In the Bombay University, there were twenty nine (29) members of whom five were Indians. In the Madras University - there were forty (40) members of whom there were three Indians. The Governor - General was the Chancellor of Calcutta, while Governors of Bombay and Madras were the Chancellors of Bombay and Madras Universities. The territorial jurisdiction of Bombay and Madras Universities was the respective Presidencies and Native States of Western and Southern India, while that of the Calcutta University extended over the whole of Northern India, Central Provinces and British Burma.

Each of the universities at first had four Faculties, namely those Arts cum Science, Law, Medicine and Engineering, to which was added a separate science Faculty subsequently. These Universities remained Affilating and Examining bodies. The teaching was imparted in Government, Missionary and Private colleges. Some High Schools had college classes and several colleges arranged classes in school courses. Most of the colleges of this time period provided education in Arts.

As regards Technical college, there were two colleges of Engineering, one started at Roorkee in the North Western Province in 1847 and the other was the Calcutta College of Engineering, opened at the Writers' Building, Calcutta in November 1856, amalgamated with the Presidency College in 1865, and then shifted to Shibpur (Howrah) Bengal in 1880. The Overseer's School of Poona was raised to the status of Poona College of Engineering and affiliated to the Bombay University in 1858. In Madras Presidency, the industrial school attached to the Gun Carriage Factory became Guindy College of Engineering and was affiliated to the Madras University in 1858.

Medical training was being imparted in the Medical Colleges in Calcutta, Bombay and Madras and in the Lahore Medical School.

Law Departments were attached to Arts Colleges and separate Law Colleges came into existence later.

Calcutta Medical College was the first Medical College in India. In 1833 Lord William Bentinck (1833-35) formed a committee to consider the possibility of establishing a Medical College in Calcutta. The Calcutta

Medical College was founded in 1835. It was housed in a building just behind the Hindu College (turned Presidency College) In April 1838, 20 beds were set for the patients and gradually it became a Medical College and Hospital - one of the best one in India.

About the Period 1854-1882 (1)

The period of time was of Peace and tranquility compared to Company period (upto 1857) which was a period of conquest and consolidation. The Afgan and Burma wars were fought in this period though, these had very little influence and impact on the main land of India. Excepting the out break of 1857, no broad issue threatend the existence of British government. The law and order position being under control, a sense of security was felt by people. It was silently admitted by the Hindus and the Muslims that they had to live under British domain.

A better attention was given to the issue of education and the missionaries with great Zeal converted Hindus to Christians along with their educational activities. Unless a good number of people know English, the Bible cannot be read by them.

For education, cesses were introduced. The urge for education encouraged local rich men to establish institutions and private enterprise in education increased.

There were less controversies and more achievements.

In Between 1854-1882 (2)

Education in india under the East India company may be taken to have ended with the Despatch of 1854. The outbreakof 1857 all over India, of the Sepoys under Mangal Pandey, dealt a blow. So before any further action to be taken on the terms of the Despatch, the Company ceased to be Political Power in 1858. The Government of India came directly under the British Crown.

Lord Canning was the Governor General (1856-58) when British Crown took over. After taking over Lord Canning was retained as Governor General from 1st November 1858 to 1862 March.

The Govt. of India appointed a commission with Sir W. W. Hunter as its President on the 3rd Feburary 1882 when Lord Ripon was the Governor General. This Commisson is known as Hunter Commission. It was an Education Commission.

Though the Company lost Political power almost after the Despatch of 1854, the recommendations, as were adopted, continued before any change or revision was made after the recommednations of Hunter Commission.

During this period there was an increase in the number of colleges and students in the three universities. At the first Entrance Examination of the three Universities out of 244 Candidates, 219 came out successful, Calcutta - 162, Bombay - 21, Madras - 36.

In 1882 out of 7429 candidates (Entrance Examiantion) 2778 came out successful.

Number of Colleges in 1857 were 27,

Number of Colleges in 1882 were 72.

During the first 14 years (1857-1871) F.A. - First Arts (later I.A. meaning intermediate Arts) passed 2666, B.A. passed 850, M.A. Passed 151.

During the next 11 years (1871-1882) F.A. - 5989 candidates passed, B.A. 2434 candidates passed, M.A. - 345 candidates passed.

Considering the growth of numerical strength of students, two other Universities were established - Lahore University and Allahabad University in 1887 i.e. after 1882, but the Preparations started much earlier.

Lahore University was backed by the Lt. Governor Sir Donald Macleod. Some influential persons started the Movement to establish an Oriental University, which besides promoting the study of Eastern Classics and Vernacular languages of the country, was also to encourage study of English language and Western Sciences. In 1869, The Govt. sanctioned Lahore University. A large number of institutions were affiliated to Lahore University. After a decade another University at Punjab was demanded. The Govt. of Lord Ripon accorded to the demand and the notifiation, dated the 14 Oct., 1882, formally constituted the Punjab Unviersity.

It was at the same time declared that 'every encouragement would be given to the study of the English language and literature, and in all subjects which cannot be taught completely by vernacular, the English language would be regarded as the medium of instruction and Examination."

In August 1867, the British Indian Association of the North-Western Province (U.P.), submitted a petition to the Governor General indicating of the defects of prevailing educational system and recommended the establishment of a University in which "the English Classics and the

Vernacular would be duly encouraged side by side with English Education." The Govt. of India did not agree to the demands. The Allahabad University (U.P.) was incorporated by an Act, dated 23 Septemebr, 1887, with a constitution closely resembling that of the university of Calcutta.

The Despatch of 28 April 1858 From Lord Ellenborough

This Despatch was written shortly after the outbreak of 1857. Ellenborough was the President of the Board of Control. This document, probably being 7 affected by the Revolution of 1857, proposed to reverse the recommendations of 1854 Despatch. It was thought that the Revolution of 1857 was the effect of 1854 Despatch. However, this Despatch was not given effect to.

The Despatch of 1859

The Despatch of 1859 is known was Stanley Despatch. This was the first Despatch after the change of Company to Crown. It was necessary to undo the Despatch of 1858 of Ellenborough.

Lord Stanley was the Secretary of State of India. He reviewed the whole position and confirmed the recommendations of 1854 Despatch.

Hunter Commission 1882

On 3rd February 1882, the Govt. of India appointed a commission with Sir W. W. Hunter as its President "to enquire particularly in to the manner in which effect had been given to the principles of the Despatch of 1854, and to suggest such measures as might seem desirable in order to further carrying out the policy laid down there in."

Though the chief object of enquiry of this commission [popularly known as Indian Education Commission] was to enquire chiefly the state of elementary Education and the means by which this can be extended everywhere, it collected plenty of useful information about collegiate education, its attendance, fees, discipline and later career of the students.

Lord Ripon was then the Governor General (1880-1884). He noticed that the Missions started an agitation to the effect that the educational system of India was not being conducted in accordance with Despatch of 1854. though this agitation was mainly in England, it had its effect upon the Christian Missioneries of India.

Again, during the Company period at the time of Renewal of Charter, roughly at 20 years interval, there was scope to review the situation since there was no company, no renewal of charter needed. But the review was needed. So Lord Ripon took the initiative to appoint this Hunter Commission, say, after 30 years.

It is held that the Despatch of 1854 and Report of Hunter Com were complementary to each other.

Recommedations of the Commission

The Hunter commission made many recommendations. Some of the important recommednations were.

(1) Withdrawal of State from direct management and support of the institutions for higher education should be by slow and cautious steps,

(2) provision should be made for ordinary financial aid and special grants to colleges,

(3) in order to encourage diversity of culture, both on the literary and on the physical side, there should be provision in all the larger colleges, Government and aided, for more than one of the alternative courses laid down by the Universities.

(4) an attempt to be made to prepare a moral text book based on the fundamental principles of natural religion, such as may be taught in all Government and non-Govt. Colleges.

(5) the Principal or one of the Professors in each Govt. and aided College to deliver to each of the college classes in every session, a series of lecture on the duties of a man and a citizen.

(6) Observance of certain general principles for college fees and exemption from this and attendance.

(7) framing new regulations for grant of scholarship.

As principle, the Hunter Commission observes "it is no less essential to the welfare of the community that provision should be made for the maintenance and development of colleges and schools of the higher class."

The Hunter Commission made 23 recommednations on the subjects of Secondary Educaiton. The more importants were :

1. "In the upper classes of High Schools there should be two divisions - one leading to Entrance Examination of the Universities, the other of a more practical character intending to fit youths for commercial or other non-literary persuits.

2. Provision should be made in respect of grant for the formation and maintenance of libraries in all High Schools and for furniture and apparatus of instruction,

3. New rules should be framed for charging fees from students and for grant of scholarships to them.

4. It be distinctly laid down that the relation of the state to secondary is different from relation to Primary Education, in that the means of primary education may be provided without regard to the local co-operation, while it is ordinarily expedient to provide the means of secondary education only where adequate local co-operation is forth coming, and that, therefore, in all ordinary cases, secondary schools for instruction in English be hereafter established by the State preferably on the footing of the system of grant-in-aids."

Hunter Commission on Education of Muslims

The Hunter Commission of 1882 reviewed the subject of Muslim education. It was then very much open that as a community the Muslims of India did not get interested in Modern or English education. Maktabs, mostly at the precints of the Mosques and several Madrashahs were continuing mainly Quranic education and they did not care to divert their attention to English education, though to the converted Indian Muslims Arabic was neither their vernacular nor mother tongue.

The Hunter Commission made important recommendations in their respect, some of which may be noted :

(1) "That the special encouragement of Mahamedan education be regarded as a legitimate charge on Local, on Municipal and on Provincial Funds."

(2) "That Higher English Education for Mahmedans, being the Kind of education in which that community needs special help, be liberally encouaged."

(3) "That where necessary a graduated system of special scholarships for Mahamedans be established" for award in schools and colleges.

(4) "That in all classes of schools maintained from public funds, a certain proportion of free studentships be expressly reserved for Mahamedan students", and

(5) "That Association for the promotion of Mahamedan education be recognised and encouraged.

With regard to the recommendations of the commission relating to this matter, the Govt. of India observed in a Resolution, dated 23rd October, 1884.

"The Governor General in Council has the subject of Mahamedan eduction at present order separate consideration, and will mainly say here that, in view of the backward condition into which in some provinces members of that community have fallen, he thinks it desirable to give them in some respects exceptional assistance."

Prior to this Resolution in July 1883, there was another Resolution of the Govt. which runs as follows :

1. "The Mohamedans cannot hope fairly to hold their own in respect of the better description of state appointments but by frankly placing themselves in line with the Hindus, and taking full advantage of the Govt. system of high and specially of English eduation."

2. A special section should be devoted to Mahamedan education in the Annual Reports of Public Instruction.

3. "For the attraction of Mahamedan to higher educaiton, a liberal provision of scholarships is essential and their wants must not be overlooked in the framing of any general scheme of scholarship for any province."

4. "Special Mohamedan Inspecting Officers to inspect and enquire into Mahamedan education generally, may be appointed in places where the Mahamedans are very backward."

[Ref. : History of English Edcuation in India by Syed Mahmud, P-175, Also in HCIP Vol-10, P-79-80].

Pan Islamic

In the meanwhile a momentons step had been taken by Syed Ahmed (1817-1898) an eminent Muslim. He founded Anglo-Oriental College at Aligharh, which later turned to Aligarh Muslim University. The foundation stone of this college was laid by Lord Lytton on 8th January 1877. He wanted it to be a university like Oxford and Cambridge. But ultimately it turned to be the Chief advocate of Two-Nation Theory.

However, The Pan-Islamic influence on the muslims of India was quite clear to the British rulers. Lord Hamilton, the Secretary of State, wrote to the Vice Roy Lord Elgin about this. [Aga Khan's India in Transition]. He wrote, "We have, however, a new element of intrigue and commotion introduced into India by the Pan-Islamic Council in Constantinople and the close connection which is being established between the sultan and the Indian Mahamedan [Ref. unpublished record of CRO, London Page-304, HCIP Vol-10].

This Pan-Islamic influence can be traced from the demands made by the Muslim leaders before the Hunter Commission. They demanded entirely separate arrangements for the Primary education of the Hindu and Muslim and insisted upon Urdu as a medium of instruction even in a province like Bengal where 90 percent of the Muslims were ignorant of that language, and their spoken language Bengali, had always been the medium of instruction. [Ref. : Adam's Report P-248].

This Pan-Islamism was also evidenced in the fact that the muslims did not take part in organisation led my Hindus - be it political or social. There was hardly any muslim in the political organisation, committee of Landholder society, Bengal-British India Society, British Indian Association, to name a few.

The position of the Muslims in educational centres was more than weak. When the Hunter Commission was declared in 1882, the picture was:

In college studies

　　Presidency of Bengal 106 Muslims

　　Presidency of Madras 30 Muslims

　　Presidency of Bombay 7 Muslims

　　N. W. Provinal (U.P.) 24 Muslims

　　Oudh 7 Muslims

　　Punjab 13 Muslims

In High School studies

　　In Bengal 3831, Madras - 177, Bombay - 118. N. W. Prince (including ME) 697, Punjab - 91.

　　By 1893 (from 1858), that is in 35 years, the number of Muslim graduates were 553 - C.U. - 290, Madras - 29, Bombay - 30, Punjab - 102, Allahabad University - 102.

　　[Ref. : B. B. Majumder, History of Political Thought, P-395].

　　In 1881-1888 the percentage of Mahamedan students of India receiving English education in College was 3.6 percent in proportion to the total number of students in such Institutions. Mahamedan students in High and English schools was 9.2, though the percentage of Mahamedans to the population of the different provinces was 22.8 [Ref. : Rechey's selection P-259. Quoted in HCIP Vol-10, P-80].

　　There was no appreciable progress of Mahamedan education during the next 35 years. From 1858 to 1893, only 546 Mohamedans succeeded in obtaining University Degrees in the various branches of learning as against no less than 15081 Hindus. the Proportion 1 to 28 [Syed Mahmud, P-186, History of English Education in India].

University degree 1858-1893, Muslims - 546, Hindus - 15081.

Here one idea must be made clear that by "Mahamedan educaiton" is meant education of the Muslim students. Education of Mahamedans and Muhamedan education do not connote same meaning.

Religious Education

Religious education was an issue during the period. Religious education was very dear to missionaries and their enterprise in the development of education demands. They always put forward the view :

(a) That the company's policy of religious neutrality was wrong. Since they are Christians they should spread Christanity by allowing the missionaries to convert Hindus to Christian and education should be the means.

(b) That as all true education is inseparable from religion, every school and college conducted by the company must impart instruction in religion i.e. Christanity

(c) That the missionaries should have full freedom, even if they receive Govt. aid, to teach the Bible compulsority to all students who may join their school.

The Brahmo Samaj, the Prarthana Samaj, the Arya Samaj demanded the same. They demanded that the school should combine instructions on the principles of Hindu religion with Western Science and literature.

The Muslims demanded that Quran must be taught. By 1882, such feelings and demands became very vocal.

The commission could not accept these demands on administrative and financial ground. It reiterated the Principle of neutrality in religion.

The Govt accepted the views of the commission and decided

(a) That, private schools may be permitted to impart such instruction as they choose,

(b) That, the Govt. would ignore such religious education

(c) That, the Govt. would pay grant-in-aid on the basis of secular education.

Private Enterprise during the period

Though the Govt's aim to spread education in India was very much appreciable, its miserliness was evident. So Govt. enterprise was never satisfactory. The demand for education and the Govt's failure due to miserliness to meet the demand, opened a big field to private Indian enterprise which was really very eager to spread English education mainly through vernacular medium.

As a result, we can record establishment and development of education in India through private enterprise.

Institutions	*Conducted by Private effort*	*1882 Conducted by Govt. effort*
Arts Collge	5	18
Secondary Schools	1341	757
Primary Schools	54662	1842
Profession College and Schools	10	18
Total	66618	2365

Primary Education

The subject of Primary Education figures prominently in the Report of the Hunter Commission. It made significant recommendations for the spread of Primary Education in the country.

(1) On the policy of education, the Govt. should adopt, he recommended vernacular as through this, one will fit for a position, life, taking it for granted that all of a Primary school will not go upto University education.

(2) That the Govt. should devote streunous effort for this in a larger scale than heretofore.

(3) That in selecting person to fill the lowest offices in the Govt. preference be always given to candidates who can read and write. [as Lord Hardinge said in his Resolution 11 Oct. 1844].

(4) That Primary education be extended to backward areas, inhabited mainly by aboriginal races.

(5) That the control of Primary Education should be made over to District Boards and Municipalities.

(6) That indigenous schools should be encouraged though, those were comparatively inferior. Attempt should be made to improve the teaching in such schools gradually and steadily.

(7) On the subject of the internal management of Primary Schools, the commission recommended that there should be no attempt to achieve uniformity of standard in all the provinces. The managers should be free to choose the text books, time of the schools and holidays to be observed. The instruction should be through mother-tongue and the schools should be inspected.

(8) The Commission recommended that a specific fund should be created for Primary education. Money meant for the rural areas should not be spent in Municipal areas, so the fund should be separated. The commisison said that local fund should be utilised for the primary educaiton and it was the duty of the Govt. to assist the local fund by a suitable system of Govt. aid.

(9) The main responsibility of providing Fund to Primary Educaiton rests with the local fund, the Provnicial Govt. plays a secondary by giving suitable Grant-in-aid to local fund.

(10) The ideal to be kept in view by the Provincial Govt. is the Govt. of India letter No. 63, dated 11 Feb. 1871 issued by the Home Dept. which lays down that Govt. Grant to local funds should be at the rate of half of the total assets or one third of the total expenditure.

The total expenditure on Primary education in 1882 was Rs. 16.77 lakhs from Provincial fund and Rs. 24.88 lakhs from local fund. Thus the total amounts to Forty One lakh sixty five thousand i.e. Rs. 41.65 lakhs.

As it is observed by J. P.Naik in his referred to book - Under the proposals of the Commission, expenditure on Primary Educaiton from Govt. Fund would have been Rs. 112 lakh (not 16.77 actual) and that the expenditure from local fund would have been Rs. 224 lakhs (not 24.88 lakhs - actual) and the total amount would have been 336 lakhs (not 41.65 lakhs actual). This account of Mr. Naik is based on the calculation that - Total poulation of British India 2000 lakhs, if 15 percent attend the school, taking 15 years of age as school going age, the number of pupils come to 300 lakhs and the expenditure on each student, if taken at the time of that period and if the total 15 percent of total population were of school-going age the cost would have been about 337 lakhs.

But at the time 1881-82, hardly 17 percent of the school going age attended school. Here is a statistic on attendance of pupils of school-going age.

Province	Percentage of Male Children	Percentage of Female Children
Madras	17.78	1.48
Bombay	24.96	1.85
Bengal	20.82	0.80
N.K. Province+Oudh	8.25	0.28
Punjab	12.11	0.72
Centra Province	10.49	0.44
Assam	14.61	0.46

(Contd...)

Coorg	22.44	2.86
Hyderabad Dists.	17.10	0.22
Total Average for India	16.28	0.84

In case of Madras and Bombaty the Native states are taken into account [Ref. : Naik Nurullah P-220].

Growth of College Education between 1857 - 1885

During the 28 years of this period from 1857 when 3 universities in three Presidencies - Calcutta, Bombay and Madras were established till the education commission of 1882, numbers of colleges increased and a tendency was found for higher education which was sure to give material advantage.

As already mentioned only 219 students passed the Entrance Examination in the first of such Examination. But after 25 years in 1882, out of 7429 who appeared in the Entrance Examination, 2778 passed and large number of them sought admission in colleges. The colleges could admit those who passed the Entrance / Matriculation Examination held by the universities. The colleges were to be affiliated to Universities and could impart instructions which were prescribed by the university.

In 1882 the number of colleges in India was 72, against 27 in 1856.

The point to be noted is, private enterprises for establishing college was very much eager, not that as business, but as love for higher education of Indian youths.

Province	*No. of Colleges in 1856*	*No. of Colleges in 1882*
Bengal	15	27
Bombay	3	6
N. w. Province (I.P.)	5	11
Madras	4	25
Punjab	-	2
Central Province	-	1
Total	27	72

Recommendations of the Commission 1882

The Govt. Resolution appointing the commission almost precluded the commission to study and survey in this field as the universities were being run by separate bodies comprising representatives of classes and the result of their improvement might be collected from their reports.

But within 20 years from 1882 i.e. in between 1882 and 1902, there was a noticeable growth of colleges and pupils attending those. But those were mainly Arts colleges which taught literature, history etc. and had very rare scope of learning science subjects.

During this twenty years there was a rise in professional colleges. And number of interested students in Law and Medicine was promising. Even engineering college attracted roughly 1000 pupils.

Below is the table

	No. of Institution	No. of Pupils
(1) Arts College		
English	140	17048
Oriental	5	503
(2) Professional College		
(a) Law	30	2767
(b) Medicine	4	1466
(c) Engineering	4	865
(d) Teaching	5	190
(e) Agriculture	3	70
Total	191	22909

University

Three universities in three Presidencies - Calcutta, Bombay and Madras were established with a view to ascertaining, by means of examination, the persons who have acquired proficiency in different branches of learning, and rewarding them by Academic Degrees, as evidence of their respective attainments.

After 1857, Punjab University was founded and it has also been noted that in 1887, Allahabad University came into being.

In 1860 Indian Universities (Degree) Act was passed empowering the Universities to confer such Diplomas or Degrees or Licences as might be approved by the bye-laws or regulations.

In 1884, the Indian Universities (Honorary Degrees) Act was passed which empowered the three Universities of Calcutta, Bombay and Madras to confer the Honorary Degree of L.L.D.

Secondary Education 1857-1882

Soon after the receipt of Despatch of 1854, Department of Public Instruction, created by the Despatch, took part in rapid expansion of Secondary Schools. On the one hand, the people were ready to get English education and the larger grants placed under the disposal of D.P.I., influenced the growth.

Between 1857 to 1874, there was a large increase in the number of secondary schools directly conducted by the Govt. The number of Govt. secondary schools in 1882, was 1363 with 46,605 pupils (Ref. Indian Education Table). But in 1855, the number of schools was 169 with 18335 pupils. So in 25 years (1857 to 1882) number of Govt. schools increased by 1194 and no of students by 28270.

Every Provincial Govt. framed the rules of grant-in-aid as was suggested by the Despatch of 1854.

Private enterprises also took part. Formerly, the missioneries were, so to say, pioneers, but now Indian effort defeated the missionaries.

The Hunter Commission of 1882, was of the view that the Govt.'s responsibility to primary education was more than its responsibility to secondary education.

So it recommended that the main agency of expanding secondary education should be private enterprise. But in each distict there must be govt. school. But govt. secondary schools may be instituted in a place where the private enterprise is not advanced or wealthy enough to run a school with a grant-in-aid.

So by 1901, number of secondary schools increased and Indian private enterprise was evident.

	1882	1902
1. Total No. of Secondary School	3916	5124
2. Total No. of Pupils	214077	590129
[Commissions Report P-193]		

It is to be remembered that these statistics of secondary education have certain defects. The term secondary education is not interpreted in the same sense in all provinces. [Ref. : Naik, P-197].

Teacher's Training Institution

As to the question whether Training was necessary for teachers, the Hunter Commission was not very much expressive. It recommended :

(1) That an examination in the Principles and Practice of teaching be instituted, success in which should thereafter be a condition of permanent employment as a teacher in any secondary school, Government or aided.

(2) That graduates wishing to attend a course of instruction in a normal school in the principles and practice of teaching be required to undergo a shorter course of training than others.

The progress in training secondary teachers was very low in the twenty years following the Report of this Commission in 1882.

In 1901-1902 (20 years after 1882) there were only six training colleges - Saidapet, Rajamahendry, Kurseong, Allahabad, Lahore and Jabbalpur. Besides this six colleges, every province in India had organised a certificate examination for teachers. Madras university had instituted the L. T. Degree. By 1902 Bombay was the only major province that had not organised a training institution for secondary teachers.

Vocational Education

The Despatch of 1854, advocated Vocational Training, though this particular term was not used. The Despatch said that instructions in secondary schools should be practically useful to people of India in their different spheres of life and proposed new schools should provide more opportunities than now exist for the acquisition of such an improved education as will make those who possess it, a more useful member of the society in every condition of life."

But the commisison of 1882, neglected this salutary advice. In 1882 it was only in the province of Bombay that some provision was made for vocational education by grant of few scholarships of Rs. 4.00 per month to children of agriculturists in order to encourage them to attend model farms connected with High schools, for instruction in practical agriculture.

Lord Curzon : Education 1900-1921

Lord Curzon was the Governor General of India from 1899-1905./ The period of administration was marked by some striking changes in the sphere of education as in the other branches, with all his great intellectual powers, infinite capacity to work, strong sense of duty, intense desire to serve the people of India and magnificients in almost all fields of adminitration. Curzon committed the blunder of wounding the educated intelligentsia beyond hope of reconciliation. And he attempted to partition Bengal. It is no wonder that Curzon was not only the ablest but also the most hated Viceroy that ever came to India.

Education in India as Curzon saw it

Though there is a narrative of expansion of education, education had been muddling for years. In Primary education, four out of every five Indian villages were found to be without a school, three of every four Indian boys grew up without education and only one Indian girl in every forty (40), attended any kind of schools. Curzon realised (i) that primary education was languishing nearly everywhere for want of funds. (ii) secondary schools really sapped the brain power as well as the physical strength of rising generation. (iii) the position of the higher education seemed to him still worse. (iv) the standard of teaching and learning were equally low. [Raligh as referred to in HCIP, Vol-10, P-57].

Curzon saw in his mind's eye the students driven like sheep from lecture room to lecture room and from examination to examination. On the whole, Curzon drew a very depressing picture of the state of education in his time, the text books were badly chosen, degrees were pursued for their commercial value, the senates of the universities were over swollen with members of unacademic nature and the syndicates were devoid of statutory powers.

Only 2.5 percent of the female population of school going age attended schools. there was too Slavish an imitation of the European model. The members of the Indian Univesities admitted that teaching had been made subsidiary to examination. Instead of thinking only of the mental and moral development, teachers were preoccupied with percentages, passes and tabulated results.

To Curzon the whole system was at fault and reminded him of the days of Hebrew judges when there was no King in Israel. [Raleigh : as quoted in Vol-10, HCIP, P-56].

The above facts of education fired him with a burning zeal to take up the subject of educational reforms. He sought to reorganise the educational system and to effectively control the educational institutions of the country.

After a preliminary survey the Vice Roy summoned in September 1901, a conference of Chief Education officers at Simla "to consider the system of education in India."

On 27the January 1902, his Govt. appointed a Universities Commission "to enquire into the conditions and prospects of the Indian Universities, to report upon proposals which might improve their constitution and working, and to recommend such measures as might tend to elevate the standard of University teaching and to promote the advancement of Learning."

[Ref. : Lovat Fraser - as quoted in P-56, Vol-10 of HCIP].

Raleigh Commission 1902

The commission was presided over By Mr. Thomas Raleigh, Legal member of the Vice-Roy's Executive Council. The members included Mr.

Syed Hussain Bilgrami, Director of Public Instruction, to the Nizam's dominions, Mr. Justice Gurudas Banerjee, a judge of the Calcutta High Court. (He was taken after the protest of the Hindu).

The Commission visited all the Universities and a number of affiliated colleges during its three months tour and submitted its Report in June 1902.

The Principal recommendations were :

(1) The legal power of the older Universities should be enlarged so that all the Universities may be recognised as Teaching Bodies, but the local limit of each University should be more accurately defined and steps taken to remove from the Calcutta university the affiliated colleges in the Central Provinces, United Provinces etc.

(2) The Senate, the Syndicate and the Faculties have to be re-organised and make more representative than before.

(3) More stringent conditions were to be imposed for the recognition of affitiated institutions, and there should be insistence on the better equipment of affiliated colleges and supervision of the discipline of students and their places of residence.

(4) There should be a properly constituted Governing Body for each college.

(5) Suggestions were made for important changes in the courses of study and methods of Examination.

(6) That a minimum rate of college fees should be fixed.

(7) That second grade colleges (teaching only to the I. A. Standard) should be gradually abolished.

(8) That the system of teaching Law by law classes attached to Arts Colleges should be modified.

It was of utmost importance to Curzon that the quality of educaiton must be improved. His view was by this time education had not materially advanced in quality but had definitely deteroriated in quality. On the basis of this analysis. Curzon started a drive for qualitative reform.

The Govt. expressed general approval of the commission's recommednations except the last three (6.7.8), on which further enquiries were to be made before coming to a final decision. The Report and the Govt's comments were published in October 1902.

Opposition

Indians of all classes objected.

The objections were on the grounds that - (1) Syndicate and Senate would be officialised. (2) the universities would practically be Govt. Department. A big public meeting was held in Calcutta Town Hall opposing the recommendations. Phiroj Shah Mehata took the leading part. Indian National Congress in its Ahmedabad Session in 1902, passed a resolution to the effect that if the recommendations were accepted, the policy of education persued in the last 50 years would be reversed and the spread of education would be checked. The Congress strongly objected to the last three recommendations.

Indian University Act - 1904

Lord Curzon did not pay much heed to the objections raised by the National Congress or any else.

The Indian Universities Act was passed on 21 March 1904. It based mainly on the recommendations of the Raleigh Commission.

The Act fixed that Ordinary Fellows should not be less than fifty and more than hundred for the three Older Universities (Calcutta, Bombay, Madras), for the other two the minimum was forty and maximum was seventy five. These numbers were excluding the Chancellor, the Vice-Chancellor, the Rector of the Calcutta University. The tenure for the Ordinary members was fixed of five years.

The Syndicate of the universities was to consist of the Vice-Chancellor, the Director of Public Instruction and not less than Seven and not more than fifteen fellows elected by the Senate or by the Faculties in such manner as may be provided by regulations. Adequate representation of the University teachers was to be provided. The University was to have more powers of supervision over the affiliated colleges and conditions for the affiliation of new colleges. All affiliation or disqualification of colleges were to be settled by the Govt., the appointment of Professors, Readers and Lecturers were subject to approval of the Govt. Many other details of the university policy were subject to Govt. supervision practically nothing was to be done without the approval of the Govt.

An important feature of the Act was provision by the Universities for the "instruction of students, with power to appoint university professors and lecturers, to hold and manage educational endowments, to erect, equip and maintain university laboratories and endowments, to make regulations to the residence and conduct of students and "to do all acts which tend to the promotion of study and Research." The Calcutta University under the guidance of its most distinguished Vice-Chancellor Sir Ashutosh Mukherjee started post graduate teaching in the university within a few years. The Act was severely critised by Indian Public. The Indian National Congress in its session in Madras in 1903 entered a protest against the general principles of the Bill by saying that if the Bill was enacted would destroy the independence of the Universities. The Congress also made several suggestions for modifying the Bill.

Lord Curzon paid no heed to anything or anybody. He defended the Bill and defended the Act. He believed that this Act had put educaiton on a Sounder basis.

The Public criticism was not duly tempered by the consideration of actual state of things.

The Senate of Calcutta, Madras and Bombay University had 180, 197 and 310 Senate Members who were called 'Fellows'. The Fellowship in those days was regarded as an honour as Justice of Peace and academic accomplishments were hardly considered. So some of the Fellows could hardly sign their names. [Ref. : Lovat Fraser in his Book]. Again it was found that even in those days some institutions were run more as profitable business than as an academic institutions.

The enactment of 1904 tightened the control of Govt. over higher education.

It is true that all the universities had not been transformed as was envisaged by Lord Curzon, but the example of Calcutta University during the first twenty years showed what great improvements were possible within the framwork of the Act of 1904.

Mr. Chairley, a Frenchman and an Unprejudiced Commentator observed that the Act of 1904 "Constitutes the real charter of present day education in India." [Ref. Lovat Fraser as quoted in Vol-10, HCIP P-60].

Lord Curzon reversed the doctrine of State withdrawal in the field of education. He held that it was the duty of the Govt. to maintain a few institutions of every type as models to private enterprise. The Inspection system was strengthened and a policy of inspection of Private School was adopted.

Between 1854 and 1902, the principal object was expansion and not improvement. This outlook was changed by Lord Curzon.

N.B. : Figures of 1902 include figures for Burma and Some Indian states, while the figures of 1921-22 are for British India only exclusive of Burma. [quoted from J. P. Naik & Nurullah's Book P-243].

Progress of Education 1902 to 1922

Type of Institutions	No. of Institutions		No. of Students	
	1901-02	1921-22	1902	1922
Arts College	145	165	17651	45418
Professional College	46	64	5338	13662
Secondary Schools	5493	7530	622768	1106803
Primary Schools	97854	155017	3204336	6109752
Special Schools	1084	3344	36380	120925
Total	104627	3886493	7596560	7396560
Unrecognised	43081	16322	635407	422105
Total	147708	182452	4521900	7818725

No. of Universities 5 10 Figures not available

Reforms in Collegiate Education

As Lord Curzon emphasised on quality rather than quantity, he wanted that colleges should have better libraries, better laboratories and hostels for the students. Therefore he enhanced the grants for colleges. He approved an additional grant of Rs. 13.5 lakhs for colleges.

Secondary Education

There was a great expansion of Secondary Schools between the period 1882 to 1902. Both in college and school education private enterprise took the largest part in the field. Of course, all the institutions did not run satisfactorily. Lord Curzon adopted the same policy, as he had taken in cases of collegiate education.

The new policy of Curzon was that the Govt. would control all types of aided and unaided secondary schools. The Govt. Resolution of 1904 explained the policy.

The system of Govt. Recognition of Schools was introduced. The Recognition depended on some conditions as : whether -

(1) There is a necessity of such school

(2) Education provided is sound

(3) Its financial stability is assured

(4) The Managing Body, if any, is properly constituted

(5) The subjects are taught in proper standard

(6) Due provision has been made for instruction, health, recreation and discipline

(7) Teachers are suitable as regards character, number and qualification.

(8) Fees to be paid by pupils are justified.

Such Recognised schools only are fit to get grant-in-aid

Point to be noted that as in Sec-21 of the University Act Conditions were laid down for affiliation to a college, almost same are the provisions for Recognition of a secondary school.

On Recognition depended not only fitness of grant, but mainly the permission to sit for the Matriculation Examination.

To enrich the quality of educaiton (a) Large sums were sanctioned to Govt. Schools that could serve as a model to private schools. (b) Large fund was also sanctioned to private schools so as to enable them to come to the standard of Govt. schools. (c) The necessity of Training to Teachers was emphasised. (d) A change was made in the curriculum. (e) It was recommended that mother tongue should be used as medium of instruction upto middle stage. An attempt should be made so that the pupil may have a better mastery in English which will be the medium of instruction in the next stage of secondary schools. (f) The inspection of schools was given much importance.

Curzon on Primary Education

In the field of Primary Education Curzon emphasised expansion first and improvement second. He held that the need for Primary education was greater than any time in the past. For the expansion of Primary Education which he thought, did not expand for want of funds, he sanctioned the povision of non-recurring grant. This liberal policy had its effect.

	1881-82	*1902*	*1912*
No. of Primary School	82916	93604	118262
No. of Pupils there	2001541	307667	4805736

[The statistic is from J. P. Naik's book P-263].

N.B. : The year 1911-12 is taken because the full effect of Curzon's policy was noticeable. Figures include some Indian states, excluded Burma.

Curriculum : Curzon was not in favour of simplifying the curriculum as was recommended by Indian Education Commission. He desired an enrichment of the curriculum.

Curzon emphasised establishment of Training colleges for the training of teachers of the Primary Schools. He fixed 2 years for training of teachers.

369

Other Educational Reforms of Curzon

1. Schools of Art - There was a controversy that whether schools of art should continue or clsoed as those have failed in their primary object of promoting Indian Art.

Curzon directed that the schools should be continued with certain modifications in their objects, method and organisation.

2. Agricultural Education : Agricultural Education was hardly known to India though it is an exclusively agriculture dependent country. Curzon caused to organise an Agriculture Department. He also created a central Research Institute at Puna with the object of giving training in agriculture. He also laid down that every important province of India must have its own Agricultural College. He directed that agricultural eduation among the people may be broadcasted and Agriculture as a subject be introduced in Secondary Schools.

3. Foreign Scholarship : He instituted scholarship for sendning Indian students for technological studies abroad.

4. Moral Education : Indian Education Commission, 1882 - Prescribed that for this purpose moral Primer of text books should be introduced. The problem was how this could be done in a secular system of education. The view of Curzon on this topic is described in his Resolution on Education Policy (1904) which reads : para 25.

25. "In Govt. Institutions the instruction is, and must continue to be exclusively secular. In such cases the remedy for the evil tendencies noticed above is to be sought, not so much in any formal methods of teaching conducted by means of moral text books or primers of personal ethics, as in the influence of carefully selected and trainied teachers, the maintainance of a high standard of discipline, the institution of well managed hostels, the proper selection of text books, such as biographies, which teach by example and above all in the association of teachers and pupils in the common interests of daily life."

5. Creation of Archeology Department : He was the person who caused to pass the Ancient Monument Preservation Act of 1904.

6. Appointment of Director General of Education : One of the greatest contribution of Curzon was to create the post of a Director General of Education for India. The Despatch of 1854, created Department of Education in the Provinces. The credit of creating a post in an all India basis was Curzon's idea. The first man who was appointed in this post was H. W. Orange.

The Period from Curzon to Chelmsford 1905-1921

Lord Curzon was succeeded by Lord Minto II (1905-1910), then came Lord Hardinge II (1910-1916) and he was succeeded by Lord Chelmsford (1915-1921) as Governor General of India.

During this period Four very important factors caused a rapid development in the field of Education. These are :

(1) Resolution on Education Policy adopted by the Government.

(2) Sadler Commission or The Calcutta University Commission (1917-1919).

(3) Govt. of India Act 1919

(4) First World war (1913-1919).

The proposal of partition of Bengal made Lord Curzon very unpopular though his steps on Education in India were very significant. Moreover, he had little respect for Indians. But his policy on Educaiton was continued by the successive Governor Generals with little Changes.

Upto 1910 - the subject of Education was under the Administrative control of the home Department. Now the Govt. showed their sense of the greater importance of Education by creating a new Department of education under a separate member of the Vice-Roy's Council. At the Durbar of 1911-12 the Govt. announced an annual grant from imperial funds of 50 lakhs of Rupees for Popular education.

The next important land mark in the history of higher education is the resolution of the Govt. of India on Educational policy issued in 1913. This observed :

At present there are only five Indian universities for 185 arts and professional colleges in British India besides several institutions in Native states. The day is probably far distant when India will be able to dispense altogether with the affiliating University. But it is necessary to restrict the area over which affiliated universities have control by securing, in the first instance, a separate university for each of the leading provinces in India, and secondly, to create new local teaching and residential universities within each of the provinces in harmony with the best modern opinion as to the right road to educational efficiency."

The first Universities of this type were to be located at Dacca, Benaras and Aligarh. The Govt. further urged the necessity of multiplying and improving facilities for the training of teachers for Primary and Secondary schools, reaffirmed the policy of relying mainly on Private efforts in

Secondary Education with the assistance of a more elastic system of grant-in-aid.

Sadler Commission

In 1917, Government appointed the Calcutta university Commission, better known as Sadler Commission, as the Chairman of the Commission was Dr. M. E. Sadler, the Vice-Chancellor of the university of Leeds. The other members of the Com. were Sir Ashutosh Mukherjee, Dr. Gregory, Mr. Philip Hartog, Professor Ramsay Muir. The Commission submitted a voluminous report in 1919 dealing with practically, every problem of secondary and university education. It endorsed the policy laid down in the Govt. Resolution on Education 1913. Although the Commission dealt with Calcutta University only, the problems it had dealt with are more or less common to the other Universities.

Before going to details, we should note the following four recommendations :

(1) The Intermediate classes of the University were to be transferred to Secondary Institutions, and the stage of admission to University should be that of the present Intermediate examination.

(2) Secondary and Intermediate Education was to be controlled by a Board of Secondary Education and not by the University.

(3) The Govt. of India should cease to have any special relationship to the university of Calcutta and the Govt. of Bengal should take its place.

(4) The duration of the Degree Course should be three years after the Intermediate stage. The provisions being applied immediately in regard to Honours courses and soon after to Pass courses.

This was readily accepted by the Government in view of the constitutional changes introduced by the Government of India Act, 1919.

Two important consequences followed. A number of new Universities of affiliated type as well as a number of a new type of unitary, residential and teaching universities were established. This policy was followed even after the constitutional changes of 1919 and 1935 by which education was placed in change of Indian Ministers. The Indian states also adopted the same policy. Seven new Universities came into existence.

(1) Affiliating Universities : (a) Agra (1927), Utkal (1943).

(2) Affilaiting and Teaching : (a) Patna (1917), (b) Rangoon (1926), (c) Nagpur (1923), (d) Andhra (1926), (c) Saugor (1946).

(3) Teaching : (a) Lucknow (1920), (b) Dacca (1921), (c) Delhi (1922), (d) Allahabad (1927), (e) Annamalai (1929), (f) Osmania (1918).

As a result, expansion of education was like this in 1941-42 :

Number of students :

(1) Intermediate   - 85072 (Male - 77313, Female - 7759)
(2) Under Graduate   - 32972 in Arts (Male 28950, Female - 4022)
(3) Under Graudate   - 10770 in Science (Male - 10039, Female - 731)
(4) Post Graduate   - 6085 in Arts (Male - 5437, Female - 648)
(5) Post Graduate   - 1347 in Science (Male - 1266, Female - 81).

In Indian states also there was an impetus :

Intermediate   - 8571 (Male - 7654, Female - 917)
Under Graduates in Arts   - 1364 (Male - 1226, Female - 138)
Under Graduates in Science   - 1350 (Male - 1178, Female - 172)
Post Graduates in Arts   - 90 (Male - 76, Female - 14)
Post Graduates in Science   - 57 (Male - 55, Female - 2)

The number of students in Law   - 7555 (Male - 7438, Female - 117), in Medicine - 6531 (Male - 5788, Female - 743) in Engineering - 2278 (Male - 2277, Female - 1).

[Souce - Report 1944 (P-89) as quoted by R. C. Mazumder in Vol-XI, P-882, HCIP].

The number of Research students in Arts - 336 (305+31), in Science - 164 (152+12).

Five Universities not included in the above list, deserve special notice. Those are:

(1) Benaras Hindu University (1916), (2) Aligarh Muslim University (1920), (3) Serampore college (1818), (4) Viswabharati (1922), (5) Sreemathi Nathibhai Damodher Thackersey Indian Women University, Bombay.

Some other institutions belonging to the type of Universities are not included in the above list.

Swadeshi Education

The Swadeshi movement in Bengal and growth of national sentiments led to the foundation of the National Council of Education in Bengal.

As a part of National Sentiment the Nationlists resolved to boycott Calcutta University which they described as Golam-khana (House of manufacturing slaves). At a conference attended by a very large number of eminent men of Bengal in different walks of life held on 10 November 1905 (the year of declaration of partition of Bengal, by Lord Curzon), it was decided to establish at once a National Council of Education in order to organise a system of education - literary, scientific and Technical - on National lines and under National Control. Raja Subodh Chandra Mallick had promised One lakh of rupees, Brajendra Kishore Roy Chowdhury - a Zaminder of Maymansing had promised five lakhs of rupees (to be paid in cash or in property yielding Rs. 20,000.00 per year), third gentleman, whose name was not disclosed, offered two lakhs in cash and a large house with compound, while a fourth donor was likely to make an endowment of Rs. 30,000.00 a year [I am not sure whether the mentioned gentlemen were present in the meeting, but the organisers announed these.]

The number of Naitonal Schools also grew apace, and in 1908, there wer 25 secondary schools and about 300 Primary Schools.

The Gurukul Kangra of Hardwar was also independent of the system of education controlled by the Govt. as was the National Council of Education. The Gurukul Kangra of Hardwar was started in 1902 by Swami Sraddhananda, with the same object which was professed by the Beneras Hindu University as its aim, but carried it out more faithfully and with greater sincerity. But its ideal to revive the old Hindu culture by imparting educaiton of a special type and in an artificially created environment suitable for it, has not evoked much enthusiasm outside a very limited circle.

The college of Enginering and Technology founded about 1921, by the National Council of Educaiton, continued its useful career as a Technological Institution which was developed in to a full-fledged University at Jadavpur, then a suberb of Calcutta, after the achievement of Independence. The Arts section and the affiliated schools affiliated to the National Council languished soon.

Research Institutes : There were many institutions for advanced studies and research of university standard which formed a class by themselves. Those cannot be regarded as Universities or ordinary colleges affiliated to the University. The followings deserve special mention.

1. **Indian Institute of Science, Bangalore :** The Institute began work in July 1911 and its laboratories provided facilities for post-graduate work in Physics, General Chemistry, Organic Chemisty, Bio Chemistry and Electrical Technology. This should be

mentioned that it was the dream of J. N. Tata and after his demise his two sons - Dorabji Tata and Ratanji Tata gave effect to their father's wishes. This institution was supported by the Govt. of India and the Maharaja of Mysore.

2. **Bose Research Institute** : Calcutta. This institution was founded by Acharya Sir Jagadish Chandra Bose on 30 November, 1917. Here Sir J. C. Bose carried on his fundamental investigations on plants. He also wanted to train up a band of able and devoted workers who would continue this line of work after him. At the time of his passing away in November 1937, facilities for investigation in the following subjects were provided :

   (a) Plant physiology and Genetics

   (b) Bio and Agricultural Chemistry

   (c) Zoology and Animal Physiology

   (d) Anthropology

   (e) Theoretical and Experimental Physics

3. **Forest Research Institute and College** : Dehradun. The first Forest Research Institute was opened in 1914 on the Chandbag Estate, Dehradun. In 1929 it was shifted to Kaulagarh Estate, a few miles away of Dehradun.

4. **The Harcourt Butler** : Technological Institute, Kanpur, founded in 1921. It was intended to be an Institute of technological research, for promoting industrial development.

5. **The Imperial Agricultural Research Institute, New Delhi** : An Americam named Mr. Henry Phipps donated 1 30,000.00. From this fund Pasteur Institute at Coonoor, South India, was founded and the balance was for an Institute for experimental cultivation founded at Pusa under the Control of the Central Govt. A farm of 830 acres was attached for this purpose.

   In the earth quake of January 1934, Phipps Laboratory was destroyed. The Institute has been rebuilt in a new site at Delhi.

6. **Indian school of Mines, Dhanbad** : This was opened by this Govt. of India in 1926 to provide high grade instruction in Mining Engineering and in Geology.

7. **Thomason College of Civil Engineering, Roorki** : It was opened in 1847 and has been converted to a University after independence.

For Oriental Learning

1. **Bhandarkar Oriental Research Institutes Poona :** It was inaugurated in July 1917, to commemorate the 80th birthday of great Oriental Scholar Sir Ramkrishna Gopal Bhandarkar. The Govt. of Bombay transferred to this Institute the Manuscript Library, formerly at the Deccan College, Poona and also entrusted it with the publication of the Bombay Sanskrit and Prakrit series. Its monumental work is the publication of a critical edition of the Mahabharata. It is now recognised as an international centre of Oriental research.

2. **Indian Institute of philosophy Amalner, East Khandesh :** This institute of research in Philosophy was founded in 1916, by Seth Motilal Maneekchand of Amalner and his friend Seth Ballavdas. The object is to encourage persons who have already studied Western Philosopghy to get a first hand acquiantance with Indian Thought in general and with Advaitic Philosophy of Sankaracharya, in particular.

Inter University Board

With the increase of the number of Universities the Govt. of India felt the need of an agency to coordinate the works of the Universities (15) of that time. In May 1924, at Simla a conference was held. Indian Universities Conference was the name of this meeting. A resolution was unanimously passed recommending the establishment of Inter University Organisation.

The functions assigned to it were :

(i)   To act as an Inter-University Organisation and Bureau of Information.

(ii) To facilitate an exchange of Professors

(iii) To serve as an authorised Channel of Communication and facilitate Coordination of University works.

(iv) To appoint or recommend where necessary a common representative of India at an Imperial or Internaitonal Conference on Higher Education.

(v)   To assist Indian Universities in obtaining recognition for their degrees, diplomas and examination in other Universities.

It was suggested that expenses would be equally shared by the fifteen Universities then in existence. But only twelve universities agreed to join the Board and made preliminary contribution.

In 1926 the fist conference was held at Delhi. Since then in addition to annual meeting, other meetings were held.

The University Education Commission (1948-49) known as Radhakrishnan Commission made an observation on the Inter University Board.

"The Board has acted as an advisory body but its influence has not been as potent as it might have been. The universities have not always inclined to follow the advice given by the collective body of the vice-chancellors. The Board has, however, acted as a forum for discussion of University problems."

[Ref. : The report fo the Com. P-29].

Central Advisory Board of Education (CABE)

Another important body composed of experts on educaiton was the Central Advisory Board of Education India, constituted in 1920-21. It was presided over by the Education Member of the Governor General's Executive Council. Its members were also from Govt. of India, Provincial Govts., Inter-University Board and such other important ones. It held periodical meeting to discuss educational problems and advise the Govt. on them.

Research

The most remarkable progress in eduation during the period was the advanced study and research. Diverse branches of knwoledge both in arts and science made quantitative expansion and the Research aspect strengthened the qualitative expansion.

Valuable research work was undoubtedly conducted by a large number of individuals on their own initiative in the 19th Century both in Arts and Sciences. Cunningham Fleet, Kielhorn, Buhler, R. G. Bhandarkar, Bhagwanlal Indraji, Rajendralal Mitra, Haraprasad Sastri and many others in the field of Indological studies, Sir J. C. Bose and Sir P. C. Roy in sciences were pioneers of research works in India. But there was no organised attempt to train students in methods of research at any University before 1904. The University Act of 1904 laid down that teaching and research were the proper functions of the Universities in addition to holding examinations.

The Act of 1904 was strongly condemned by the Indian public. Only one man realised the potentialities of this Act and he was Sir Ashutosh Mukherjee. So when the post of Vice-Chancellor of Calcutta University was offered to him by Lord Minto II, ssuccessor of Lord Curzon, he readily accepted it in order to reconstitute the University in accordance with the Act of 1904.

Calcutta University and Sir Ashutosh

He served as Vice-Chancellor from 1906 to 1914 and again from 1921-1923. Even in the intervening period he was the defacto Vice-Chancellor. Through out the long 17 years Sir Ashutosh devoted his time, energy and resourcefulness in transforming the Calcutta University into the most important teaching Universitgy and the greatest Centre of research in India. Though the same Act was in operation in the other four Bombay, Madras, Allahabad and Lahore Universities, progress in them came later. The Calcutta University was gradually transformed from an examining body to a centre of reserch.

This was accomplished in three stages during 1906-1914. In the first stage instructions were given to M. A. students by University lecturers, most of whom were college lecturers giving only part-time service. Eminent scholars were appointed as Readers in order that associaiton with them might stimulate the advanced students. In the second stage distinguished scholars were appointed whole time professors. In the third stage, there was a regualr staff of whole time professors, Readers and lecturers, though the part-time service of eminent professors of colleges were not altogether dispensed with.

Huge sum of money was required for all these and the Govt. was not so responsive. But Sir Ashutosh was undomitable. He induced wealthy persons to make rich endowments to the University. Taraknath Palit, Rash behary Ghosh made substantial donations and endowments to the University. Many others followed the suit. Ashotosh could realise his dream of the Calcutta University inspite of the non-co-operative attitude of the Govt. But from Lord Hardinge he secured special endowments for four professorship. He adopted various means to promote research in the University.

Not only the University of Calcutta but the world of science should ever remain greatful to Sir Ashutosh for this great change over.

One great aspect of Sir Ashutosh is seldom appreciated even by Indians. That was his spirit of Indian Nationalism. He was the first to make provision for the study and research in Ancient Indian History and Culture, the history of the Sikhs, the Rajputs and the Marathas. He made Bengali and other major languages in India and their literature full fledged subject of study for the M. A.Examination. He thus laid the foundation of nationalism and national integration when nobody dreamt of utilising the Univesity for such purposes. His appointment of university teachers from all parts of India was also a grant step towards national integration.

The University Grants commission 1948-49 (Radhakrishnan Com.) give a fair outline and estimate of the subsequent progress of the research work.

"It was only in 1914 that Sir Ashutosh Mukherjee founded the first post graduate departments at the Calcutta University and placed post graduate training and research there on a proper footing. Promising scholars from all parts of India were appointed to Professional Chairs and in a few years Calcutta had produced research work of a high quality, both in Humanities and Sciences, and several of its professors won international recognition. After the First World War (1913-1919) several new Universities came into being of these, the teaching universities started post-graduate training and research from their very beginning, while some of the affiliating, new as well as old, started post graduate departments in certain fields of study. These new schools attracted a number of young and promising teachers who organised research and raised the level of post graduate teaching at several univesity centres. The degree of Ph.D., D. Litt., and D.Sc. were instituted and were awarded to students on successful completion of their researches. In a few departments of some Universities, the teaching staff came to consist largely of men with research degrees. A number of professors ful-filled their promise of leadership in research and their work brought them international recognition like the Nobel Prize, the Felloship of British Academy, the Fellowship of the Royal Society or higher Doctorate Degrees of Oxford and Cambridge. It may rightly be said that both in quality and quantity the level of scientific research was at its best in Indian Universities between the years 1920-1945. While before 1920 scientific research was mainly a monopoly of Scientific services, after 1920 the leadership in fundamental research in most of the sciences passed over largely to the universities."

[Ref. : Radhakrishnan Report P-145 as quoted by R. C. Majumder].

Outside the University, the research work was promoted by a number of learned societies, both old and new. The most important of these conferences is the Indian Science Congress founded in 1914. There were also the Oriental Conference, the Indian History Congress, the Political Science Conference, Educational Conference and Indian Historical Records Commission, all of which are All-India in Character.

With the growth of Scientific research, several scientific societies have also been formed. The socieites like the National Academy of Sciences, The Indian Academy of Sciences and the Naitonal Institute of Sciences, provided facilities for publication of scientific papers in their journals and thus have substantially encouraged the growth of research in the country. Similarly there are several societies, looking after special subjects of studies, like Mathematics, Chemical, physical, Geological, Botanical and Zoological Societies.

But the research works by brilliant scholars had come to a declining stage as had been observed by the Radhakrishnan Commission and reported in Page 147-48 of the Report of the Commission.

"Unfortunately there are signs of a steady decline in the quality and quantity of research at our Universities. There are several causes, but the most important is that most of the leaders of research in different fields have either left the Universities or are on the verge of retirement and the Universities have not been able to find suitable successors to continue the research tradition intiated and fostered by these pioneers. Ever since the higher administrative services were thrown open to the Indian graduates, the Universities have had to compete with the Govt. which is the largest employer in India, for recruitment of their teaching staff. The universities could not attract the best men to their staff and during the last ten years, a number of brilliant teachers have left the Universities for Govt. service, as they were offered better salaries and prospects there."

Professional Education and Research

1. Agriculture and Commerce Education : In 1928 the Royal Commission of Agriculture was appointed. In 1929 the Imperial Council of Agricultural Research was incorporated. Twenty Institutions for higher educaitonal works in Agriculture were established during the period under review. Only five were established in the forties and five in 1947.

The Govt. Commercial Institute in Calcutta and the Sydenham College of Commerce and Economics in Bombay (1914) were the oldest institutions of this kind. Since then every University has either a Faculty or Department of Commerce.

For training of School teachers Degree Colleges were started in Calcutta in 1908, in Bombay in 1922 and also at other places. Govt. colleges were established at Patna and Allahabad for Diploma Courses. But Nagpur, Benaras, Aligarh and Lakhnow had University Training Colleges. All these admit only graduates and award them the Diploma or Degree after training for one academic year.

Engineering and Technology

There were three Engineering Colleges in three Presidencies - Shibpur (Bengal), Poona (Bombay) and Guindy (Madras) and during the Swadeshi Period one at Jadavpur (Bengal) for Engineering and Technical Education.

In 1915, the Indian Institute of Science at Bangaloe opened electrical engineering Classes.

In 1917, the University of Benaras first started the degree classes in mechanical and electrical engineering and metallurgy.

In 1931-32 Shibpur College started mechanical Engineering and in 1935 electrical Engineering Courses, courses in metallurgy in 1939-40.

More or less about the same time these three courses - Mechanical, Electrical and Metallurgy were started at Guindy and Poona.

Thus including 4 established in 19th Century, 19 Engineering Colleges came into being within this period.

There were 15 Institutions or Departments for training in Technology. Thus Civil, Mechanical, Electrical, Metallurgy, Chemical, Mining and Communication were the courses of study in these institutions.

Advanced studies deserving Master's Degree were not provided for. India had to depend on foreign experts for designs of important works such as - water supply, sewerage, bridges, railway lines and factories. Dependence was also there in the machines for textile, sugar, jute. For all those India was completely dependent on foreign organisations.

The need for improving tenchnical education was realised and two British experts - Messrs A. Abbott and S. H. Wood were invited to advise the Govt. of India. They submitted a Report in June 1937. But little effect was given to this Report.

Law

Though there were many distinguished Lawyers and Jurists in India, there was no adequate provision for advanced studies. There were faculties of Law which prescribed courses of study and attendance at Law Classes. Practising Lawyers were employed as part-time Lecturers. After passing Examination the graduates were allowed to practise in any court. There was also lower courses for non-graduates. who after passing in an examination could practise as a pleader or Muktear.

Some improvement was made during this time. A Law college was started in the Calcutta University in the time of Sir Ashutosh Mukherjee. The advanced studies in Law were recognised by the award of M. L. or D. L. Degrees. In Calcutta University Tagore Lecturership was introduced.

Medicine : The indigenous system of medicine such as Ayurvedic, Unani and Homoeopathic were very popular with large section of people. But a regualr study of these was not felt necessary and so no provision was made either by the University or the Government. There were a few private institutions for teaching.

As in Law, so in Medicine also there were graduate and non-graduate courses. Advanced studies and researches were encouraged by awarding M. D. Degree. Both theoretical and practical trainings were arranged in Medical Colleges and Schools. Though there were very eminent practioners, little has been done in the field of research and discovery.

Only the name of Dr. U. N. Brahmachary may be mentioned as he had discovered a specific remedy for Kala-jar (Black-fever).

Religious Education : Before the advent of British, religious education was treated with utmost importance by the Hindus, Muslims and other communities.

The British adopted the policy of religious neutrality and therefore, scrupulously forbade any form of religions training, direct or indirect, in schools and colleges getting support from the Govt. Only the missionaries imparted religious education in their institutions.

The Education commission of 1882, Indian Universities Commission 1902, the Sadler Commission 1917 did not contradict this policy of religious neutrality in educational institutions.

Mr. R. T. Telang who was a member of the Commission of 1882, summarises that "There are only two possible modes, which can be adopted, in justice and fairness, of practically imparting religios instruction. Either you must teach the principles common to all religions under the name of Natural Religion, or you must teach the Principles of each religious creed to the students whose parents adopt that creed. At all events on this, I am quite clear, that our institutions for secular instruction should not be embarassed by any meddling with the religious instruction, for such meddling among other mischiefs, will yield results which on the religious side will satisfy nobody and on the secular side will be distinctly retrograde."

There was serious division of opinions among the prominent individuals, Muslim Organisations, Arya Samajis and the like.

In January 1944, the Central Board of Education appointed a Committee to examine the desirability and practicability of providing religious instruction in educational institutions.

The Committee met in November 1944 under the Chairmanship of the Right Rev. G. D. Barne, Bishop of Lahore. Out of 11 members 7 members attended the meeting. With a single dissent, the meeting adopted a Report. The Board referred the matter to a reconstituted Commitee of 14 members. The Committee held its meeting in October 1945. 8 out of 64 attended the meeting and adopted a Report with 2 members dissenting.

Finally, the Central Advisory Board of Educaiton resolved. "After fully considering all the aspects of the question, the Board resolved that while they recognise the fundamental importance of spiritual and moral instruction in the building of character, the provision for such teaching, except in so far it can be provided in the normal course of secular instruction, should be responsibility of the Home and the Community to which the pupil belongs."

Detailed Study : period from 1905-1921

As an important factor of the period under review, Government Resolution on Educaiton Policy 21 Feb 1913 has been referred.

We are to note that the period from 1903 to 1913 was of great importance in the history of British Universities. Most British Universities were reconstituted according to the need of that Country. It had an influence on India too. The Govt. of India had to review the University Act of 1904.

The Govt. Resolution on Education Policy of 1913, declared that there would be a University in every province of India, that the colleges located in mofussil towns would be developed into teaching universities, etc.

But no action was taken as it was thought that an expert enquiry should be made before taking long-lasting measures. The second reason was the First World War which kept England engaged.

Yet, during this First World War Period, the Govt. appointed the Calcutta University Commission know as Sadler Com. as the president of the com. was Dr. M. E. Sadler. (The names of other members have already been mentioned). Though the Com. dealt with Calcutta University, the problems it tackled covered all universities of the time.

We have referred to the main recommendations (see Supra), now we may note the details.

(1) The Commission studied the problems of Secondary education along with University as secondary edn. was the foundation of

University education. So in the Report there were Radical recommendations on secondary schools.

(2) The Govt. should establish Intermediate colleges where teaching would be provided in Arts, Science, Medicine, Engineering Teaching etc. and the admission test for Universities should be the passing of the Intermediate examination.

(3) Such colleges might be a separate Institution or might be attached to selected seconary schools.

(4) A Board of secondary and Intermediate Educaiton should be established and be entrusted with the controlling authority. In the Board the members should be from Government, University, High Schools and Intermediate Colleges.

(5) A University should be established at Dacca to lessen the darden of Calcutta University. (Dacca Univesity was established in 1920]

(6) Honours Courses, distinct from Pass Courses should be introduced for abler students.

(7) The duration of the degree courses should be three years.

(8) Steps were to be taken to encourage Muslims to schools for education.

(9) Physical Training should be introduced. A Director of Physical Training should be appointed.

(10) A student's welfare Board should be organised.

(11) Appointment to Professorship and Readership should be made by special selection committees, including external experts.

(12) Female education should be organised and subjects pertinent to women should be introduced. Purdah Schools should be organised both for Hindu and Muslim girls. A special Baord of Women Education should be established.

(13) Education as subject should be introduced in Intermediate, B. A. and M.A. Examinations. The number of trained teachers should be increased.

(14) Technical, Professional and Vocational Educations being very much important, provisions for these should be made.

New Universities : Since 1887 i.e, after the incorporation of the Allahabad University, no new Univesity was established till 1916. The Govt. Resolution on Education 1913 and the Report of Sadler Commission led to the establishment of several new Universities.

(1) In 1916 Mysore University of the State was incorporated to lessen the load of Madras University.

(2) In 1917, Patna University was established.

(3) Delhi University 1922.

(4) Benaras Hindu University 1915, which owes its existence to the great work of Pandit Madan Mohan Malavya.

(5) Aligarh Muslim University in 1920. This too owes its existence to Syed Ahmed.

(6) In 1920 Dacca university

(7) In the same yer, Lucknow University (1920).

(8) The Nizam of Hydrabad established Osmania University at Hydrabad in 1918. The medium of Instruction was Urdu.

Finance

Lord Curzon sanctioned a gratn of Rs. 5 Lakhs a year for College and University Education in 1904. In 1921-22, the Govt. grant had risen to 20 lakhs 54 thousands.

College Education 1905-1921

There was a remarkable improvement in collegiate education. The standard increased, the colleges were better staffed, better housed and better equipped. The finance of the colleges also bettered through collection of higher fees from pupils and increase in government grants. That the number of students also increased a lot. [The most significant aspect is of Bengal. Though backward than United Kingdom in the aspect of Literacy Percentage, yet the number of Bengal's University students (Intermediate, B. A., M.A. combined) was higher than U.K.] That the number of college students increased can be seen from the following table.

Students at Intermediate Exam.	*1904*	*1917*
Madras University	2430	5424
Bombay University	457	1481
Calcutta University	3832	8020

Within 13 years (1904-1917) the number of students appearing at the Intermediate Exam. increased 2.5 times in Madras, 3 times in Bombay and almost 3 times in Calcutta.

Secondary Edn. (1905-1921)

Since 1904-1905, the Govt. always insisted on the quality rather than the quantity in education. This was evident in the Resolution on Education Policy 1913. It insisted on

(1) Graduate and or trained teachers

(2) Teachers of English of higher standard - minimum salary Rs. 40, maximum Rs. 400

(3) Hostel facilities

(4) Improved science teaching and manual training

(5) To found Govt. schools in required places

(6) The Govt. schools playing the part of Model Institution - Model to the private institutions.

(7) To divert studetns to various walks of life by opening avenues for different courses after Matriculation or an alternative exam.

Though the idea in total was appreciable and the Govt. alloted more grants for secondary Edn. but all the ideas could not be realised.

On the other hand, private enterprise for expansion of education increased and centreing the issue of the proposal of partition of Bengal, a political and social awakening took place. It can be roughly measured from the following data.

	1905	*1921*
No. of Secondary schools :	5124	7530
No. of Pupils :	5,90,129	11,06,803

The expansion was roughly double.

Primary Education

Though Lord Curzon took the Policy of larger grants to Primary education, he was always in favour of qualifitative education and never accepted the policy of compulsory primary educaiton. In 1906 the Gaickwar of Barodo introduced compulsory primary education in his state. People wanted that what Gaickwar had effected in his princely state, could be implemented all over the country if the Govt. could be persuaded. The great exponent of this demand was Gokhale. On 19 March 1910, he moved a resolution to this effct in the Imperial Legislative Council. The point was, making primary education compulsory and free through out the country. This was withdrawn as an assurance on the part of the Govt. was given that the whole question would be examined most carefully. But nothing happened. Gokhale then again introduced the resolution in the form of a Bill on 16 march 1911. The bill was circulated and came for discussion on 17 March 1912. The debate lasted for 2 days but he was defeated as the Govt. was then not prepared to accept the bill.King George V came to visit

India in 1911-12. At the coronation of His Majesty, a recurring grant of Rs. 50 lakhs was assigned to popular educaiton.

This was followed by the Govt. Resolution on Educational Policy 1913. For financial reasons as well as qualitative education, the Govt. policy did not introduce free compulsory primary education but for expansion of education steps would be taken to double the number of Primary schools. But it was not materialised.

In 1918 Vithalbhai Patel introduced in Bombay Legislative Council a bill introducing compulsory Primary education in Municipal areas. It was accepted and the Bombay Primary Education Act of 1918 (known as Patel Act) came into being for the Municipalities.

This example was taken up by many and such provincial attempts were made for compulsory education.

Acts For Compulsory Primary Education

Year	Province	Name of Act	Compulsory for Boy or Girls or Both	Applicable to Rural or Urban
1919	Punjab P.E. Act	Boys	Both	
	United Province	"	Both	Municipal Area
	Bengal "	Boys, Extended for Girls 1932		"
	Bihar and Orissa		Boy	Both
1920	Bombay City of Bombay P.E. Act		Both	City of Bombay only
	Central Province	P.E. Act	Both	Both
	Madras Elementary Edn. Act	Both	Both	

Source : Students' History of Education in India by J. P. Naik Nurullah, P-292].

Remuneration of Primary teachers

Bombay or other provinces where the area of compulsory education was municipal area, the remuneration was Rs. 33 p.m. with increament benefit. But in Bengal it was only Rs. 8 p.m. as because most schools were private and the Govt. did not pay adequate grant. (From Adam's report we come to know that in Bengal a Primary teacher got about Rs. 3 to Rs. 5 p.m. in 1835.)

Curriculum : The curriculum of primary education originally devised to convey Western knowledge through mother tongue. Later two objectives came - (1) to prepare students for secondary education (2) to secure lower grade jobs where English was not required. School gardening and nature - study were introduced in several provinces.

387

Building and Equipments : To be very brief, both the school house (Building) and equipments were poor and chances of improvement, except in very special case, were not visible.

Indianisation of Edn. Department : Indian Education Service (I.E.S.) was controlled by England and mainly Europeans were recruited for the posts of Education Department. The recruitment was also done in England. There was heavy opposition to this system. This system implied the moral and intellectual inferiority of the Indians. It was argued that Indianisation of services was a step towareds self-government. It was also objected on the ground that a large sum of money was drained through salaries to Europeans. Moreover, the bureaucrates created through the system were die-hard anti to national inspiration.

In 1917, on 20 August the Secretary of States announced that increasing assocation of Indians in every branch of Indian Administration was the policy of His Majesty's Government in England and the Govt. of India was in complete accord with the policy.

In 1921-22 it was found that some Indians were the I.E.S. of the total posts (IES) for Men of 373, 200 were Europeans, 120 Indians and 53 vacant. Of the total 42 posts for women - 31 were Europeans 2 Indians and 9 vacant.

Govt. of India Act 1919

It has been already noted that during the period under review, one important event in the political history of the country was this Act of 1919 which had a remarkable effect on the progress of Education in India. The very basis of this Act of 1919, was The reforms suggested by Montagu, the then Secretary of State and Lord Chelmsford, the then Governor General of India. By this Act the Department of Education was transferred to the Control of Indian ministers subject to certain reservations.

The Montagu-Chelmsford report in its Para 238 states that - "guiding principles should be to include in the trasnferred list those departments which afford most opportunity for local knowledge and social service, those in which Indians have shown themselves to be keenly interested, those in which mistakes which may occur though serious would not be irremediable, and those which stand most in need of development."

This manifesto implies that the education would be classed as a transferred subject. But there arose considerable differences of opinion regarding the complete transfer of the entire control of education to Indians.

The Anglo-Indians and Europeans demanded that the subject of their education should be in the hands of the centre.

The opinions of the Provincial Governments also differed. Bengal, United Province, Punjab, Bihar, Orissa, Assam, Madras, advocated different principle and opinion on the complete transfer of the subject.

Ultimately, the whole of the Education Department was transferred to Indian ministers subject to reservations. The list of reservation became long as below :

1. The Benaras Hindu Univesity and the like as would be decided by the Governor General, would be under Central Control for their All-India character.

2. Colleges for Indian Chiefs and educational institutions maintained by the Governor General in Council.

3. The education of the Anglo-Indians and Europeans

4. The authority of legislation on several subjects were also reserved. Those were:

    (a) Questions regarding the establishment, constitution and function of new Universities.

    (b) Questions affecting the jurisdiction of any University outside the province concerned.

    (c) Questions regarding Calcutta University and the reorganisation of Secondary education in Bengal (for a period of 5 years).

Thus the total subject of education was partly All-India, partly reserved, partly transferred with limitation and partly transferred without limitation. Yet it was a workable compromise between and among various conflicting opinions.

Before we pass to the next section of our discussion - the period from 1922 to 1937, we can have a look at the development from 1854 Woods Despatch to 1921-22, a period of roughly seventy years.

		1855	*1921-22*
1.	Universities	-	10
2.	Arts College	21	165
3.	Professional Colleges + Schools	13	64
4.	Secondary Schools	281	7530
5.	Primary Schools	2810	1,55,017
6.	Special Schools	7	3344

(Contd...)

7.	Total No. of Recognised Inst.	3132	1,66,130
8.	No. of scholars in Recognised Inst.	135079	73,96,560
9.	Total Expenditure on education	Rs. 9,99,898	Rs. 17,35,88,099
10.	Govt. expenditure on education not known but		Rs. 8,56,01,368

most of the above amount
was spent by Govt.

[*Source :* The figures for 1855 are taken from the Report of the Indian Education Commission, General Table no. (a) those for 1921-22 are for British India only excluding Burma - as quoted in Page 309 of J. P. Naik's Book, referred to]

From 1921 to 1937

The total period under review witnessed two big movements, both unsuccessful, under the leadership of Mohandas Karamchand Gandhi. One was Khilafat Movement expressed through non-cooperation in 1921 and the other was Civil Disobedience Movement in 1930-32 (which was a bit success) expressed through salt movement. The attention of the public and the Government was so concentrated on the two that there was practically, none had the time and intention to look for education.

The problems of dyarchy

The Report on the Indian Constitutional Reforms by Montagu and Chelmsford was published on 8 July, 1918. But there was considerable delay in Passing of the Act. There were reasons of course. The Bill of Indian Constitutional Reforms, after amendment was passed by the House of Commons on 5 December. The House of Lords passed it on 18 December and Royal assent was received on 23 December 1919. Again it took time to settle the financial relations between the centre and the provinces. This procedure being completed, elections to the new Legislative Councils, set up by the Act were held in November 1920. The New Reforms Scheme came into operation on the first day of the year 1921 which again was the year of Khilafat Movement or Non-Cooperation Movement and Civil Disobedience Movement.

This book has no scope to comment on the provisions of this Act of 1919. But this must be mentioned that the most special feature of the Act was the introduction of 'Dyarchy' in the provincial administration. The subjects to be dealt with by the provincial Govts. were divided into two parts called 'Transferred and Reserved'. The Reserved subjects were to be administered by the Governor with the help of the Executive Council, and the Transferred subject were to be dealt with the help of Council of Ministers. This was a hardle to fight out and overcome.

Another hardle was that the character and organsiation of the Department had undergone a vital change. Fresh recruitment to the I.E.S. was discontinued in 1924. The subject education was now not in the hands of the centre in toto. the Provincial Govts. had to deal with transferred subjects and education was in a big form was in its perview. After the Hartog Committee report on this issue on 1929, the Provincial Governments became active, and by 1937, a Provincial Service had been created in all the Provinces except Madras and North-Western Frontier.

Anotther remarkable issue was the sudden cessation of financial assistance and interest in the education of the provinces of the Central Govt. The Central Govt. had so long showed much interest and had taken much initiative in the qualifitative expansion of education in India and a good fund in the form of grant and recurring grand had flown from the source. With the introduction of Dyarchy, the Central Govt. ceased to take any notice of education in Indian Provinces. The Hartog Committee in its report had referred this as 'Unfortunate'.

The financial problem that arose of dyarchy was somehow solved by the Royal Commission of superior Civil Service in India (1923-24), popularly known as Lee Commission. But the other problems remained.

National Education 1921-37

We have already recorded that a National Education system was sought to be developed when the anti-British sentiments and activities developed in the Country.

The promise of the political leaders of whom M. K. Gandhi was all in all that Swaraj will come within a year, proved to be a false one. The call of coming out of the Golamkhana (schools and colleges then prevailing) had lost its charm when it was found that the Khilafat and the Civil Disobedience movements could not achieve anything and Swaraj was at a very long distance. As it was evident, the Britishers had no intention to leave India and if it was to be done, a very strenuous long fight was necessary, The concept of running a parallel education system in the name of National Education was no more tenable and acceptable. So this idea was almost given up. Lala Lajpat Rai very clearly uttered that National Education could only be provided by a free country only.

Jamia Milia Islamia : But Jamia Milia Islamia continued and shifted its location from Aligarh to Delhi in 1925. This institution did not seek any Govt. grant for its running and maintenance.

It professed to broaden the education of the youth on their own cultural heritage. Being exclusive an Institution of the Muslims, for the Muslims and by the Muslims it laid more importance on Arabic. It ran secondary and Primary units also where modern language, social science were taught.

It had a chemical Industry attached to Jamia Science Laboratory. It had a library of about 20,000 volumes. The Urdu Academy of Jamia made publicatons of literature in Urdu.

About 400 hundred students from various parts of India and other Asiatic lands had been studying there.

Viswa-Bharati

It was after the educational concept of Rabindranath Thakur. It was of all India character and the poet thrived and was partly successful even at that time, to give it an international character. It was not on Govt. grant that it depended. It had many departments such as, Vidya-Bhavana, China-Bhavana, Shiksha Bhavana, Kola-Bhavana, Silpa Bhavana, Sangeet Bhavana, Sri Niketan.

The Gurukul University was another to foster national education. It was established by Arya-Pratinidhi-Sabha, Punjab in 1902. It began as a small elementary school and had grown into a full-fledged University. It was not in favour of receiving government grants and was independent of Govt. influence and control. In 1924, it was shifted to Kangri, free from all uneducational influence in sylvan solitude as was the education centres of ancient India. Students of age group 6 and 8 years are admitted. The course is of 14 years and at the end, a student becomes a Snataka (graduate). Then after a training of 2 years, one becomes a Bachaspati (Doctorate). The Gurukul system has wing for girls also. In Dehradun a college for girls has been running since 1923.

The speciality of Gurukul system is, it tries to revive certain ideals of ancient Hindu education.

Syllabus : The syllabus of Gurukul is very interesting and one may designate it as scientific. In the first four years in four classes Sanskrit, Hindi, Arithmatic, Geography, History, Drawing, Religion and Morality are taught. Lessons in hand and eye training, clay-modelling, mat-weaving, spinning etc are included in the curriculum.

After passing Adhikary (Matriculation), students join university classes - which are divided into three colleges - Veda Mahavidyalaya, Sadhana Mahavidyalaya and Ayurveda Mahavidyalaya.

The speciality is, education must be imparted in residential institution which will combine the home and the school in one.

Education must be free including lodging and boarding. Birth or status is not a discriminating factor. Greater emphasis is laid on character, hardship, sublimation of sex-instinct i.e. Brahmacharya of the ancient education.

Darul-Uloom, Deoband : It is a Muslim University conducted on orthodox lines of Islam and was established in 1864 (at Deoband). It attracts students from all parts of India and even from other Muslim countries. It is the 4th Muslim University in the world the other three are Jamia Azhar, Jamia Zetuna and Jamia Tunis.

This is a residential University. The courses are in Arabic, Persian, Tajveid, Tybb, Tabligh (Muslim missionery to Preach Islam). It has departments of Arts and Crafts, Physical Training etc. Its alumni, after passing out, suffix the term 'Deobandi' to their names. They are awarded the degree 'Fazil'. It has about 1600 students.

Darul-Uloom Nadwatul Ulema : It is at Lucknow and was established in 1898. Its stand is between the orthodox university of Deoband and the modern university of Aligarh Muslim University. This institution also attracts students from all over India and other Muslim Countries outside India. The suffix, the alumnis add to their names, in 'Nadvi'. The number of student were 300 during the period under review.

S. N. D. T. Women University : Shrimati Nathibai Damodar Thackersey.) This Univesity owes its origin to a school for Hindu Widows started by Prof. D. K. Karve at Poona in 1896.

The headquarters of the University were removed to Bombay in 1930. The name of the University bears the name of the mother of a famous Bombay merchant who donated a very large sum in the memory of his mother. The Govt. of Bombay had given statutory recognition to the University in 1951. It runs colleges at Bombay, Poona, Baroda, Surat, Bhabnagar and Ahmedabad. It has many a number of schools scattered in Maharastra and Gujrat. It has also made provision for the training of Primary and Secondary Teachers.

The small school of 1896, developed into a big institution with the combination of a Hostel, a primary school, a secondary school and a training school for Primary teachers.

D. K. Karve bent upon to a devise a new scheme of higher education for Indian girls. He believed that the education of men and women was entirely different, since they have to play different roles in life.

He drafted a curriculum well suited to Indian girls as future wives and mothers and the course should be completed before they reached the age of 18, after which an Indian girl seldom remained unmarried, at least in those days.

The Indian women's university was started in 1916 and shaped according to the ideas of Prof Karve. The ideal institution attracts students not only from different states of India but also from abroad.

The special features of this University are :

(1) It is mainly concerned with the higher education of women.

(2) The medium of instruction is mother tongue.

(3) The courses of study include music, drawing, painting and home science.

(4) It has a system of external examiantion for private students who can not join as regular students.

Sir Aurobindo International University Centre, Pondichery

The famous educational Centre was inaugurated on 6th January 1952 at Pondichery. Sri Aurobindo founded an Ashram school here in 1943.

The Centre consists of three educational divisions - Primary, Secondary and Higher Admission is open to all irrespective of caste, creed, sex and nationality. Education is provided free of charge. Even the teaching and non-teaching persons are not formally remunerated. The centre, however, provides lodging and basic personal necessities for each active member of the staff and his family, on a standard similar to that of the Sri Aurobindo Ashram.

The main purpose of the University Centre is to provide for an integral education along the lines envisaged by Sri Aurobindo. The centre does not aim at competing with other universities. It conducts the following courses:

1. **Infant :** Starting at the age of 4 for 3 years developing through games and activities.

2. **Primary :** It is 4 years course with French, English and mother tongue and lessons in elementary, science, mathematics, social studies and drawing as general subjects.

3. **Secondary and Higher secondary** : It is a 7 year course including 2 years of intermediate course with languages as in primary course and Mathematics, Physics, Chemistry, Botany, Zoology, Physiology, Hygiene, Geology, Social Studies, Drawing and any one of the technical subjects. (as per in the list in 5)

4. **University** : It is a 3 years degree course followd by a two-year course in higher studies.

5. **Technical Training Courses are** : Carpentry, eletrical, mechanical engineering, photography, painting, dramatics, short-hand type writing, commercial correspondence and such others. Now computer is introduced.

6. **Language classes for Adults** : English, French, German, Hindi, Tamil, Sanskrit.

There is no religious teaching as such, the Ashram is not related to any religion. The aim of education is to help the student towards an all round development.

College and University Education

A significant advance was made in collegiate and University education during the period under review.

(1) To coordinate the works of the Universities of India

Inter University Board was created. It was the result of the recommendation of the university Commission and an All india conference of Indian Universities held at Simla in 1824.

New Universities : The Resolution Education Policy 1913, wished that there should be at least one University in each province. During this period five new Universities came into being.

(1) Raja Sir Annamalai Chetter University at Chidambaram, Madras.

(2) Andhra University for Telegu speaking areas of Madras Presidency

(3) The Delhi University

(4) Agra University

(5) Nagpur University

The Hartog Committee in its report, after appreciating the progress and expansion of education in general and particularly by the Universities, criticised that the Universities were not producing leaders of society both from qualitative and quantitative points of view. It also commented that due to indiscriminate admission the quality was affected. It observed that the Honours courses were not properly organised. It ultimately suggested that steps should be taken to make the Universities more useful and fruitful and less a disappointing agency.

Secondary Education

In the field of secondary education there was expansion no doubt but the medium of instruction and qualified trained teachers created hurdle.

The expansion of Secondary education, during the period under review, can be gauged from the following data in British India excluding Burma.

	1921-22	*1936-37*
1. No. of recognised secondary schools	7530	13,056
2. No. of scholars in those schools	11,08,803	22,87,872

A special feature in secondary education was that a proficiency in English was desired by brighter students, while the less ables considered English a fearful subject.

The Hartog Committee 1929, marked the number of failure candidates in Matriculation examination. As the cause of this, the committee observed that laxness in promotion in lower classes was the principal reason of the failure. It suggested that all students need not prepare for Matriculation, so diversified curriculum in school was necessary to chanalise the pupils to different persuits. It also recommended the necessity of improvement of the service conditions of teachers.

Primary Education

We have noted that there was a craze for expansion of Primary education. A demand was made that Primary Education must be free and compulsory. As a result Primary Education Acts were passed in many provinces by 1921-22.

In 1923, 1926 and 1930, P.E. Acts were passed, In 1926 Bombay enacted making it compulsory for whole of the Povince.

In 1926 Assam made the Act applicable both to Municipal and Rural areas.

United Province enacted for Rural areas only in 1826.

In 1930, Bengal enacted both for rural and Municipal areas. The Hartog Committee observed that the position was not as rosy as the figures would lend one to infer.

The Committee pointed out that 87 percent people live in rural areas. They are poor, conservative and illiterate. The schools were so sparesly situated that the pupils had to cover long distance to reach a school. Hunger was a problem for poverty. To employ a boy of 14 to house-hold work was more useful than sending him to school. Non-attendance in schools and drop outs were many.

The committee made some recommendations, some of which are;

(a) Policy of consolidation rather than expansion should be followed.

(b) The minimum duration of the Primary course should be four years.

(c) The standard of teachers should be raised. The remuneration should be attractive

(d) School hours and holidays should be adjusted to seasonal and local requirements.

(e) The inspecting staff of the Govt. should be strengthened.

Position of Primary

	1921-22	1926-27	1931-32	1936-37
No. of Recognised Primary Schools	155017	184829	196708	192244
No. of pupils in above schools	6109752	8017423	9162450	10224288
Total direct exp. on P. Education	Rs.49469080	Rs.67514802	Rs.78795236	Rs.81338015

[Source : Book of Naik Nurullah p-349]

The point to be noted is, number of Primary School decreased in 1936-37 in relation to 1931-32. It is also clear that though the P.E. Acts were passed in favour of compulsory Educaton, it did not materialise. This may be attributed to the fact that the social leaders were busy politically. They gave more attention to Civil Disobedience than to compulsory Primary education.

Adult Education

During the period under review a new outlook was evident and relates to adult literacy. According to 1921 Census it was known that the illiteracy percentage was 93. The Indian ministers took an interest in removing illiteracy. In 1927 as many as 11205 adult education centres were running with an enrolement of 290352. But it decreased. In 1936-37, the number of centres were only 2027 with an enrolement 63637 only.

Data on Progress

1921-22- 1936-37

Types of Institution	No. of Insitution		No. of students	
	1921-22	1936-37	1921-22	1936-37
University	10	15	unknown	9697
Arts College	165	271	45418	86273
Professional College	64	75	13662	20645
Secondary Schools	7530	13056	1106803	2287872
Primary Schools	155017	192244	6109752	10224288
Special Schools	3344	5647	120925	259269
Total	166130	211308	7396560	12888044
Unrecognised Institution	1632	16647	422165	5101530

Summary : The period of 16 yrs. from 1921 to 1937, had several novel things to reckon with and notable progress in education, though not all satisfactory.

1. The Education Department was Indianised to a great extent
2. I.E.S. was discontinued in 1924 and a new Provincial Class-I service' was introduced
3. Adult literacy was taken note of.
4. Initiative for women education grew.
5. Primary Education Acts were passed and compulsory Primary Education as an ideal to be achieved was realised.
6. Expansion of education in all levels - university to Primary was remarkable, though not satisfactory.
7. Some improvement in qualitative education was made by opening Research avenues, new Faculties and new courses of study.
8. Physical Training was considered to be important.
9. The Muslim Community so long enamourned and satisfied with their religious education, now got up to have English education.
10. The education in vocational subjects got greater importance.
11. The Hartog committee after necessary enquiries made some important recommendation on all levels of education.

Education During the period from 1937-1947

During the period India was ruled under three Governors - Lord Linlithgo (1936-1943), Lord Wavell 1943-1947 March), and Lord Mount Baten (1947 March to 14 August 1947). Of these the last one tackled only the transfer of power from British hands to Indians and to effect the partition of India in full consultation with and approval of the then Congress leaders including M. K. Gandhi the top most one. So he was not concerned with any development issue of the country. But the other two had their roles to play.

This is the period when the second World War was fought and the Congress fought their last fight in 1942. The First fight for the Independence of the Country was fought by Subhas Chandra Bose challenging the British force with his own regiment Indian National Army, after the last fight of the Congress and Gandhiji.

The Dyarchy introduced in 1919 Act was done away with along with the abolition of 'Reserved Subjects' and 'Transferred subjects'. Provincial administration became the responsibility of the Provincial Ministry answerable to legislature.

The period under review, thus had very significant facts in its womb.

(1) The second World War.

(2) The last and final political movement Quit India - which was initiated by Gandhiji and who did not take the minimum responsibility. The violent Indian patriots did what they themselves planned and paid heaviest toll for their urdent desire for independence of the country. This was in August 1942 and the Govt. finished this unplanned political adventure of Gandhiji within two months.

(3) Preparation of Subhas Chandra Bose with his Indian National Army for an armed war with the British which failed factually after the defeat of Japan, but created the spirit of defying the orders of the British, among military, Navy and Air-force.

(4) The Govt. of India Act 1935 was passed on 2 August 1935. This Act separated Burma from India and created two new provinces - Orissa and Sindh, Dyarchy was abolished and all the provincial subjects were trasnferred to popular control. This new system of Governance, popularly known as Provincial Autonomy came into operation in 1937. Elections were held and congress leaders came to power in many provinces. But all resigned in 1940 after holding the office for roughly three years. From 1940-1945, the caretaker Govts. were in charge. The second World War broke out in September 1939. The popular ministry came to power again in 1946 and remained in power roughly for two years i.e. upto 15 August 1947 when the Britishers transferred power to Indians - which is popularly known as Independence.

(5) The horrible riot occured centering the Partition of India. The Calcutta Riot of Aug 1946 culminated in the riot on Partition of India - which the national leaders with Gandhiji at the top watched helplessly and abused the Muslim leader Jinna for all the massacre. The Govt. remained as aloof as the Congress.

So for these troubles and turmoils, education had the least scope to make a head during the period under review.

But one thing must be noted that the Congress under the leadership of Gandhiji devoted a lot for (a) Basic education (b) adult literacy and (c) abolition of untouchability

The subject - Education got a definite outline in the Act of 1935. While the Act of 1919 made education a subject "Partly all-India, partly reserved, partly transferred with limitation and partly transferred without limitation", the Act of 1935 divided the subject - Education in two categories - Centre's sphere of activity on education and the sphere of the Province on education. Thus the great thing done was the anomalous position was cleared out.

(1) Within the sphere of the Centre

   (a) Education in Centrally administered areas.
   (b) The Benaras Hindu University and the Aligarh Muslim University
   (c) Education of Defence forces
   (d) Archeology, Historical places and monuments, the Imperial Library, Indian Museum, Victoria Memorial and such others - maintennance and development.

(2) **Province :** All matters regarding educaiton excepting those which are listed as Central subjects.

University Education

During this period four new Universities were established. The University of Travancore 1937, the University of Utkal 1943, the University of Saugor 1946 and the University of Rajputana 1947. Thus the total number of Universities rose to 19. Along with, the number of pupils in the University naturally was higher.

The World War II, increased the demand for trained personnel and the Govt. therefore, increased grant for University education. Many new colleges and Faculties were opened. But though the expansion was remarkable, yet in the basis of comparison with other countries, this expansion was negligible.

It is learnt from the Report of Commission, that the number of University going pupils in relation to the total population of the country, India's position was very poor.

Germany : of 690 people one is a univesity student
Great Britain : 1 in 837 people
U.S.A : 1 in 225 people
Russia : 1 in 300 people
India : 1 in 2220 people

Population and no. of Universities

England	41 million	12 Universities
Canada	8.5 million	13 Universities
Australia	5.5 million	6 Universities
U.S.A.	130 million	1720 Universities
India	400 million	19 Universities

The Indian University commission was appointed by the Govt. of India in 1948 in order to report several important aspcts of University education in India. This Commission was presided over by Dr. S. Radhakrishnan and so popularly it is known as Radhakrishnan Commission which submitted its Report in August 1949.

The Report of Radhakrishnan Commisison, we shall discuss in the next chapter Education from 1947 onwards, i.e. the period after transfer of power.

While concluding the discussion on Univesity Education, we must comment that though the enrolement was higher, the percentage of University going pupils was not at all proportionate to the number of population of the Country. Since education was modeled according to the foreign rulers, the nationals had little to perform in the field of University education. But one thing was evident that quality of education was not so improved as the admission to university education was open to all economically equipped ones. The scholarship system was not so broad as to accommodate poor but meritorious pupils.

Total enrolement was higher but progress in professional branches like science, technology, agriculture etc was much less satisfactory.

Adult Education

Considering the illiteracy percentage and consequent developments in the fields of social and economical to be made in a just born independent country, that is India, the issue of Adult Education must be of highest importance. We have discussed earlier that the number of school going children was only 7 in 100 and the presence of girls was very insignificant. The illiteracy percentage was as high as 93. In 1941 Census the illetaracy was 88 and literacy 12 per cent. The foreign government took some care in the University, College, Secondary and Primary educaiton. University education, particularly qualitative output of the universities, they needed for their administration. The numbr of personnel required to administer such a big country were not available in their own land - England. So they filled up the highest and higher posts with men of their own land. But the thousands required next to those highest and high posts, were to be filled up with the natives. So University education and that too of quality was of most importance to them. So the university and education of lower rank were their necessity. Illiteracy of India was more a boon than a liability to them as in administration 100 percent people were not required and illeterate mass was easier to govern. So Adult education was never an issue to the foreigners ruling this country.

The Central Advisory Board of Education (1939) appointed an Adult Education Committee, nearly after 190 years of the foreign rule. The chairman of this Adult Education Committee was Dr. Syed Mahmud who was a Congress leader and minister of Education in Bihar. The Congress took the issue in right unrest.

From the report of the Adult Education committee, it is learnt that Dr. Syed Mahamud, as the Chairman, delivered a very significant lecture in the meeting emphasising the importance of adult education for the development of this independent country. He proposed to formulate plans for the promotion of literacy on a nationwide basis. Syed Mahmud told that no Govt. can succeed in its socio economic plans of development, until and unless people co-operate intelligently. He also said that expansion of Primary education was dependent on adult education or so to say, literacy of the people.

It was found that the Congress and the Congress led provincial govt. took up the issue in 1937-38 when they formed the provincial ministry after the election under 1935 Act. But a time came when the leader of the Congress men felt that ministry and adult education were of less importance to Politics. So in 1940 the Congress ministers resigned and the adult education issue stumbled till 1946 when the Congressmen resumed the ministry. Thus the whole matter was, though taken ardently, dealt with half-heartedly. This was the fate of Basic Education issue too.

Basic Education : This is also named as 'Wardha Education', as it was the brain child of Gandhiji while in Wardha and published his scheme in his paper Harijan, in 1937.

There was a universal demand that free and compulsory Primary Education should be introduced as soon as possible. This demand got momentum when Education turned an issue of the province and in the election of 1937. Congress men formed ministry in many provinces.

At that juncture of time that Gandhiji gave birth to his child - Basic Education or Wardha Education. He knew that his ministers in different provinces would rear up his child and such education centres would come up which would produce goods and pass the examination i.e.produce and perform. The products of the Basic education centres would be sold nation-wide, the centres would be economically fortified and sound requiring no aid from any source and literacy would develop as it would have developed in free, compulsory, universal primary education scheme.

The concept of Basis Education propounded by Gandhiji may be summed up as follows :

(1) The course of Primary education should be extended at least to 7 years and should include the general knowledge gained upto the matriculation standard less English, plus a substantial vocation.

(2) For the all round development of boys and girls, all training should so far as possible be given through a profit yielding vocation.

(3) This primary education beside training of the mind, should equip boys and girls to earn their bread by the stage guaranting employment in the vocations learnt and by buying from the schools their products at prices fixed by the state.

(4) Such education taken as a whole can and must be self-supportig.

(5) Higher education should be left to private enterprise and the state universities should be purely examining bodies.

On the chairmanship of Gandhiji an All-India National Education Conference was held at Wardha in 1937, to consider his proposed scheme, which passed the following resolutions :

(a) That free and compulsory education be provieded for seven years on a nation-wide scale,

(b) That the medium of instruction be the mother tongue.

(c) That the Conference endorses the proposal made by Gandhiji that the process of education through out this period should centre

403

round some form of manual and productive work and that all the other abilities to be developed or training to be given should as far as possible, be integrally related to the central handicraft chosen with due regard to the environment of the child.

(d) That the Conference expects that the system of education will be gradually able to cover the remuneration of the teachers.

The age of entry to school should be 7 years and the standard attained at the end of 7 years' schooling should appoximate to the Matriculation (excepting English).

The Original scheme of Gandhiji and the resolutions of the Conference evoked strong criticism. The scheme if undertaken would please Gandhiji but preclude people from education. The criticism and the displeasure led to further modification of substantial nature for which a committee was appointed with Dr. Zakir Hossain as the Chairman. The committee was entrusted with the job of preparing a detailed scheme of Basic education.

Dr. Zakir Hossain was in a fix. He could realise the hollowness and imperfection of the scheme on the one hand and the over zealous Gandhians on the other, who believed more in holiness in Gandhi than his hollowness.

By the rhetoric of language he tried to avoid the blame that might be put on him that he had deviated from Gandhi. Yet he declared the absurdity of the economic aspect of the Scheme and proposed central and provincial Govts', financial aid. He also repudiated many points of the scheme and proposed acceptable and practical suggestions. The Central Advisory Board of Education gave its general approval with some changes. It did not approve the financial proposal of Dr. Zakir Hussain.

This scheme was nurtured like a hot house plant in a few areas, out of devotion to Gandhi but did not make any appreciable impact on Primary Educaiton. The ministers resigned, the ministers re-instated but the concept of Basic Education breathed its last before Gandhiji.

Teachers : It was always urged that qualified teachers were necessary in Primry level. The teachers must be trained and qualified. In the field of education, quality of teacher is, no doubt very important. Though the issue of qualified teacher was always raised, their remuneration was never to any body, excepting the teacher themselves, an issue to ponder over. Though a comparative study is not possible for want of data, yet the data Hartog Committee mentioned in its report may be mentioned. Salary of Primary Teachers per month in the period under review :

1.	Madras	Rs. 15.25
2.	Bengal	Rs. 8.50
3.	United Province	Rs. 18.50
4.	Punjab	Rs. 25.50
5.	Bihar and Orissa	Rs. 11.40
6.	Central Provice	Rs. 24.50
7.	Assam	Rs. 14.25
8.	Bombay	Rs. 47.00

(anna converted to Paisa)

The salary of Primary teachers of Bombay probably may not be correct. It was better than all, no doubt, but not that much.

In 1929 there was World-wide economic depression, there was cut in salary. How far the primary teachers were affected, whether there was cut in this poor salary, we cannot say definetely. The Sargent Report advocated better salary for teachers. The Primary teachers were hard-hit by inflation during the post-war period.

In 1946, in Bombay Province the Primary teachers went on strike, 45000 Primary teachers participated and it continued for 54 days.

A better pay and dearness allowance was sanctioned to the Primary teachers but the inflation was the blotting paper to dry the increase.

Primary Education (1937-1947)

Primary Education was imparted by Lower Primary and Upper Primary schools. The number of Primary schools in British India

in 1939	-	189751
No. of Pupils	-	11,445,392

According to Census of 1941 the literacy percentage was only 12.1. In comparison to previous census in 1931, it was an increase of 4 percent. So Indians were the most illeterate in the whole world. Out of the total population 389 millions only 47 millions could read and write in 1941.

So the issue of Primary eduction was of considerable interest. Even now when the percentage was so low, the problem of drop-outs made it darker. The description in the following table will show the problem of drop-outs.

The year 1937

Class I	52 lakhs attending school
Class II	24 lakhs attending school

Class III	17 lakhs attending school
Class IV	12 lakhs attending school
Class V	7 lakhs attending school

Class IV, at which permanent literacy was likely to be attained, was covered by only 12 lakhs while 52 lakhs joined Class I i.e. less than one out of Four children came upto Class IV. Mostly it was due to poverty and distance to school from home. Parents considered it more profitable to use the child as a working unit rather than a school going unit.

The primary education and literacy could only be achieved if it was made free, compulsory and universal. Gokhale's initiative on this issue was negated. The Govt. was reluctant to spend on Primary. It better thought to spend on university, that would give them good crop. In the Basic Education scheme, the Govt. was exempted from any financial liability.

The compulsion of Primary education produce better results was proved by the Province of Bombay. A big area of the province was covered by the compulsion of Primary education both for girls and boys by enactments, and the result was both noteworthy and praiseworthy.

Expansion of Primary (1937-47)

Year	No. of Schools	No. of Pupils
1881-82	82,916	2061541
1901-02	93,604	3076671
1921-22	155017	6109752
1936-37	192244	10224288
1945-46	167700	13027313
1946-47	134866	10525943

The difference between 45-46 and 1946-47 may be attributed to partition of Punjab and Bengal

[Source ; The data is from P-375 of the book of J. P. Naik and Nurullah]

Secondary Education (1937-47)

The picture of secondary was not all satisfactory though the universities qualified pupils who would be prepared to match the need of the time.

As we have noted in the beginning that this period was a disturbed one from the national political and international angles. And for this disturbance, however, no one was responsible. It was the sum total of circumstances and situations which contributed to this. Even from economical point of view, this period was very much stern and negative.

Yet progress in the secondary education took place but the pace was not so fast. More so, this progress, along with it, carried the defects which were pointed out but not remedied. The teachers who were the backbones of the system, were very much dissatisfied as they were helpless under the economic condition which situation and circumstances had thrust upon them and there was no authority who cared their misfortune. The Primary teachers could attract attention by the strike in Bombay Province but nothing of that kind did happen in their case.

The Number of university students was almost doubled between 1936-37 and 1946-47, inspite of the establishment of Pakisthan i.e. Partition of India, but the number of secondary students did not double.

So many reasons for this slow progress have been advanced. But only one was significant and the other was partly significant.

The number one reason is the economic situation hard-hit the middle class-who was most interested in education. The cost of education became higher and not affordable to many. The lower group of middle class was helpless regarding where from they would get money for payment of fees and buying books and other equipments.

The second reason was that the war needed some technically trained people. So education for non-literary course, some vocational training which enables to earn became attractive. The provincial Governments started technical, commercial and agricultural schools and larger grants were made available to non-Govt. institutions of this type. So a one way road to pass matriculation through secondary schools lost its lusture a bit. Education was needed for employment and if that was available being non-matric, does not matter. So the picture of secondary education was not so brignt, as was the university and primary education during the period under review.

The following is the picture of secondary education of the concerned period 1941-47.

Type of Schools	Schools			Pupils		
	Boys	Girls	Total	Boys	Girls	Total
Middle English Schools	4169	620	4789	540441	85484	625925
Middle Vernacular Schools	2914	567	3481	404377	92300	496677
High Schools	3061	576	3637	1381038	178341	1559379
Total 1946-47	10144	1763	11907	2325856	356125	2681981
Total 1936-37	-	-	13056	-	-	2287872

(The data is from P-370 of J. P. Naik and Nurullah's book)

Training of Teachers

The number of Training Colleges for secondary teachers was considerably increased and the number of women teachers undergoing the training had an increase. In 1946-47 the total out put of trained teachers was 3417 of whom 2110 were men and 1307 were women.

Women's Education

Women's eduation made steady progress though slow, during the period inspite of predicaments discussed above. Though in Primary schools the number of girls was encouraging, in higher classes only in middle class and upper middle class could be found. The early marriage of girls was a factor though, the syllabus which was more intellectual and theoretical, did not attract the guardians as these did not help a girl in her father-in-law's house in future. Moreover, during that period of time, a highly educated i.e. matriculate or college girls were not so favourite with the old fashioned father-in-laws and mother-in-laws who were habituated to avoid such girls as their daughter-in-laws. So a girl's father had to face problem to get her daughter married.

As compared with the previous period, the number of girls students increased in every stage. But the total number of girls was very small compared to boys.

In India the ratio of male female was - male 1000, female 935 in 1941 census. The number of women who could read and write was only 1.1 percent and male 11.3 percent in 1911. In 1921 it was female 1.8, male 13.6 percent.

The reservation regarding girls' education in the minds of the people (young and old) began to dilute gradually. So the position was found improved in this period. Let us consider the following figures.

Total No. of girls under Instruction
1937-38	3012212
1941-42	3726876
1946-47	4297785

	No.of girls colleges [General and Professional]	No. of girls students
1937-38	41	3810
1941-42	58	6072
1946-47	91	10315

[Source : HCIP Vol-XI, Page-903]

A new feature in women's education developed and that was co-education. Divergent opinions were expressed in favour and against this new feature. The general trend of opinion seems to have been that girls of the age group 13-18 should be educated in separate institutions. Many favoured the idea of separate colleges also.

The Hartog Committee (An auxilliary com. appointed by Simon Commission which was presided over by Sir Philip Hartog) in 1927-28 observed -

"In recent years repeated demands have been made by representative Women's association for the differentiation of the curruculum in girls schools from that adopted in boys' schools. The first All-India Women's conference on Education Reforms, held at Poona in 1927, recommended alternative courses for those who do not want to take up college education - domestic science, fine arts, handicrafts and industries. Similar recommendations were made by other conferences. In Primary Schools separate optional for girls are common. In secondary schools separate alternative courses are less common. Little has been done to provide alternative courses in the universities."

The Radhakrishnan Com. observed : Some of the arguments given are a women cannot develop her personality in the man's college : that there is no need for women to undergo the nervous strain of examinations : that women's education should be more in keeping with the temparament and needs of women as wives and mothers : and that over crowding is more serious for women than for men."

On the other hand it was argued that separate college for women would mean unnecessary increase in expenditure and were likely to be, in many cases, poor or inferior duplicates. Further, a healthy association and competition of grils with boys in academic fields would perhaps be beneficial to the development of personality and character of both. As a matter of fact, both the systems, separate college for girls and co-education were in vogue during the period under review. Co-education was almost a necessity in the post-graduate stage and number of girl students in post graduate as well as Degree classes had been steadily on the increase. But co-education being, comparatively speaking, a recent innovation, the system had many defects at the end of the period under review, as would appear from the following observations made by the Radhakrishnan commission.

"There are truly few co-educational colleges in our country. Rather, there are men's colleges to which women have been admitted as students, which is a very different matter. Quite frequently in co-education colleges nearly all the facilities are for men and women are little more than tolerated. Often sanitary facilities for women are totally inadequate and sometimes wholly lacking. Recreation space and facilities for women similarly are inadequate or lacking."

[Ref. : Radhakrishnan Com. Report P-399]

Question was raised about the common curriculum for men and women. Here again, the opinions sharply differed. The commisison in its report cited several opinions on the issue. The Principal of a college wrote : "Women's present education is entirely irrelevant to the life they have to lead. It is not only a waste but often a definite disability." Another wrote, "The present system of women's education, based as it is on man's needs, does not in any way make them fit for coping with the practical problems of daily life. Their education should give them a practical bias, specially from the point of view of families, for making them good mothers, doctors and nurses." (Radhakrishnan Committee)

On the other hand, among girls gradually growing tendency of being equal to men, or to surpass them was found. But women who were of advanced age, were in favour of a special curriculum suitable for women. We have already cited the observation of the Hartog committee.

It is not easy to reconcile the two objectives that (1) the education of the grils will be similar to that of the boys and (2) the girls should have a separate curriculum. The solution may be this that subjects said to be suitable for girls be included in the curriculum and allow the girls and their families to select the subjects. One important but often unnoticed fact is that in 1928 there were in British India nearly 600 Companies and Flocks with an enrolement of 10 thousands Guides and Blue Birds - it was the result of Girl-Guide Movement in the country.

Education of the Muslims

'Education of Muslims' should not be a topic for discussion. Yet it is always discussed as a separate topic because of the backwardness of the said community. This backwardness is their own contribution to their own community. No one else is responsible or can be accused to be responsible.

The Muslims always suffered from the pride, if you call it so, or arthodoxy, if you call it so, that they were the progeny of the ruling class - the Nawabs and Emperors who invaded India, ascended the throne, were in power for nearly 500 years, were partly successful in their object of

Islamaisation of the country in a bid to bring to the true religion to the idol worshippers of the country through horrible conversion process.

The Britishers or the Christians were more acceptable to them as they were People of the Book than the most-hated idol worshipers - Hindu. The term 'Hindu' they invented to distinguish the Indians from themselves - the Muslims - the followers of the only true religion Islam.

When the Britishers (Christians) came to power, the Muslims heaved a sigh of relief that the Indians or Hindus or the idol worshippers were not on the throne.

But their pride or arthodoxy prevented them the education system enunciated by the christian Britishers. To them nothing was better than Arabic and Persian and nothing is higher than Quran - which contains everything from A to Z.

They were not all interested in modern education system which the British Christians introduced. They continued their education in Maktabs - generally attached to a mosque and Madrasahs.

So when social leaders like Raja Rammohan Roy, Iswar Chandra Vidyasagar and the like urged for English education and Western knowledge, the Muslims did not show any interest. People like Syed Ahmed of their community took interest in English education, though late, could not make the muslims nod from the immobility.

When they could realise that the English education or the system of education introduced by the Britishers was much needed for their living, they began to take interest. As they were late, they turned Backward. The opportunity was open to them always but only a few took advantage of it. The whole community remained absorbed in the glory of their reign and pride of their doctrine. So, that happened which was very much natural to happen. They as a community lagged behind. They were late enough to start.

Thus, the education of Muslims happens to be a separate topic for discussion. And now the situation is, the Muslims demand special advantage in every sphere for the 'backwardness' which they themselves imposed on themselves.

Whatever be the psychology, you agree or disagree does not matter. We are here to deal with facts which history endorses.

During the period under review the happy feature is the rapid progress in education made by the muslims - who had been very backward in this respect.

During the decade 1917 to 1927 the total number of Muslim pupils in colleges and Universities rose from 5212 (1917) to 8456 (1927). In Primary and Seconary stages the number increased from 1552142 (1917) to 2437373 (1927). The total number in all rose from 1593528 to 2589836.

[Source : R. C. Mazumder's article in HCIP, Vol-XI, P-905]

In his studies and Reports Sir Philip Hartog observes :

"In all important Government reports on education you will find special chapter devoted to the education of the Muhamedans. Of late years the total number of Muslim pupils has grown faster than the rest of the school population. Between 1917 and 1927 it increased by 62.5 percent, or almost a million. the ratio of the Mohamedans and non Muhamedans was 24:7...."

An analysis of the figures for the different stages shows, however, that at every stage going upwards, the proportion of Mohamedans unfortunately diminishes. The wastage of both boys and girls are appalingly heavy. Only 17 percent of the boys and less than 6 percent of the girls reach Class IV. In the 'high stage' of secondary education Muslims only form 15 percent of the total. But it is clear that in the high schools they are making up Iceway, for between 1927 and 1932 the number increased nearly by 50 percent from 32000 to 47000 and in the collegiate and university stage they are also beginning to make up Iceway, though less rapidly. In 1935 they still formed only about 14.5 percent of the university population (male - students)."

The observation of Hartog Committee that "only 17 percent of boys and less than 6 percent of girls reach Class IV' - regarding this it may be mentioned that - the number of earners in a mohamedan family being less than the number to be fed, muslim boys enter into some works which make them earning boys. So they leave the school - which gives no earning directly. The muslim girls are given to marriage a bit early and they are very much needed in the family works as also with the case of non-muslims. So the girls are made to discontinue school education which in no way help the girls in their married situation.

The progress of education of the muslim girls was not satisfactory. The pupils in Class I of the Primary school in 1927, represented 35.50 percent. But in Class V, it came down to 5.8 percent.

In 1917 there were only 6 muslim girls in Arts Colleges, in 1922 it increased to 25 and in 1927 to 30. In 1935 there were only 300 Muslim girls out of the total 5500 students.

Expenditure on Education

Statistics

Expenditure on education from all sources

1937-38	Rs. 26 lakhs 98 thousands
1943-44	Rs. 34 lakhs 46 thousands
1944-45	Rs. 39 lakhs 6 thousands
1945-46	Rs. 46 lakhs
1946-47	Rs. 57 lakhs 66 thousandss

Institutions and Enrolment figures

	1936-37		1945-46	
	No. of	Pupils	No. of	Pupils
1. Universities	15	10139	16	15693
2. Arts, Sc. & Inter College	279	101182	454	175509
3. High Schools	8416	117991	4949	1978546
4. Middle Schools	9889	1274897	12120	1626000
5. Primary Schools	189601	10516358	167841	12103203
6. Engineering + Technical	9	2426	12	4789
7. Training College	23	1785	38	2550
8. Other Professionals	43	17907	73	31489
9. Engi+Tech. Scholls	558	33368	654	35619
10. Training Schools	537	26019	588	31388
11. Other Spl. Schools	4847	218641	9255	362589

Literacy 1947 (Excluding Pakisthan)

	Population	Literate	Percentage
Male	183333874	45610431	24.9
Female	173545520	13650683	7.9
Total	356879394	59261114	16.6

[Source : R. C. Majumder P-910 Vol-XI, HCIP]

Literacy Excluding Pakisthan 1941 Census

1.	Travancore	47.8 Pc
2.	Cochin	35.4 Pc
3.	Baroda	23.01 Pc
4.	Madras Presidency	13.01 Pc
5.	Bombay Presidency	19.5 Pc
6.	Bengal Presidency	16.1 Pc
7.	United Province	8 Pc

[Source : HCIP Vol-XI P-910, R.C. Mazumder]

General Review of the British Education of roughly 150 years

What the Critics Say :

1. the Principal charge against the British educational system followed in India is that it failed to create a national system of education for this country.

2. It did not prepare India in that way in which this country could establish itself as a self-respecting nation in the comity of Nations.

3. The Christian missioneries took up education as a means to the end of proselytisation. They believed that Christanity and Western culture were inseparable and the natives, if were to bring to a mark, must be christanised. But when the East India company was somehow compelled to take a bit of responsibility of the education of India and when from 1858 the British Govt. took the responsbility, it took no step to bring about a synthesis between the East and West.

4. The next criticism advanced is, the British educational system failed to formulate aims of education.

5. The non-formation of aims led to adoption of wrong methods. It neglected indigenous system of education and depended on English system. Adoption of Downward Filtration theory and negligence to make Primary Education Compulsory were the Chief faults of their method.

6. The British education system failed to develop India socially, economically and politically. Certain aspects of British Rule were inimical to such advancement.

7. As there was no aim so there was no plan. Their system did not know what goal was to be achieved and how.

8. The progress of education was not commensurate with the needs of the reasonable expectations of the country and this is particularly applicable to such Primary Education as would increase the percentage of literacy.

9. The educational system was not related to unemployment problem.

10. The nationalists, marked so, of our country criticise that the British education system "was divorced from the actualities of Indian life. It did not give a true picture of Indian life of the political servitude and of the real causes of the economic and cultural backwardness of Indian society. It gave a distorted account of India's past history, glorified the British conquerers of

India and portrayed the British as Civilizers of India. It tended to weaken national pride and self respect" (A. B. Desai Social Background of Indian Naitonalism P-139)

Before I submit my criticism of the criticisms advanced against British system of education, we must note the contribution of the system to India. They ruled the country for nearly 200 years and tackled the issue of education for nearly 150 years. So some good must have resulted. Let us consider those.

Contribution

1. The most important achievement was to introduce India to English language and lierature and through them, to all the thought, the scientific and industrial development, and the social and political philosophy of the West. Raja Rammohan, Pandit Iswar Chandra and other respectable Indians who were with Rammohan and Iswar Chandra, wished this development of India and did their best in their capacity with this end in view.

2. India owes the scientific and critical study of her ancient times to European scholars. The Oriental languages were also benefitted. The officials and missioneries studied the modern Indian languages, wrote their grammer, compiled dictionaries and in many cases published books. India is indebted to Sir George Griempson for his Linguistic survey of India.

3. Indian Art, Architecture and Archeology were much benefitted though those were not an important part of their education policy.

4. Western system of Law and Medicine have come to Indian perception through their education policy.

5. Increase in the number of pupils receiving education specially among women, Muslims and Depressed classes was tangible contribution of the British system of ducation.

6. There was a large variety of subjects in which instructions were provided.

7. Trend towards study of science, Technology, Law and Medicine got impetus.

8. Steady growth of Research in both science and Humanity subjects took place.

9. The necessity of training of teachers was urgently felt.

10. Establishment of Unitary, residential and teaching universities, as were in Buddhist system of education, was given much importance.

Criticism of the Criticism of British Education Policy in India

The most important and the most vocal criticism of the British system of education is made by the nationalists of India. The criticism is, it failed to create a national system of education and that it was divorced from the actualities of Indian life.

Let us admit the truth in the charge and let us question -

(1) Was any concrete form of such a 'national system of education' was proposed to be substituted ?

(2) Was the educational ideas of Sri Aurobindo, Rabindranath, Gurukul Kangri or any of that type accepted by the nationalists as national education system?

(3) Do the critics of the system agree with each other about their views on 'national culture' or for that matter 'national education'?

(4) Has any uninanimous definition of National Culture and National Education at all emerged and percieved even after these 70 years of Independence or Transfer of Power ?

The point is, the slave mentality which the Britishers starting from Macaulay, Bentinck and Wood wanted to inculcate among the nationals and national leaders still persists. Are we sure that we have advanced from what was in the Despatch of Wood in 1854? Have we been able, even after that 70 years to have the foundation of our education on an Indian basis. Is the education system of India is now based on Indian life as was wanted by Nationalists ? Is it not true that while the slogans of national culture and 'National Education' are put forward as the basis of all kinds of reforms, a few have so far analysed the contents of what they mean by it ?

It is very easy to detect the defect but very difficult to remove.

The 'Slave mentality' inculcated, still is there. The leadership of the country is still under foreign influence and control. So there is no unanimity regarding national culture and national system of education. We are following the steps dictated in 1854.

The nationalists' charge that the British education system 'gave a distorted account of Indian's past history, glorified the British conquerers of India and portrayed the British as civilizers of India'. Though the history of India is distorted althrough, at least from 1000 AD, yet has the history of India been re-written setting aside the distortions, in this long 70 years ? Did any body dare ?

The cause of this failure or non-functioning was due to the fact that the leaders on whom the responsibility devolved, "Were indians in blood and colour but were english in their taste, in opinions and in morals and in intellects."

The Britishers were not Maurya or Gupta emperors who were benevolent and looked after the well-being of the people and progress of the country.

The Britishers were not Indians. They were interested in exploitation, through trade and commerce. They cared education only to that extent to which they could extract from Indians. The number of Europeans fell short for the need of governing this so big a country. So what they needed was expressed by Macaulay just before the time when British Emperor took the administration from the hands of the East India Company. Lord Bentinck and Wood did the job.

Can anybody seriously challange that the education system of Independent India is not running in the same line detected by Sir Charles Wood, President of the Board of Control, in his Despatch No. 49 dated 19th July 1854? This Despatch, described as the 'Magna Carta of English Education of India', formed the land mark in the history of Education in modern India.

Thus, Thomas Babington Macaulay's Minutes (2 Feb 1835), Lord Bentinck's Resolution (7 Mach 1835), Lord Hardinge's Educational Despatch (10 October 1944), culminated in the Despatch of Wood (19 July 54).

Whatever the British education system, the ultimate target was to smoothen the Imperialist interest of Great Britain. The benefits the Indian enjoyed was only normal and natural. As they were foreigners and had a country of their own, they had little interest in total development and welfare and for this the Britishers cannot be blamed. They did that which they needed.

But the question is, did the national leaders did what the nation desired and needed? Had they any programme on national system of education ? Have they even now a plan on education centreing the ethos of the country and touching Indian life ?

This we shall examine in the next part, where we shall discuss education in the post independence period and the place of education in the five years plans prescribed for the development of the country.

The pity with the national leaders, as has been revealed they are good immitators. And everybody knows that immitators cannot be inventors.

Part - XI

1947 - 1975 A.D.

Education in Independent India [First Phase]

Historical Perspective

At last in 1947, the Britishers transferred power to Indians after partitioning the country as Hindusthan and Pakisthan. 15th of August was marked as the day of Independence of Hindusthan and 14th August as the day of Independence of Pakisthan.

The schedule of the British govt. was to transfer power by June 1948. On 20 February 1947, Attlee the Prime Minister of the British Govt. in England made his historic announcement :

"The present state of uncertainty is fraught with danger and can not be indefinitely prolonged. His Majesty's Government wish to make it clear that it is their definite intention to take necessary steps to effect the transference of power to responsible Indian hands by a date not later than June 1948.

Admiral the viscount Mountbatten was appointed as viceroy in succession to Lord Wavell. Mount-batten assumed the office of the viceroy of India on 24 March, 1947.

A cabinet was formed to administer so called Independent India. Sri Jawaharlal Nehru was the Prime Minister. Maulana Abul Kalam Azad was the minister in charge of education.

Azad convened an all India Educational Conference in 1948. Prime Minister Nehru inaugurated the conference. In his inaugural speech he said:

"When ever conferences were called to form a plan on education of India, the tendency, as a rule, was to maintain the existing system with slight modifilatiions. This must not happen now. Great changes have taken place in the country and the educational system must also be in keeping with them. The entire basis of education must be revolutionised."

When the Prime Minister himself feels the necessity and so declares that "the entire basis of education must be revolutionised," it was very rightly expected that a National system of Education would succeed an imperial and colonial system of eduation. And that 'revolutionised' education system must start from 1950 if not from 1947. The appointment of Radhakrishnan Commission in 1948 was expected to serve the purpose of 'revolutionising the entire basis' of education in India, as announced by the Prime Minister. But that did not happen.

Our education system, the system of education of Independent India has still its basis on the imperial and colonial education system introduced as early as in 1854 on the basis of Macaulay's Minute and Wood's Despatch. The policy of education adopted by the British Govt. in India is based on the basis of those document.

Those two famous documents which formulated Indian education and whch are still being followed had basic intentions -

(1) To initiate a sense of superiority of English people who were governing India, in the minds of the Indians whom they named 'Natives' and there by justifying their right to treat India as one of their colonies and govern it.

(2) Produce an army of clerks, petty officials and public men who will always feel themselves inferior to their rulers and shall even remain 'your most obedient servant.'

It is true that a good number of Hindu Indians were eager to have contact with English Education and acquaintance with Western Philosophy and science. But they did not dream that they would be contemptuously named 'Natives', would be treated as inferior and less dignified, their professors in the colleges and universities would get lower scale of pay than an English professor of equal qualification. In short, they did not think that they had to get everything at the cost of national honour as well as self respect.

So when the power was transferred to Indians like Prime Minister Nehru, all expected that henceforth education conferences and commissions would not maintain the British system with little modifications, but a national system of education would supplement the existing one.

But that did not happen even after 70 years of 15th August, 1947. The arena of education has expanded but not the national pride and individual self-respect. Money has become the sole purpose of education, as it was true to great extent in British period.

That the present education system should be radically overhauled and entire basis of education should be revolutionised, are being felt by the small circles of educationist and the public at large. But the Govt. remains unconcerned. That which was easy in the middle of 20th Century, has now become difficult and complicated in the 1st quarter of the 21st Century. Expenditure on education has increased but the philosophy has not changed.

Several Commissions such as Radhakrishnan Commission, Muduliar Commission, Kothari Commission have been appointed but those have made modifications and never touched the basic system.

Education in the Constitution

The constitution of India has given the issue of Education mainly in the charge of the states. But no state alone can revolutionise the basis of education as was desired and announced by Nehru in 1948. The formation of the education policy should be a charge with the Central Govt. and it is not a provincial issue, it is a national issue. The Central Advisory Board of Education should be newly constituted and be given the task of revolutioning the basis and / or overhauling radically the education system of the country. It must be done within a specific time limit. This Board must be (1) bereft of political inclination, (2) free of Political influence and interference and (3) immune from the semetic influence prevalent in Indian political and academic world. National Education system should be outlined by such men who have regard for Bharatiya ethos, secular and progressive in attitude.

As has been mentioned, the constitution of India (1949) makes education a state subject. The Central Govt. took a very limited part in the system. The Central Govt. concerned it self only with.

(1) Benaras Hindu University, Aligarh Muslim University, Delhi University.

(2) Institutions for Scientific or technical education financial by the Central Govt.

(3) Professional, Vocational or technical training, including training of police officers.

(4) Promotion of special studies or research

(5) Scientific or technical assistance in the investigation or detection of crimes.

(6) Education in Union territories and centrally administered areas.

(7) Co-ordination and determination of standards in institutions for higher education or research and scientific and technical education.

The state was given the charge of education including universities excluding the areas mentioned above (entries 63, 64, 65, 66 of List 1), Ref. Constitution of India.

The third list is concurrent list. Entry 25 of this list - Vocational and technical training of labour was not handed over to the state.

Realising the importance of Universal Primary education, article 45 of the Constitution provides that, "the state shall endeavour to provide, within a priod of ten years from the Commencement of the Constitution, for free and compulsory education for all children until they complete the age of 14 years." May it be noted that this Article 45 is a directive Principle only which is not a compulsion.

But before the commencement of the constitution (November 1949), the National Govt. which was formed after the transfer of power, two major steps were taken - (1) the creation of a Ministry of Education and Scientific Research and (2) appointment of a University Education Commission under the Charimanship of Dr. S. Radhakrishna in 1948. This is known as Radhakrishnan Commission which submitted its report in 1949.

Then a Secondary Education Commission was appointed in 1952, under the chairmanship of Dr. S. Lakhsmanaswami Muduliar. This commission is known as Mudaliar Commission.

In 1964 another Commission was appointed to review education in all respects and to make recommendations for future development. The chairman of the Commission was Dr. D. S. Kothari and this Commission is known as Kothari Commission.

In the meantime the University Grant Commission (UGC) was created in 1956 under the Chairmanship of Dr. C. D. Deshmukh. At first a non-statutory body was set up under an Executive Order in 1953 and in 1956 a Statutory Body was created by an Act. of Parliament.

So, during the premiership of Nehru so mamy Commissions were appointed - Radhakrishnan, Mudaliar and Deshmukh but no revolution in the entire basis of education materialised. Even the Kothari Commission appointed after the expiry of Nehru, which was advised to recommend for future development failed to revolutionise the entire basis of education.

As a result, education in India expanded largely, though very low in companison with other countries like U.K., U.S.A. Germany, Japan and there was disparity between the output and its absorbtion in the economy. Unemployment, therefore, became an issue. The growth of national cconomy and the growth of education were disproportionate The economy developed in its own way. The education developed in its own way and the twine did not meet.

The education system having no basis on national ethos, pride and honour, the employed educated ones never took into consideration that their service had some relation with nation i.e. the country's development. So those who were employed, earned for his ownself without any attitude that he is one of the nation. Thus not the country's but self development became the target of an individual. Consequenty corruption became the rule of the day. Corruption infiltrated downwards. Not the country but the material development of the individual became the target. The wave still continues.

Radhakrishnan Commission 1948

The first commission after transfer of power (independence), was Radhakrishnan Commission. It was felt by the Govt. that a reconstruction of University education was essential for a national cultural resurgence as well as for meeting the requirements of scientific, technical and other man power required for the Socio-economic development of the Country.

Important Recommendations :

1. Universities be constituted as autonomous bodies.
2. University education should be placed in the third list - concurrent list.
3. The Central Govt. has to take the responsibility of finance.
4. For allocating grants to universities a central university grants com. should be established.
    [U.G.C. was constituted by an Act of Parliament in 1956]
5. There should be no only affiliating University.
6. The Salary scale of teachers should not be much less than those in Central or Provincial services, that the qualified ones could be attracted to teaching services of the Universities.
7. It recommended silent prayer at the beginning of the day and in the first year teaching of the lives of great religious leaders, in the second year some selection from the scriptures and in the third year central problem of the philosophy of religion.
8. The medium of instruction should be Western Hindi but English will continue to occupy an important place in intellctual and academic life.

9. In order to meet the need of rural reconstruction in industry, agriculture and various walks of social life, rural universities surrounded by a ring of rural colleges doing undergraduate work, should be established.

10. The total duration of the school course should include intermediate stage and should cover a period of 12 years. (Class I to Class XII, as it is now. The same recommendation was made by the Commission in 1917-19 - Sadler Com. referred to earlier]

11. Importance on research in the fields of industry, administration, scienfitic organisations.

12. Importance on quality as well as quantity education.

The recommendations of the Radhakrishnan Commission (1948) were mainly on University education. Many of the recommednations were implemented though not all.

In the meantime the Govt. resolved to develop the country through 5 year plans. Briefly speaking the period of the plans were

(1)	1950-1955	First Plan
(2)	1955-1960	Second Plan
(3)	1960-1965	Third Plan
(4)	1965-1970	Fourth Plan

In the meantime, another Education Commission was appointed in 1952 within the First 5 year plan period, to reorganise the secondary, which was not given due attention since 1881-82. This secondary education commission was appointed under the Chairmanship of Dr. A. L. Mudaliar. The Commission is known as Mudaliar Commission. It presented its report in 1953.

It must be noted that though Secondary Education was not looked after by any authority, its expansion was remarkable which may be by force of circumstances.

The position in 1950 was :

1. No. of boys Schools - 5685

2. No. of Girls Schools - 997

3. Enrolemebnt Boys - 9.05 Lakhs

4. Enrolement Girls - 1.40 Lakhs

5. Percentage of enrolement at the secondary stage in relation to the total popualtion in the age-group 14-17, was 4.8 (Boys 8.2, Girls 1.3).

Mudaliar Commission 1952, was for the secondary education only as the Radhakrishnan Commission 1948, was for the university education only.

The main recommednations of the Mudaliar Commission were :

1. The school course should be reduced to 11 years from 12 years. [On this basis XI Class schools known as Higher Secondary Multipurpose Schools grew up later with various streams like - Humanities, Science, Commerce, Agriculture, Technical, Fine arts, Home Science]

2. Regarding curricuta, the Com. proposed :

    (i)   3 languages - Mother Tongue, English and Hindi. Children whose mother tongue was Hindi were to take up one modern Indian language other than Hindi.

    (ii) Social studies and general science

    (iii) One craft

    (iv) Three additional subjects from prescribed seven groups - Humanities, Science, Agriculture, Commerce, Home Science, Fine Arts and Technical.

The object of these Multipurpose school was to divert the students at this age of 17 to different walks of life that they can earn livelihood and put less pressure on University education.

3. Examination reforms were also suggested

4. Teachers - More qualified teachers were to be employed

5. The com. proposed that steps should be taken to provide educational and vocational guidance to pupils

6. Strengthening libraries and laboratories, introduction of audio-visual aids etc. were recommended.

This XI class school system was introduced late and died early. The scheme was introduced in 1959 and in 1976 XII class school system with 3 years Degree Course was introduced.

Kothari Commission

In 1964 another Commission on Education was appointed under the Chairmanship of Dr. D. S. Kothari to review education in all its aspects, and to make recommednations for future development of education (Discussed - post).

National Policy on Edducation 1958

After examining the recommednation of the Education Com., the Govt. of India issued an important statement on the National Policy of Education. This became the basis for educational development in 4th and 5th 5-year plan.

Women's Education

In the post-independence period the issue of women education received an impetus, and a good deal of progress was made. The enrolement of girls in 1960-61, was considerably higher than 1949-50.

In 1949-50, enrolement of girls per 100 boys was 33 but in 1960-61 the enrolement of girls per 100 boys increased to 42. The enrolment increased not only in Primary sector, almost in all sectors - Primary, Secondry, University, Professional and Vocational.

But before 1960, Govt. of india appointed a National Committee for Women education under the Chairmanship of Smt. Durgabai Deshmukh. The committee was advised to go deep into the difficultires that deterred the progress of female education and to make recommendations regarding the manner in which the education of girls could be brought at per with the boys, specially at the primary and secondary stages.

The Committee recommended, among others, the following most important ones :

(1) The eduation of women should be regarded as a special issue and for some years special fund to be provided.

(2) There should be a National Council for the Education of women at the Centre and similar Council in states, and Union Territories. the main object of these councils will be to eduate the public and advise the Govts the measures to be taken.

(3) There should be a special unit in the Govt. of India to look after the programmes of girls education and in each state Department of education, a special officer should be appointed at the Directorate level. The existing Inspectorate for Girls schools should also be considerably stengthened.

(4) It is necessary to develop a large number of special programmes for bringing about a rapid expansion in the education of girls. The most important of these are the preparation and employment of women teachers and provision for special amenities for girls, such

as grant of free books, writing materials, scholarship, clothing or provision for mid-day meals.

The major recommednations have been accepted by the Govt. In 1959 a National Council for the Education was set up under the Chairmanship of Smt. Durgabai Deshmukh. Most of the State Govts. have appointed Asst. Director or Deputy Director incharge of Women education. The strength of Inspectress has increased. Special fund has been allotted.

The Central social welfare Board has adopted a scheme of condensed course for adult women (18-35 age group) who once had to give up education but now had been interested. Through this condensed course such intending women may qualify themselves as teachers, nurses, midwives etc. The training is of two to three years.

Data on Women Education
Enrolment in Institutions

Institution	1921-22	1931-32	1941-42	1946-47
Primary School	10871312	1944070	3123643	2715230
Secondary School	124959	196170	410333	442403
Arts & SC Colleges	1207	2685	11778	16284
Professional Colleges	266	521	1725	2468
Profession Schools	19570	17568	40869	38375

[Source : Indian Edu. quoted from S. N. Mukherjee's Education in India Today and Tomorrow P-255].

In 1904 Mrs. Annie Besant established Central Hindu Girls school at Benaras with a view to impart Western Education to girls. In 1916 Lady Hardinge Medical College was established in Delhi. The S. N. D. T. university (see Supra) for women was established. In 1917 there were 12 Arts Colleges, 4 Professional Colleges and 1656 Secondary Schools for girls.

The women's movement in contemporary Europe had an influence. Mrs. Annie Besant and Mrs. Margaret Cousins founded Women's Indian Association in 1917. In 1925 the National Council of Women was established. It flourished and got affiliated to Internaitonal Council of Women.

In 1927 was held for the first time, All India Women's conference. this conference agitated issues like equal opportunities of education, education of women and amilioration of women's social position.

The National Movements in India and participation of Women in large numbers, highlighted the issue of Women education.

No. of girls Institutions & enrolment

	1947-48	*1960-61*
Institutions	16951	41674
Enrolment	3550503	14259047

From the data available from Govt. of India - programme for Educational Development 1961-66, it will be evident that there was a rapid progress and girls were enrolled in different institutions.

	1949-50	*1959-60*
1. Research	85	657
2. M.A., M.Sc	1656	7679
3. B.A., B.Sc, Intermediate	23540	76643
4. Prof. Edu.	4055	22246
5. Spl. Edn.	771	6570
6. Vocational Edn.	35760	78097
7. School Edn. different stages	575553	12464688

Droup-out is a serious problem in Indian Educational frame. It causes wastage. But the socio-economic condition compels pupils to drop from school education in every stage. This is more evident in girls cases. If the drop out is the result of poverty, the girls drop out is the result of social system i.e. to give them in marriage at an early age. This affects the number of women's availability as teachers, nurses etc.

A meeting of Education Ministers of India was held (may be in 1961 or 1963, the report was published in Times of India on 15 Nov, 1963). The conference suggested:

1. construction of quarters women teachers
2. hostels for girls in rural areas
3. free education to girls at least upto secondary stage
4. improvement of training facilities for women.

and so many such suggestions. In case of drop-outs (discontinuance of study) it was learnt that 100 pupils admitted in Class I and only 41 of them reached Class IV. This wastage was more prominent in case of girls.

The initial inspiration of getting admitted to school and having education of the girls, was remarkably encouraging which is evident in the following data :

Enrolment Picture

Year	Class VI-VIII	Class IX - XI
1950-51	5.3 lakhs	1.90 lakhs
1955-56	8.7 lakhs	3.32 lakhs
1960-61	14.7 lakhs	5.27 lakhs

[**Source :** Education in India 1959-60]
Output of Girls in University Examination

	1949-50	*1959-60*
Intermediate	8252	25091
B.A. and B.Sc	4694	18554
M.A and M.Sc	744	4186
Professional Subjects	1232	6166

[**Source :** Edn. in India 1960-61]

Besides, the S.N.D.T. Women University, The Prayag Mahila Vidyapith, Allahabad, had separate special courses for girls and Degrees it offers are also different. It was established in 1922 and aimed at spreading girls education. The examinations held by the Vidyapith are : Pravesika, Vidya-Vinodini, Sugrihini, Vidushi, Saraswati and Bharati. The Arya Kanya Mahavidyalaya at Baroda is a residential one. It lays great stress on physical activities.

It was felt that girls should have a special type of course of study. So, Home Sciences as a subject was adopted in 24 Universities.

During the period under review there were 75 colleges teaching this subject. In 8 colleges, Post-graduate courses in the subject are taught. Those 8 are : Faculty of Home Science, Baroda, Lady Irwin College, New Delhi, St. Thresa Colleges, Ernakulam, Queen Mary's College, Madras, Women's Christian College, Madras, SIET Women's College, Madras, Sri Avinashilingam Home Science College at Coimbatore and Maharani's College for Women, Bangalore.

Though Women are receiving and have been receiving training in various subjects, their largest enrolment can be found in teachers' training institutions. In the professional field Nursing is practically a monopoly of women. In 1946, two colleges were set up. The Nursing Council was constituted under the Nursing Council Act of 1947. The third and fourth nursing colleges were set up in 1959 and 1961. Now many Nursing Colleges for training have been set up.

A scheme for technical education and vocational training for girls has been drawn up by the Govt. of India under which competent authorities may establish - polytechnics, technical schools and integrated institution for girls.

Women workers are needed in community Development Project. Each Block needs one Mukhya Sevika, two Gram Sevikas, one Health Visitor (lady), four midwives. Centres for their training have been set up. The training period is of few months only.

Lastly, we must be very much clear about the ideals of women education. The old idea is a women's place is home and hearth and they should be so educated. The modern view is, women are equal with men. So they will cover all aspects and not be confined to home and hearth.

Whatever view is taken, one thing must be kept in mind that women in India, have some traditional ideals to guide and inspire them. Probably, there are a few country in this world which have this heritage. Moreover, in India marriage is not a contract, as it is found else where. Modernity should not mean that one has to give up one's own national cultural heritage and immitate a foreign culture. The Indian women must be Indian and the content of education should be such that they do not fall prey to foreign culture in the name of modernity.'

Adult Education

If we take into account the literacy percentage of adults in India now, it will come at best to 74 percent. In 1947 our literacy was 14 percent and in 1971, it was 29 percent. So after Independence upto 1971, the growth was less than 1 percent a year. The percentage has fallen in Independent India. This may be for two culpable reasons.

1. Adult Education issue did not get the importance
2. Increase of popualton beyond control, at least in one community. In the constitution of India Article 45, directs, primary education to be imparted to all within ten years i.e. by 1959. We have failed to achieve that. But in the constitution, there is no provision for adult education or literacy.

We have noted 'Adult Educaiton Centre' here and there. But in most cases those are more bluffs than real. By literacy we mean very cheap a thing - Reading, Writing and Arithmatic and we have failed to make the adult popualtion literate. The society in which these illeterate adults live, if not take interest and make the illiterates aware of their drawbacks, they cannot be brought to education centre. The Govt. should take the lead and should direct every NGO to take up literacy campaign as one of the basic object of that NGO.

Among the adult illiterates, there are men who once was enrolled in a school, but as they dropped out they have managed to forget what they had learnt once upon a time in their lives.

So the programme of adult literacy should receive a carefuld and serious attention of the Govt and the society at large.

Agricultural Education

It must be admitted that the cultivators, now-a-days, are more or less well informed about agriculture and agricultural products. Rain, Water, Seed, Fertiliser, Season and Variety of agriculture are not now very unknown to peasants directly related to land.

Radio, Television, Block Agriculture Offices and experience have made the peasants informed. But coming to the formal education of the subject of Agriculture our progress should be analysed.

The University Education Commission had stated that - "education to promote the interest of agriculture is extremely inadequate and agricultural education should be recognised as a major national issue." This statement was seriously taken up. This led to reorganisation of agricultural education and expansion of the existing facilities. In 1947 there were only 17 agricultural institutions offering higher education in the subject. After a period of roughly 25 years, the number of agricultural colleges reached 93. In 1965-66 the enrolment was 11,562. But the encouragement of students to receive agricultural education had a set back. And the cause was unemployment of educated youths. To give more impetus Agricultural Universities were established - where education, research and expansion was integrated.

There are now nineteen such Universities and there is a target to establish one Agriculture University in every state.

With the object of 'Green Revolution' the Indian Council of Agricultural Research (ICAR) has been a major contributing factor for the development. Agricultural polytechnics to impart techniracy i.e. the essential technical know-how of agriculture to all farmers has been in action. Consequently we find peasants are now very much accustomed to use technical machineries in agriculture.

Medical Education

We have touched the subject while discussing the history of education during the British period in India.

Till 1946, there were 15 medical colleges with an annual enrolement of 1200. Training of specialists and scope of research was almost little. During the post independent period under review, emphasis was laid on this aspect of education. Health Survey and Planning Committee (1959-69) examined different aspects of the matter. Study in medical colleges turned to be an ambition of meritorious students. Within the period under review 100 medical colleges with an annual enrolement of more than 12000 grew up. Medical colleges under private enterprise took a major part. Number of Doctors has increased considerably. Training of para-Medical persons has expanded. Different disease prevention programme have been taken up by the Govt. Post-Graduate teaching and research have developed. All India Institute of Medical Sciences have been created by an Act of Parliament. Indian Council of Medical Research is looking after medical researches.

Technical Education

During the period under review i.e. 28 years of independence, a major advance in the field of Technical Education has been effected.

Indeependent India in 1947, faced a great challenge in this field. In 1947, the country produced only 930 graduates in Engineering and 320 graduates in technology. Facilities were meagre.

There are now five Institutions of Technology and fifteen Regional engineering colleges. There have grown up Polytechnic Institutions. In this field also private enterprise has played a role. New colleges and polytechnics were established.

Consequently, the annual admission to engineering colleges increased from 3000 in 1947 to 25000 in 1965-66 and in Polytechnic from 3700 to 50000. The post independent period saw a spectacular development in Industry for the contribution of these institutions in this field. [Source : J. P. Naik]

In the present day, after 70 years of independence, the nature of economy has changed. There has been spectacular change in the field of science and Technology including electronics. Knowledge of Computer technology is a must now in every field and employment. So there is a phenomenal growth in Computer technology and its utilisation.

Kothari Commission 1964

This education commission was appointed after seventeen years of independence. It opined that "the existing system of education, designed primarily to meet the needs of an imperial administration within the limits set up by a feudal and traditional society, will need a radical change if it is to meet the purpose of a modern democratic and socialist society - changes in objectives, in teaching methods, in programmes, in the size and composition of the student body, in the selection and professional preparation of teachers and in organiation."

Kothari Commission, with a foresight, devised a picture of national system of education and a programme spread over next 20 years, i.e.upto 1986.

It happens to be the third Education Com. within 17 years of Independence and the sixth since British Colonial rule in India.

The first two - Radhakrishnan and Mudaliar were on University and Secondary education respectively. But this commission under Dr. Kothari was comprehensive as it dealt with all aspects and sectors of education. The other special feature of this Commission was along with 11 Indian members it included one each from five other countries - France, Japan, U.K., U.S.A. and U.S.S.R. This Commission submitted its report in 1966.

As in 1948, the then Prime Minister Nehru felt, this commisison also came to a conclusion that drastic reconstruction of the system, amounting to a revolution was needed if India had to reach its goal. This revolution or drastic reconstruction was to be done in three aspects:

(1) Education should be so transformed as to relate to the life and aspiration of the nation.

(2) Qualitative improvement of the standard in general and in few sectors the standard should be international,

(3) Expansion and equalisation of educational facilities.

This committee was vocal that no reform in education is more urgent than to relate it to the aspiration of the people and their lives and needs. So internal transformation is needed. Educaiton is the powerful instrument to effect the social, economic and cultural changes needed for the country. This transformation was to be done rapidly by expanding education. The delay may make this transformation more difficult as more delay will make more people accustomed to traditional system which is targetted to be reformed.

The commisison, to bring about this internal transformation suggested ten programmes.

(i) Science education must be an integral part of school education. In University level research should be emphasised.

(ii) Particularly in secondary stage of education, vocational education should be provided at least to 20 percent in age group 11-16, at higher secondary stage age group 17-18, at least to 50 percent and in higher education, about one-third of the total enrolement may be in vocational course.

(iii) A common school system of public education should be introduced,

(iv) Some form of social service should be obligatory at each level,

(v) All modern Indian languages should be developed and used as media of education. Though English is the window to the World and should be taught, Hindi should be developed as link language of the country.

(vi) Through curricular and extra curricular means national unity and national consciousness to be created and developed.

(vii) The existing education system is rigid. It has to be elastic and dynamic.

(viii) It is necessary to develop a large programme of part-time and own-time education.

(ix) The Commission proposes that 10 percent of the enrolement at higher primary and lower secondary stages, 25 percent of the enrolement of Higher Secondary stage and about one-third of the enrolement at University stage should be in part-time or self study courses.

(x) The education system should emphasise the development of fundamental social, moral and spiritual values, there should be provision for giving some instructions about different religion.

2. For qualitative Improvement, the commission, along with other recommendations, suggested :

(i) Increase in the number of working days

(ii) lengthening the duration of the working day,

(iii) Proper use of vacations.

(iv) The first ten years of school education should be a period of general education. Specialisation after Class X. The H.S. stage should be of two years and located in schools. This will be followed by a 3 year first degree course.

(v) Substantial improvement in the remuneration of teachers should be made. The gap in the remuneration of teachers at different stages should be abridged. There must be parity and uniformity in respects of pay, allowance, retirement benefit of teachers working in all types of institutions - Govt. Private local authority. If this is implemented best persons may be recruited which ultimately will help to achieve better standard.

(vi) Drastic changes in curricula, teaching method and examination have been suggested.

(vii) The commission is of opinion that since the resources available in men, material and money are not enough during the next 10 years, 10 percent of institutions should be upgraded. At the primary level these institutions should be distributed equally to all parts of the country. In the secondary and H.S. stage, at least one in every block, and one college in every district. At the university stage five or six universities are to be selected.

3. On expansion of education, the Commission wants that it should be taken up after internal transformation and improvement of standard as suggested be achieved.

The expansion programme will constitute,

(i) Adult education & literacy

(ii) Primary education to all

iii) Expansion of secondary and Higher secondary will be on selective basis.

The Commission visualises that by 1985, the total enrolement in national system of education will rise by 100 million i.e. 70 million in 1965 will come upto 170 million in 1985. This will largely depend upon equalization of educatinal opportunities. Good and effective primary education to all children will be first major step. In secondary and Higher Secondary stage, scholarship and placement should develop and admission to quality institutions should be made on the basis of merit.

The budget on education will rise by 8 times i.e. Rs. 6000 million in 1965 to Rs. 470000 million in 1985 which is 6 percent of national income.

The Kothari Commission is to be praised and appreciated at least in two aspects :

(i) It is for the first time realised that education of a nation should be based on national aspiration and realities and needs of life. By immitation you can not transform. For transformation you need invention.

(ii) The commisison by its recommendations has emphasised the msot important requirements of a good life - (i) science and (ii) spiritualilty. The education system, to be a National system of Education, particularly for India, a blend of science and spirituality must be there.

[Indebted to J. P. Naik and Syeed Nurullah's Book for this part - Kothari Commission].

We have noted that after the tansfer of power in 1947, Radhakrishnan Commission was appointed in 1948 to consider University Education. After that Mudaliar Commission was appointed to consider Secondary Education in 1952. By an Act of Parliament in 1956, University Grants Commission (U.G.C.) - a statutory Body was set up Dr. C. D. Deshmukh was the first Chairman.

U.G.C.

It consists of nine members of whom not more than three are to be Vice-Chancellors of Universities, and not more than two officers of the central Govt., the remaining members are to be nominated from among the educationists of repute. the main responsibility of the Com. is to Co-ordinate and maintain standard for which necessary statutory authority is provided. The Central Govt. places funds at the disposal of the U.G.C. After its creation in 1956, during the second 5-years plan (1955-1960) Rs. 24 crores and during the next plan, Rs. 110 crores in the 4th and Rs. 210 crores in the 5h plan period approximately 400 crores were alloted. The com. in turn allocates funds to the Universities for necessary developments.

The Commission has been rendering appreciable service. Development of Research works, better facilities for teachers, Library, Laboratory etc.

Research

The Govt. took up the issue of research very seriously in post-independence period for the socio-economic development of the country.

Govt's policy on Research

In March 1958, the scientific policy Resolution was taken by the Govt. It states :

1. To foster, promote and sustian, by all appropriate means, the cultivation of science and scientific research in all its aspects - pure, applied and educational.

2. To ensure adequate supply of scientists of highest quality,

3. To encourage and initiate training of scientific and technical personnel, to fulfill the country's needs,

4. To encourage creative talent of men and women.
5. To encourage discovery of new knowledge.
6. To ensure for the people of the country all the benefits that can assure from the acquisition and application of scientific knowledge.

Three year Degree Course

As was recommended by Radhakrishnan Com. three years' degree course has been introduced with the exception of few Universities. Radhakrishnan Com. wanted 12 years' school course. But Mudaliar Com. wanted to introduce XI-Class schools. This was introduced. Now 12-Class schools are running and college education starts after that.

Dr. K. L. Shrimali Committee

Radhakrishnan Com. proposed the establishment of Rural universities. The Govt. of India appointed a Committee presided over by Dr. K. L. Shrimali to consider the proposal.

The committee recommended to establish Rural Institute (avoiding University). The object of these institutes was to provide facilities for higher education in rural areas. In accordance with this recommendation of the Shrimali Committee eleven Rural Institutes were established.

Higher Education

Since 1947 to the period under discussion, there has been a phenomenal growth in Higher education. The progress may be seen from the given data

College Education in British India 1857

In 1857, there were only 23 Colleges for general learning, 3 Medical Colleges and one Civil Engineering College.

	Colleges of general learning	*Medical*	*Engineering*
Bengal			
(a) Govt.	7	1	-
(b) Missionaries	7	-	-
Bombay			
(a) Govt.	2	1	-
(b) Missionaries	-	-	-
N. W. Province			
(a) Govt.	4	-	-
(b) Missionaries	-	-	-

(Contd...)

Madras			
(a) Govt.	1	1	-
(b) Missionaries	2	-	-
	23	3	1

During the period 1920-1946 Pre-Independence Period

	1921-22	*1931-32*	*1946-47*
Colleges	231	417	933
Enrolement	59591	99493	199253

Figures in 1959-60

Management	Arts+ Sc College	For Spl. Edn.	Professional Edn.
Govt.	222	45	359
Local Bodies	3	2	3
Private Bodies			
Aided	635	48	271
Unaided	128	15	92
Total	988	180	725

It will be clear from the given data that Private enterprise was very remarkable : (1) Two out of three colleges were managed by Private bodies and many were unaided by the Govt. (2) Only about half of the Professional Colleges were under Govt. Control.

By this time 1961-62, number of Universities was 55 and the total enrolement was more than 10 lakhs. State-wise number of Universities was :

Andhra - 3	Asam - 1	Bihar - 6
Delhi - 1	Gujrat - 3	J.K. - 1
Kerala - 1	Madhya Pr. - 5	Madras - 2
Maharastra - 5	Mysore - 2	Orissa - 2
Punjab - 4	Rajasthan - 3	U.P. - 9
West Bengal - 7		

The U.G.C. appointed a committee in September 1961 to examine the question of establishment of new Universities and to suggest broad outlines for future.

The committee recommended that, where ever resource and circumstances make it possible, it would be advisable to adopt a federal type of organisation for a university. A federal type of university provides greater possibilities, scope and incentives for imprroving the quality of higher education, specially at the post-graduate and research levels. This is our most precious need.

It also recommended that there is a limit of size of a University. The pupil enrolement in a University should not exceed 10000. India needs new types of Universities as well. There is enough room for developing single faculty universities, specialising in one particualr branch of learning.

But there is a need for proper planning while starting new Universities. Since independence, thirty five new Universities have been established. For a few the ground was no doubt prepared. The rest, would be justfied by local needs and facilities. A few have been brought into being in order to satisfy regional patriotism or to invest the institution a dignity in name and law which does not belong to it in terms of educational achievement. Before a University is brought into being, there ought to be a wide-spread net work of schools, colleges and research institutions, which can provide sustainance.

University and Governments

The Constitution of India, as mentioned earlier, has made univesity education an affair of the state, the Central Govt. retains the responsibilty of determination of standards. Only three Universities - Benaras Hindu University, Aligarh Muslim University and Delhi University are under the control of the Central Govt as per constitution. In 1951, the Viswa Bharati University had been declared by the Parliament to be an institution of national importance. So now only 4 Universities are under the direct control of the centre. The rest are under respective states.

The article 282 of the constitution enables the centre to give financial assistance to the states for any public purpose which, of course, include university education.

Indian Universities are dependent on the states in two ways -

(1) They are created by the state legislature and so they are dependent on the Govt. for their Constitution and powers.

(2) They receive annual financial aids for recurring and non-recurring expenses from the state Govt.

But for these two restrictions, the Indian Universities are more or less autonomous.

Secondary Education

It is admitted that secondary education is the back-bone of the nation. Therefore, its administration must be more than efficient and its curriculum should be most modern and the whole system must have its relation with traditional culture of the country which relates to identify of an Indian national.

Only Kothari Commission (1964-66) of the Commissions, touched the issue of national inspiration, relation to life and need of the people. The commission meant it to be one of Internal Transformatiion. We shall not differ to agree that this Internal transformation has not taken place and we cannot boast yet of an Indian National System of Education. We simply ammend and immitate. So the back-bone aspect of our education is normally and spiritually extremely weak and has failed to reach an international standard even after 70 years of transfer of power.

This invites us to look into the details of the problems of secondary education. Let us consider summarily the position from Wood's Despatch 1854, which forms the basis of our education till today.

The Despatch declared "that the people of India should be made familiar with works of European authors, and with the results of the thought and labour of the Europeans on the subject of every description and to extend the means of imparting the knowledge must be the object of any general system of education."

Thus through English education grant-in-Aid and University came to India.

Some defects cropped up. Hunter Commission was appointed which examined the position and recommended.

"That in the upper classes of High Schools, there be two divisions - one leading to Matriculation Examination of Universities, the other of a more practical character, intended to fit youths for commercial or other non-literary persuits.

This useful recommendation was ignored.

The growth of secondary education was very notable between 1882 to 1902:

	No. of Schools 1882	*No. of Schools 1902*
Schools	3916	214677
Enrolement	5124	622868

There was no consolidation and control. University recognition was loose.

Then University Act 1904 was passed. It empowered universities to frame rules of recognition of schools. Only recognised schools could present candidates for Matricualtion Examination.

The people at that period was inspired by a national sentiment centering partition of Bengal. Lord Curzon's educational policy was taken with distrust and disgust. The general public on the other hand was much interested in education and National school grew up. In summary - An open revolt against the prevailing educational system was organised in Bengal. Naitonal Council of Education was set up. Sri Goorudas Banerjee, Rashbehari Ghosh and Rabindranath Thakur were leaders. The Council drew up a very detailed programme of national education starting from the infant stage right upto university stage. A national college with Sri Aurobindo as its first principal and a technical institution (the present Jadavpur University) were started in Calcutta. Some national schools were also established. The movement did not last long. With slackening of the Swadeshi Movement, the schools, excepting Jadavpur, were closed.

Regarding medium of instruction, there was a great demand of introducing mother tongue. A resolution in the Imperial Legislative Council was moved by Shri S. Rayaningar on 17 March 1915. But English was kept as medium of instruction on the grounds that -

(i) It is inter provincial language

(ii) Mother tongues are not yet properly developed as text books

(iii) Pupils knowledge of English will deteriorate

The ultimate result was that English continued as medium of instruction.

During this period, Secondary schools had to take recognition from two agencies - (i) university for permisssion to present candidates in Matriculation Exam and (2) the education Dept. for grant-ibn-Aid. Education Dept. did not like the University as the Recognition Authority.

However, from 1917, several Commissions and Committees, tackled the problem and submitted reports

1917 - Sadler Commission report

1929 - Hartog Committee report

1937 - Abbot Wood report

1944 - Sargent Committee report

Of these Sadler Commission, we have discussed the report of the Sadler Com. known as Calcutta University Com. Sir Michael Sadler was the Vice-Chanceller of Leeds University.

In our previous discussion we have mentioned Hartog Com. practically Hartog Committee wanted to eliminate wastage caused by failure in Matriculation Examination.

The Committee suggested (1) Diversion of boys to industrial and commercial careers at the end of the middle stage. Industrial schools with courses of study were to be established. (2) Middle vernacular schoolls should have more diversified courses for pursuits of rural students.

Abbot Wood Report 1937

Two English experts Mr. Abbot and Wood were invited to advise the Govt. of India on Certain educational problems. The Report of Abbot and Wood suggested a complete hierarchy of vocational institutions parallel to the hierarchy of instiutions imparting general education.

Sargent Report - 1944

So far as Secondary Education in concerned, it recommended as follows:

(1) The High School Course should cover six years and the normal age of admission should be 11 years.

(2) Entry to high school should be on selective basis

(3) High school advantage should be made available at least to 1 of the 5 of the appropriate age group.

(4) The method of selection of High School must be very careful.

(5) High Schools should be of two types (a) Academic (b) Technical

(6) The Curriculum in all cases should be as varied as circumstances permit and should not be unduly restricted by the requirements of the universities or examining bodies.

Such were the recommendations of commissions and committes before the Mudaliar Commission was appointed in 1952 only to consider Secondary Education. There was an enormous expansion of Secondary High Schools.

	1916-17	*1947-48*
No. of Schools	4883	12693
Enrolement	924770	2953995

[**Source :** S. N. Mukherjee - History of education in India P-250]

Several improvements took place -

(1) English ceased to be the only medium of Instruction.

(2) Friction between Universities and Education Dept. was removed. The Universities automatically included all recognised departmental schools in their list of approved schools.

(3) The curricula were widened and vocational courses were provided.

(4) The standard of teaching improved owing to the increase in percentage of trained teachers.

Developments after 1947

After Independence three important bodies examined the issue of secondary education of the country

(1) Tarachand Committee 1948

(2) University Education Com. alias Radhakrishnan Com. 1948-49

(3) Mudaliar Commission 1952

(4) Kothari Commission 1964-66

Of these we have discussed the recommendatins of each excepting Tarachand Committee.

Tarachand Com

The committee made important recommendations. It suggested that the schools at secondary level should be multipurpose type, though unipurpose schools should not be discouraged. It also suggested to appoint a commission of secondary education issue.

Since the publication of Tarachand com. report, there is a strong movement for the diversification of the courses at the secondary level. Attempts are also made to materialise vocational education.

Aicse

Based on the recommendations of the Mudaliar Com., the Govt. of India established All India Council for Secondary Education (AICSE) in March 22, 1955. It served as an expert Body advising Central and State Governments on the improvement and expansion of Secondary Education.

All executive functions, performed by AICSE have been entrusted to Directorate of Extension Programmes for Secondary Education (DEPSE). It is now a department a department of the National Council of Education and Research and Training (Ncert).

Depse

The DEPSE has different units through which it functions :

Extension Services Project
Examination Reform
Basic Data
Service Education
In-Service Programme
School Experiment Project

Problems of Secondary Education

Our Secondary education system is an object of severe criticism. Secondary Educaiton is the connecting link between primary education and higher education. The three are interdependent. Without better Primary education, no better secondary education is possible and with a weak secondary education higher education cannot be upto the mark.

So the need is the strengthening of Primary Education, where seriousness and devotion are very much wanting.

However, the secondary education of our country is faced with the following vital problems :

1. Aim. the secondary education in India suffers from aimlessness.
2. its pattern
3. its curriculum
4. its need for guidance
5. administration and control i.e. management
6. fianance
7. examination system
8. Discipline - the last but the most important - just second to AIM of education.

[Indebted to S. N. Mukherjee's book-Education in India today and tomorrow].

Primary Education

Let us recapittulate what we have discussed earlier on Primary Education

1. This country had a indigenous system of Primary education from time immemorial
2. Munro, Elphinstone, Adam and Thomason were unanimous that the primary educaiton was no novel to Indian popualtion. Adam

noted in 1835, Bengal and Bihar had one lakh schools i.e. roughly 2 schools for every 3 villages and there was school for every 400 persons.

3. It was also revealed by the enquiries made during the first half of 19th century that attendance of pupils in such primary schools was, 1 in every 34 in Madras, 1 in every 36 in Bengal and 1 in 62 in Bombay. The percentage of literacy in the 1st half or 19th Century was 6.1 percent. The syllabus was of 3 R's and accounts.

4. The Missionaries of Christanity came to the country in the wake of European traders. They took up elementary education as means to their mission of conversion to Christanity. The Mahamedans were not interested as they had their own programme of conversion. So the missionaries mainly targetted the lower strata first, then to general Hindus.

5. It must be admitted that the missionaries introduced a new educational system independently.

   (a) Classes were held regualrly

   (b) There was a specific syllabus

   (c) A class system was introduced

   (d) Religious instruction on Christanity and degrading Hinduism continued

6. The charter Act of 1813, directed the East India Company which had no concern with education of the country so long, was directed to spend a sum of not less than One lakh on education every year. After 10 years, only from 1824, the company did care to spend on education though the amount of money was very poor in relation to the size and number of population of the country.

7. In 1854, extension of elementary education was advocated.

8. After the great national movement in 1857 (named sepoy mutiny by the Britishers and so followed by their Indian agents), the British Crown began to govern India directly.

9. In 1859, Stanley's Despatch admitted that it was impossible for the Govt to take the total financial burden of elementary education of the country and so it was necessary to levy cess or tax on the public and the collected money be spent on elementary education.

10. In 1864, Local cess Act was passed.

11. In 1883-84 various Municipal Acts and Local Board Acts wee passed, in persuance of Lord Ripon's policy of local self-govt.

12. The Indian Education Policy in 1904 declared.

"It is commonly reckoned that 15 P.C. of the popualtion was of school-going age, but actually a little more than one-sixth are receiving education, that the extension of Primary education has received a check during recent years. Primary education has hitherto received insufficient attention and an inadequate share of public funds."

[Source : Govt. of India Education Policy.]

13. Owing to the economic life of the people, a large number of indigenous schools were closed.

14. The Britishers having no regard for the Hindus and their idolatory tradition had scant sympathy. They crushed down the indigenous education system.

15. But Administrators as well as Educationsists - Munroe, Elphinstone, Adam, Thomason advised the Govt. repeatedly to build up public education system. But the advice remained a mere advice.

16. The British Govt. was interested in University education as that would supply them army of clerks. They decided to educate a few and that will filtrate downwrd. In the words of Mayhew.

"Education was to permeate the masses from above. Drop by drop from the Himalayas of Indian life useful information was to tickle downwards, forming in time a broad and stately stream to irrigate the thirsty plains."

17. The Britishers did not accept the theory of compulsory elementary education for all.

18. The British Govt. was unwilling to take the financial responsibility for such a scheme. It is clear from the data that the total expenditure on education in 1901-1902 was Rs. One crore 27 lakhs 8 thousand 6 hundred fifty nine (Rs. 10278659) which was .88 P.C. of the total revenue of the country.

Early Attempts for Compulsory Primary Education

1. The earliest suggestion to introduce compulsory Primary Education in India was made by Willium Adam in 1838, asking for a law that every village had a primary school.

2. In 1870, compulsory primary education was introduced in England. This gave an impetus. Vivekananda in his speeches mentioned that for social reforms, the first duty was to educate the people.

3. The first organised attempt to introduce compulsory Primary education in British India was made in Bombay under Sir Ibrahim Rahamatoolah and Sir Chimonlal Sitalwad. As a result, the Govt. of Bombay appointed a Committee to examine the issue in 1906.

4. But before that in 1893, the Maharaja Sayaji Rao Gaikwoard of Baroda introduced compulsory free Primary Education in a Taluk (Amrehi) of his state. In 1906 he extended it to the entire state.

5. In 1910 Shri Gopal Krishna Gokhale moved a resolution in the Imperial Legistature "to make bettr provision for the extension of elementary education." As expected he failed.

6. The Govt of India Act 1919 passed education for the first time in the hands of Indian ministers.

7. In 1937, Provincial autonomy was introduced with the right to control all branches of state administration.

8. It is to be noted that Shri Bithalvai Patel moved a bill in Bombay Legislature for introducing compulsory primary education in Municipal areas (excluding Bombay City). Patel's bill became an Act in 1918.

9. After this, almost every province passed acts of compulsory education.

10. In 1946-47, the compulsion existed in 229 towns and 10,017 villages for boys and in 10 towns and 1401 villages for both boys and girls.

Number of Primary Schools
10 years 1951-1960

Year	Number of Schools
1950-51	209676
1951-52	215036
1952-53	222014
1953-54	239382
1954-55	263626
1955-56	278135
1956-57	287298
1957-58	298247
1958-59	301564
1959-60	319070

It shows that number of Primary schools steadily increased in 10 years.

Enrolement

On the eve of independence, hardly 36.3 percent of the children of the age group 6-11 were in school including one-teacher school in 1952.Under the Chairmanship of B. G. Kher a committee was appointed by Indian Ministry of Education to examine the existing financial sources and suggest ways and means of raising finance required for the different stages of comprehensive education.

The committee presented a scheme for introducing eight years' compulsory education within a period of 16 years by two five year plans and one six year plan. The committee suggested that the Centre should provide 30 P.C. and the state and local bodies provide 70 P.C. of the total cost.

Enrolement 1950-51 to 1962-63

Year	Enrolement in lakhs	P.C. of Popualtion of the age group
1950-51	191.5	42.3
1951-52	198.1	43.3
1952-53	203.5	43.8
1953-54	216.7	46.0
1954-55	232.2	48.5
1955-56	251.7	52.9
1956-57	267.1	-
1957-58	281.7	56.7
1958-59	304.5	57.3
1959-60	324.5	59.5
1960-61	343.4	61.9
1961-62	378.4	65.4
1962-63	415.4	69.7

Teachers

There was a satisfactory growth in number of teachers in Primary schools. In 1953 no. of Teachers was 623 thousands (518 Men 105 Women). In 1959-60 it came to 731 thousands (606 men and 125 women)

In 1949, the average Annual (12 month) income of a Primary Teacher was approximately Rs. 480.00 i.e. Rs. 40.00 p.m. In 1957-58 it came upto Rs. 780 i.e. Rs. 65 p.m. The number of non-matric primary teachers in 1949-50 was almost 91 percent. In 1957-58 it was 71 percent.

448

Organisational Development

AICEE - All India Council of Elementary Education, has been set up by the Govt. of India in 1957 (1st July). This body has to work for the constitutional provision of Article - 45 Directive Principles of State Policy which reads :

"The state shall endeavour to provide within a period of ten years from the commencement of the constitution, for free and compulsory education for all children until they complete the age of fourteen years."

The Constitution commenced in 1949 and 10 years mean 1959. The AICEE was set up in 1957.

This body has 23 members - one representative from each state, one member to be nominted by CABE Central Advisory Board of Education. One from All India Council of Secondary Education (AICS) to be nominated by the Chairman, one principal of a training college to be nominated by Union Minister of Education, two educationists. The Chairman of this body is the Education Advisor of the Minister of Education. The head of the Basic and Social Edn. division acts as its secretary : Non-Official members hold office for two years.

The functions of this Council (AICEE)

(i)   Preparation of programme for early implementation of Art 45 of the constitution.

(ii)   To review and revise the progress made in this direction'

(iii)   Programme to expand and improve of Primary Education in each state

(iv)   Organising and assisting research in the administration finance and pedagogy.

(v)   Production of literature to improve the quality of education.

(vi)   Conducting sample survey and investigations

(vii)   To provide proper guidance leadership and co-ordination for the improvement and expansion of elementary education.

Revision : In 1957, the Educational Panel of the Planning Commission admitted that target fixed by Art 45 cannot be reached within 10 years. It, therefore, recommended children of the age group 6-11 are to be given free compulsory by 1965-66. But from the given table, it is clear that the target cannot be reached, and did not reach.

Survey : Between the years 1956 and 1959 Govt. of India carried out a survey in close co-operation with State Governments. Its objects were :

(i)   The number and population of cities, towns and villages already provided with schools.

(ii) The number and population of villages still to be provided with schools.

Teacher : The general education, training and salary must be of improved quality to ensure the achievement of the target. The pupil teacher ratio should be proper and requires more recruitment which entails more expenditure.

Mid-day Meal : It has been pointed out that one of the main causes of wastage (drop-out) in Primary education is the poverty of the parents - who make the children co-workers and the children discontinue schooling. In the third plan (1960-65), a provision of Rs. 3.2 crores was made to provide mid-day meal primarily in poverty-strcken areas of various states. It proposed to cover 119 lakhs children.

[Indebted to S. N. Mukherjee. His book Education in India Today and Tomorrow].

Educational Administration

1.   As a result of the recommendations of Wood's Despatch, in 1857 an education Branch was set up in the home Department. Departments of Public Instructions were created in the provinces.

2.   In 1901, Lord Curzon appointed a Director General of Education at the Centre and he was attached to the Home Dept. His responsibility was to advise the Govt. of India in all matters relating to Education.

3.   In 1910, an independent Dept. of Education was created at the Centre and one man was added to the ViceRoy's Executive Council. The post of Director General of Edn. was abolished.

4.   In 1915, the abolished post was revived and the name became Educational Commissioner. A Bureau of Edn. was set up with the function of publishing occassional Reports on educational matters, and publishing annual and quinquennial (five years) reviews.

5.   In 1919, with the inauguration of Mont-Ford Reforms, all Control and responsibility for education in the Provinces were transferred to the newly created Provincial Ministers of Education.

6.   In 1921, Central Advisory Board of Education (CABE) was established for the need of co-operation and co-ordination of the Provincial Govts. On financial ground this CABE was abolished

in 1923 along with the abolition of Bureau of Edn. created in 1915. The Dept. of Edn. was amalgamated with that of Health, Lands and Agriculture.

7. In 1935 CABE was revived on recommendations of Hartog Committee (1929). This Board was attached to the Dept. of Edn. Health, Lands and Agriculture. A member of the ViceRoy's Executive Council was placed incharge of that Dept.

8. In 1945, the Dept. of Health, Lands and Education was trifurcated and a separate Dept. of Education was set up.

9. In 1947, this was raised to the status of Ministry.

10. In 1958, the Ministry of Education and Scientific Research was reorganised and bifurcated - (1) the Ministry of Education (2) the Ministry of Scientific Research and Cultural Affairs.

11. In 1963 these were combined into one - Ministry of Education.

12. It may be noted that the Constitution of India scheduled Education to states, with little reservation (discussed Supra). Now, Education is administered by three distinct bodies : (1) Central Govt. (2) State Govt., (3) Local bodies.

(1) Central Govt. : Central Govt. has a cabinet Minister in charge of Edn. His dept. is the Indian Ministry of Education. Now it is named - Human Resource Development (HRD). It has an important role in formulating general policies on educaiton and ensuring the pattern of education in different states. The Minister has Deputy ministers to assist.

(2) The Educational Adviser is the administrative head of the Ministry and is the principal adviser to the Minister in all matters of policy and Administration.

The Ministry has been functioning through the following Bureau from 9 April, 1964.

Bureaus : (i) School Education, (ii) Higher Education, (iii) Language, Literature, Fine Arts, (iv) Scholarships, (v) Planning and ancillary educaitonal services. Each Bureau has been put in charge of a Joint Secretary.

School education bureau deals with elementary, basic and secondary eduation and the Central Schools. Bureau of Higher Educaiton covers univesity and Technical educaton. The scholarship bureau deals with all matters relating to scholarships internal, external, general and cultural. The bureau of planning and ancillary educational services includes National Council of Educational Research and Training (NCERT)

The Ministry is further helped by Central Advisory Board of Educaiton (CABE). All India Council of Elementary Education (AICEE), All India Council of technical Education (AICETE), University Grants Commission (UGC), Central Social Welfare Board (CSWB), National Board of Basic Education, Central Board of Sanskrit, Naitonal Board of Audiovisual Education, National Council of Women Eduation, National Council of Rural Higher Education.

Since Education is a subject in state list, the Central Govt. has a very limited control. But actually it plays a very vital role as a coordinating agency and its activities are many fold.

(1)   It fixes a general policy with an All India outlook.

(2)   Maintains cultural relation with foreign countries and UNESCO.

(3)   Grants scholarships to scheduled castes, Aboriginal and Hill Tribes as well as to overseas students from the country adn welfare of Indian students in foreign lands. There are Education Departments - Overseas Education Department in London, Washington, Bonn and Nairobi.

(4)   Co-ordinating agency of the State Govts.

(5)   Exclusively incharge of Education in centrally administered areas.

(6)   Looks after Central Universities of Benaras, Aligarh, Delhi and Viswavarati

(7)   Public Schools (Central)

(8)   Conducts Several educational and Research institutions like ITI schools of Mines and applied Geology Dhanbad, Delhi Polytechnic, Central Institute of English, Hyderabad, Training Centres for Blinds, Central Braille Press, National institution of sports.

(9)   Liberal Grant-in-aid to state Govts. and Universities for research works.

(10)   Advanced research and technical education.

There are so many such activities which are not fully mentioned here.

State Government

The State Governments are fully autonomous in regard to state-level education programmes except for those of which they receive Central grants.

The Administrative Machinery of the State Govt. consists of Minister of Education, Secretary of Education, Director of Education (DE), Inspectors of different ranks. The Minister controls the policy and directs its execution. The Secretary passes orders on behalf of the Govt. The D.E. is the permanent head of the department and is the technical adviser to the Minister. He works as secretay in some states. The D.E. is assisted by an inspecting staff. The Inspectorate has divisional offices.

Govt. shares its powers with or delegates a part of it to the Universities as regards higher education and instruction through mother tongue. There are statutory bodies like Board of Secondary Education, Board of Higher Secondary Education and local boards.

Local Bodies (Boards)

Local Boards include District, Municipal and Cantonment Boards as well as, Town Area Committees and Janapada Sabhas.

Govt. through a series of Acts, resolutions and announcements has developed a good deal of control over education on local Boards.

A new step towards Democratic Centralisation has been taken in the country as a result of recommendations of Balawantrai Mehta Committee. It recommended that not District but Block is the suitable unit of administration. It has more public touch and public has an easier access to Block than the District - The Com. recommended and proposed the establishment of a local body at the block-level called Panchayat Samiti to be elected by the village Panchayat. The Mehta Com. proposed for a Zilla Parishad with the power to approve the annual budget of the Panchayat Samiti and oversee its functions. The Panchayat Samiti at the Block level would function as an intermediary body between the village Panchayet and district body. A number of states have taken step to implement Balwantrai recommendations.

Classification of Institutions

The educational institutions are broadly classified as (i) Recognised and (ii) Unrecognised.

Recognised institutions are those which follow courses of studies which are prescribed or recognised by the Dept. of Public Instruction or by Education Board or by University and maintains a reasonable standard of efficiency. They are open to inspection and their pupils are ordinarily eligible for admisison to all public examinations.

All other institutions are described as Unrecognised Institutions. They are for the most part indigenous schools in which are taught Sanskrit, Pali, Arabic, The Quran, native systems of medicines etc.

The Recognised Institutions are managed directly by the Govt. or by a local or Municipal Board. This is called public management. Recognised schools are also managed by societies of individuals. This is known as Private managemnt. Recognised institutions may be aided or non-aided, i.e. receiving or not receiving. Institutions not getting Govt. aid are unaided recognised institutions.

In 1960-61 there were 472653 recognised institutions in the country of which 20.5 percent was managed by Govt., 46.3 percent managed by local bodies, 33.2 percent managed by Private bodies of which 30.5 percent was aided, 2.7 percent unaided.

During 1960-61, total number of pupils in recognised institutions was 4 crores 79 lakhs (Boys 3.37 and girls 1.42 crores) -

Preprimary Stage	:	0.4 percent
Primary Stage	:	71.2 percent
Secondary stage	:	21.7 percent
University Stage	:	1.7 percent
Professional and Special	:	5.00 percent

May it be cared that the picture of the period upto which we are discussing does not form the final form of the educaiton system in India. The whole education pattern underwent effective changes corresponding to the progress of the country and that of the World.

Ladder

But the educational ladder has been almost the same in future also. The educational ladder depicted here donot apply uniformly to all the states of the country. The period of ladder varies in different states. But the main structure is

1st stage Pre-Primary	:	Upto six yerrs of age
2nd stage Primary	:	Four years / five years
3rd stage Secondary	:	6+2 years
Junior		
Senior		
(Basic is included)		
4th stage University	:	3 years (for graduation)
		2 years for Master's degree

Besides there are numerous schools and colleges of varied character on professonal and vocational subjects : Commerce, Engineering, Technology, Teaching, Medicine, Law, Agriculture, Forestry and the like. But to get admission in professional institutions 12 class school course must be successfully completed.

Expenditure

Expenditure on education has been rapidly rising along with needs of time and the Nation. Avoiding the details, summarily it may be mentioned that expenditure on Education in education from different sources such as Central Govt., State Govt., District Boards, Municipal Boards, Tuition Fees and other sources, in total was :

1950-51	:	114 crores 38 lakhs
1955-59	:	189 crores 65 lakhs
1959-60	:	299 crores 66 lakhs

In the first 5 year plan the estimate of expenditure on Education was Rs. 151 crores.

In the Tenth 5 years plan (2002-2007) Rs. 43825 crores (outlay).

The expenditure on education as a percentage of G.D.P. also rose from 0.64 percent in 1951-52 to 3.98 percent in 2002-2003.

Basic Education

Basic Education is the brainchild of Gandhiji. His contact with educated youths showed him that there was something wrong in the education system. The educaton that they had received uprooted them from the soil and environment. They vainly tried to think and speak in a foreign language, they immitate the West in every respect, they know nothing about the conditions of their own country and strangers to their own land. To him it was evident that english educaiton had created a gulf between the educated and uneduated, the classes and masses.

He, therefore, thought it necessary to evolve a new type of society in which that difference between classes, masses and educated would disappear.

In July 1937, he published an article in his newspaper - Harijan. He wrote :

"By eduation I mean an all-round drawing out of the best in child and man - body, mind and spirit. Literacy is not the end of eduaiton nor even the beginning. It is only one of the means whereby man and woman can be educated. Literacy in itself is no education. I would, therefore, begin the child's education by teaching it a useful handicraft and enabling it to produce from the moment it begins its training. Thus every school can be made self supporting, the condition being that the state takes over the manufactures of those schools.

I hold that the highest development of the mind and soul is possible, under such a system of educaiton....."

Wardha

An educational conference was summoned at Wardha in October 1937 (Gandhiji's article in Harijan was published on 31 July, 1937). In this conference were present, education ministers of several provinces, congress leaders and workers including those who worked in the field of education.

In the conference Gandhiji submitted in the form of a proposal his thoughts and ideas on eudcation. The main points were :

1. The present system of educaiton does not meet the requirements of the country. English being the medium of instruction in all the higher branches of learning, has created a permanent bar between the highly educated few and the uneducated many. Absence of vocational training has made the educated class almost unfit for productive work and harmed them physically. Money spent on primary educaiton is a waste of expenditure as what little is taught is soon forgotten.

2. The course of Primary educaiton should be extended at least to 7 years and should inculcate the general knowledge gained upto the present matriculation standard less English and plus a substantial vocation.

3. For the all round development of boys and girls all training should be, as far as possible, given through a profit yielding vocation.

4. Higher education should be left to private enterprise and for meeting national requirements. The state universities should be purely examining bodies, self-supporting through the fees charged for the examination.

After the proposal was placed by Gandhiji, a sub committee was appointed to consider the new scheme of educaiton, as was proposed by Gandhiji. The sub-committee formulated the following resolutions :

1. Free and compulsory primary edn. be provided for 7 years.

2. Medium of instruction be mother tongue

3. The conference endorses the proposal of Gandhiji that the process of education throughout this period should centre round some form of manual and productive work.

4. This system of educaiton will be gradually able to cover the remuneration of teachers - is expected.

Under the Chairmanship of Dr. Zakir Hossain, a small committee of distinguished educationists, was formed in the conference.

The committee submitted its report on 2 December 1937. [Please note the time schedule (a) Article in Harijan - 31 July 1937, (b) Wardha Confernece and Com. formation - Oct. 1937, (c) Committee's report - 2 Dec. 1937 all told it took 4 months to devise a scheme of education for a country of roughly 35 lakhs sq. km. and a population of 31 crores (1937), being the 7th largest country of the World. A phenomenal efficiency of head and hand.]

Zakir Hossain Committee's report was placed in the Haripura session of Indian Naitonal Congress in February 1938 and the conference accepted the scheme.

The All-India National Educaiton Board - Hindusthani Talimi Sangha was established in April 1939 at Sevagram near Wardha, to give effect to the scheme.

What Zakir Hossain said

The Report of Zakir Hossain contained the following importants

1. A basic craft should serve as the centre of a solar system and other subjects should revolve planetwise and receive their warmth and vigour from the Central sun-craft.

2. The scheme is to be self-supporting to the extent of covering remuneration of teachers.

3. Manual labour is insisted on so that every individual may learn to earn his living through it in later life.

4. Instruction is closely co-ordinated with the child's life.

5. It also aims at training the future citizens of India to perform their duties and exercise their rights of citizenship in actual life through a scheme of social service in a co-operative community.

The courses of study in Nai Talim - New Education or Basic Education

1. Basic Craft or Sun-craft - the centre of solar system other subject to revolve round planet-wise to receive warmth and vigour.

Suggested types of basic craft - (a) spinning and weaving, (b) carpentary, (c) fruit and vegetables gardening, (d) agriculture, (e) leather work, (f) any other craft to which local and geographical conditions suit.

1. A minimum knowledge of spinning and carding
2. Mother tongue
3. Mathematics
4. Social studies outline history of India and its geographical environment
5. General Science
6. Artistic expression through music and drawing
7. Hindusthani (Urdu and Devnagri Scripts)

Basic Education in operation

The major provinces that the Congress party ruled brought Nai Talim of Gandhiji under official patronage. Bihar, Bombay, Orissa, Central Province, Uttar Pradesh opened Basic schools.

In 1942, Gandhiji gave a new interpretation of Nai-Talim. He declared, "I have been thinking hard during the detention - over the possibilities of Nai-Talim (New Education) until my mind became restive. We must not rest content without present achievements. We must pariticipate in the homes of the children. We must educate their parents. Basic education must become literally education for life."

So just after 4 years, the second chapter in the history of Nai-Talim began - "the educaiton of everybody at every stage of life."

In 1945, at Sevagram a conference was held. It was in January. Gandhiji opened the conference with following statement.

"Our field is not the child of seven to fourteen years of age. The field of Nai Talim stretches from the hour of conception in the mother's womb to the hour of death."

The conference appointed four committees to revise and prepare education for four stages of life.

(a) Adult educaiton
(b) Pre-basic education
(c) Basic education of children of 7 to 14 yrs. of age
(d) Post basic educaiton after 14 yrs. of age.

Gandhiji expired, after 3 years of this conference, in January 1948. In the meantime the Britishers have transferred power to Indian hands (all disciples of Gandhiji) on 15 Aug. 1947.

At the Basic Educaiton conference held next at Bikram, the New-Talim workers took a pledge of ideals.

Adult Education

It was held that if Nai-Talim was to be effective, it must begin not with children but with the parents and community.

Prebasic or Purva Buniyadi

This is education upto 7 yrs. of age. As soon as the child can walk upto school independent of mother, pre-basic or Purva Buniyadi starts. The aim is to develop all the faculties in cooperation with the parents and community.

Basic educaiton - Buniyadi Talim

It grows out of the Pre-basic and adult educaiton. The syllabus provided by Zakir Hossain was revised.

Revised syallabus

The syllabus was planned round the following main activities.

(1) Eastern knowledge, habits, attitude and skill necessary for clean and healthy living.

(2) Training in citizenship - practical and theoretical

(3) Capacity for self-sufficiency in food, cloth and shelter

(4) One of the following basic crafts - agriculture and gardening, spinning and weaving, wood work, house building and repair, general science and Mathematics. This plan is not of 7 years but of eight years from 7 to 15 years of age.

This eight class basic school should have 5 class rooms of 600 sq.ft. each. The remaining classes in the open. The school should have a library-cum reading room of 600 sq.ft. and an office for the Head Master, one for the teachers, an exhibition room, an assembly Hall of not less than 1000 sq.ft.

Teachers and Class

It is suggested that such an institution needs eight teachers including the headmaster. Post basic educaiton and a Diploma in basic Training should be the minimum qualification.

The strength of class should be not more than thirty.

The school may be residential or non-residential. In non-residential system the school should be held in the morning from 7 am to 11 am and 3 pm to 5 pm in the evening.

A basic school is expected to maintain (1) Teacher's Record, (2) Pupil's Records and (3) School Records.

Post Basic education (Uttar Buniyadi)

This education is in the age group fifteen to eighteen years of age. The post-basic sub-com. appointed by the Hindusthan Talimi Sangha accepted the following as the objectives of this education :

(1) Education through craft.

(2) The course should be complete in itself.

(3) All round development as an individual and as a member of the society.

(4) Courses to be diversified so as to suit different apttitudes of students.

(5) The language of instruction should be the language prevalent in the locality of the institution.

(6) The duration of the course shall vary according to the requirement of the course.

(7) Cost of maintaining themselves is to be earned through crafts practised.

University (Uttam Byniyadi)

Since 1950, there has been discussion about a university of Basic Education. The eudcation commission in 1949, had an important point on Rural University.

In 1951, Seventh All-India Conference of Basic education, this issue had an important place in discussion.

Hindusthani Talimi Sangha appointed a Higher Education Sub-Committee to consider the issue and workout a scheme.

The Committee selected 7 activity faculties for a Buniyadis Viswa Vidyalaya at Sevagram. The faculties are : Agriculture and horticulture, Animal Husbandry and dairy, Rural Engineering, Rural Industry, Rural Public Health and Nutrition, Rural Technology, Rural Education. 18 students were selected for admisison to the Sevagram Viswavidyalaya in November 1952.

Hindusthan Talimi Sangha then associated itself to Binoba Vabe's Bhoodan movement.

Basic Education and the Govt.

The Central Advisory Board of Edn. (CABE) appointed Shri B. G. Kher (Chief Minister Bombay) to examine the Wardha Scheme.

It accepted the Central Principle of the Wardha Scheme education of children through a purposeful creative activity.

Kher Com. recommended

(1) First to introduce in rural area

(2) Age should be six to fourteen years

(3) A student of basic school may divert to other kinds of school about the age of 11 plus.

(4) Medium of Instruction should be vernacular

(5) No external examination. At the end of the course, a leaving certificate based on internal examination should be given.

At their 22nd meeting, the CABE established a separate advisory com. on basic education.

The Govt. of India appointed an assessment committee in 1955 to make an on the spot survey about the development of basic education. The com. made several recommendations.

A large portion of the work of this Nai-Talim is being done by the Govt. education department. The institutions depend on Govt. for aid and recognition.

The Progress upto 1965-66

Year	No. of Jr. Basic School	No. of Sr. Basic School
1950-51	33379	386
1951-52	33751	454
1952-53	34223	655
1953-54	34940	865
1954-55	37395	1120
1955-56	42971	4482
1956-57	46681	6897
1957-58	52030	7819
1958-59	57009	8659
1959-60	61757	13554
1960-61	62591	14268

[Source : Govt. of India : Programme of educational development 1961-66]

The whole programme of Basic Education was again examined by Education Com. 1964-66, known as Kothari Commission.

Conclusion

The Basic Education has been severely and seriously crtiticised by many.

The only good aspect it proposes is a sweet and suitable understanding between and among pupil parent and society. The rest of this system is not adjustable to modern concept of education and urbanisation

The system is still tottering as it is related with the name of Gandhiji who was the Guru of all the leaders who subsequently came to power in the states and centre.

The Sargent Committee Report 1944, accepted some fundamental principles of the Wardha Scheme. But it remarked :

"Education at any stage and particularly at the lowest stage cannot or should not be expected to pay for itself through the sale of articles produced by the pupil."

While inaugurating the first meeting of the newly constituted National Board of Basic Educaiton, the ex-Education Minister Dr. K. L. Shrimali declared that basic education has been a failure. He even cited a letter written by Dr. Zakir Hossain, one of the founders of Basic Education in which Dr. Zakir Hossain the then Vice-President (1962-1967), in which he writes," basic education as carried out by the State Governments was by and large a fraud."

In 1962 December 24th, while addressing a conference of educationists at Gandhigram, the Vice-president Dr. Zakir Hossain remarked that the basic education could not develop in an atmosphere of insincerity and dishonesty. It could be more honest to scrap the system rather than try to sabotage it.

From the official reports, it has been clearly understood that the progress of this system has not been uniform in all states. While supriority of basic education over the old system is admitted, results are not commensurate with the hopes entertained with the system.

Lastly, people are not interested in basic education system which tries to run parallel with the modern accepted system, with no prospect of its own and those who propagate the system have no faith in it.

[Indebted to Sri Mukherjee Education in India, Today and Tomorrow T.S. Avinashalingam - Understanding basic Education. E. W. Aryanayakam- the Story of Twelve years.

J. P. Naik Syed Nurullah - A students' history of education. Syed Nurulah and J. P. Naik - A student's history of India.]

Part - XII

1975 to 2002 AD

Historical Perspective

This book 'Four thousand years of Education in Bharatvarsa - A History' has taken into account upto 1975 with all details and progress to end it.

But as the book is coming to light long after 1975, it is necessary that the most notable developments made in this field during this period from 1975 - 2002 should at least be mentioned if not discussed.

Notable Developments

The most notable points are two amendments of the constitution of India and steps taken after the amendments.

1. The constitutional Amendment of 1986 was a far reaching step. The Union Govt. / Central Govt. took a big share in education which happens to be an exclusive responsibility of the state Govt. with few reservations accoding to the constitution.

While the role and responsbility of the state Govts. in regard to education remained unchanged, the Union Govt. accepted a larger responsibility. This responsibility entailed (a) an integrated system of eduation (b) quality and standard (c) needs of the teachers at all levels, (d) to study and monitor the educational requirements of the country.

Naitonal Policy of Eduation (NPE) and Programme of Education (POA)

The N. P. E. - National Policy of Eduation is based on a national curricular frame work, which contains a common code alongwith other flexible, region specific components. The policy stresses on widening of opportunities to masses, consolidation of the existing system of higher and technical education and more financial provision for education at least 6 percent of the National Income. It has been proposed to constitute a fund called 'Bharat Siksha Kosh' to enlist the support of all concerned. This is to mobilise extra budgetary support in order to bridge the gap between actual requirements and available budgetary support.

Suppose, the requirement is 10, budgetary provision is 8, the Bharat Siksha Kosh will try to bridge up by providing 2.

During this period, budgetary provision has substantially increased on education. The expenditure on education as a percentage of GDP was only 0.64 percent in 1951-52. In 2002-03, it has come upto 3.98 percent.

2. The second most notable point is the 86th amendment of the constitution of India in 2002. This made Elementary Educaiton a Fundamental Right for children of the age group 6-14 years. Art 45 was a Directive which was not enforceable in a Court of law but when the amendment of 2002 made Elementary Education a Fundamental Right, now its violation is enforceable in a Court of law. 86th Amendment of the constitution was effected during the premiership of Atal Behari Vajpeyee in 2002.

A new article - article 21A is inserted after article 21. This new article deals with Right to Education. It reads :

"The state shall provide free and compulsory education to all children of the age of six to fourteen years in such manner as the state may, by law, determine."

In 1998, the State Educations Ministers' Conference recommended to persue elementary education in a mission mode.

The scheme of Sarva Siksha Aviyan (SSA) evolved from this recommendation. The scheme was approved by the cabinet in its meeting on 16 November 2000, presided over by the Prime Minister Atal Bihari Bajpayee.

The S.S.A. programme covers the entire country and addresses the needs of 192 million children in 11 lakh habitations, 8.5 lakh existing primary and upper primary schools and 33 lakhs existing teachers.

The programme seeks to open new schools in habitations where there is no schooling facilities and strengthen the existing schools' infrastructure through provision of extra class rooms, toilets, drinking water, maintenance grant and school improvement grant, strengthening teachers, training of existing teachers and development of academic support structure.

The Sarva Siksha Abhiyan covers the entire country with a special focus also on educational needs of girls, scheduled castes and Tribes.

Annual District Elementary Education Plan (DEEP) of 512 districts at an outlay of 1106 crore 26 lakhs during 2001-2002 had been approved.

New Primary Schools and Upper Primary Schools, Primary Teachers, School Buildings, Additional Class Rooms, Toilets, Drinking Water facilities were all approved and fund for this was approved.

The scheme of Non-Formal Education (NFE) was introduced in 1979-80 to target out of school children of the age group 6-14 years.

In order to make the scheme a viable alternative to formal education it has been revised as Education Guarantee Scheme and Alternative and Innovative Education (EGS and AIE). This revised scheme will cover all the unserved habitations of the country where there are no learning centres, with a radious of one k.m. and is a part of Naitonal Programme - Universal Elementary Education (UEE). The pattern of financial assistance is 75:25 i.e. the centre will bear 75 percent and state concerned 25 percent of the total cost.

Mid-day Meal : The name of the scheme is National Programme of Nutritional Support to Primary Education. This scheme was launched in 1995 when P. V. Narshima Rao was the Prime Minister.

The purposes of the scheme were -

(1) Nutritional support,

(2) Entolment increase

(3) Attendance increase

(4) Retention increase of the children of 6-11 age group in Primary School.

District Primary Education Programme (Dpep)

It is a centrally sponsored scheme launched in 1994 during the Primiership of P. V. Narshima Rao.

The DPEP is based on the Principle of 'additionality' and structured to fill in the gaps. It adopts a holistic approach admission - retention, improvement and to reduce disparities among social groups.

The programme components include construction of class rooms, new schools, opening Non-Formal/Alternative Schooling centres, appointment of new teachers, setting up early childhood education centre and so many such educational activities.

The Dpep is an externally aided project. About 85 p.c. of the Project cost is met by the Central Govt and 15 P.C. is shared by the concerned state.

Operation Black Board

The scheme of Operation Blackboard was launched in 1987-88 during the Primership of Rajib Gandhi with the aim of improving human and physical resources available in Primary Schools of the Country. Provision of at least two reasonably large rooms, at least two teachers and essential teaching - learning materials for every existing Primary school were the components of the plan.

During 1993-94 the scheme was extended to cover upper primary schools. The funds are paid to the state Govt. to provide Teaching Learning Equipment (TLE) and payment of salaries to teachers - appointed in the scheme of operation Black Board.

During the period of 1987-88 (inauguration of the scheme) to 2001-02 (roughly 15 years). TLE are provided to 522902 - Primary, 138009 - Upper Primary. Similarly 149140 for Primary, 77010 for upper primary teachers were given employment. 1 lakh 85 thousands additional class rooms have been constructed under this scheme.

Lok Jumbish

It is a project in the state of Rajasthan with assistance from Sweedish International Development Agency (SIDA) and Department for International Development (DFID) of united kingdom. The target was education to all by 2000 A.D.

Siksha Karmi

The Siksha Karmi Project (SKP) aims at universalisation and qualitative improvement of Primary education in remote and socio economically backward villages in Rajasthan with Primary attention given to girls. The project identifies teacher absenteeism is a major obstacle in achieving the goal of Universalisation of Elementary Education (UEE).

The project covers 3692 village in 150 blocks of Rajasthan.

The SKP was being implemented with the assistance from SIDA. The third phase of the project was to start from July 1998. In view of Post-Pokhran development, SIDA declined to support the project after June 1998. DFID was approached for support to phase three, planned for the period

1st July 1999 to 30 June 2003. The DFID agreed to support the project on 50:50 basis, with the Govt. of Rajasthan.

Mahila Samakhya

The Mahila Samakhya Programme (Education for Women's Equality) is a concrete programme for the education and empowerment of women in rural areas, particularly of women from socially and economically marginalised groups. It is being implemented in more than 9000 villages in 56 districts of ten states - Andhra, Gujrat, Kerala, Karnataka, U.P., Bihar, Jharkhand, M.P., Assam and may be Chattisgarh.

The objectives of the Scheme are, to enhance the self-image and self-confidence of women that they can run Mahila Samgha. The Mahila Samgha is the nodal point where all activities are planned and which provides the space where women can meet, be together and discuss their problems.

Janshala

Janshala is a community based education programme aiming at making Primary education more accessible and effective, especially for girls and children in deprived communities, marginalised groups, SC/ST/Minority, working children and children with specific needs.

This is the first ever programme in the World where five UN agencies have collaborated and pooled resources to support an initiative in educaiton. The five U.N. agencies are - ILO, UNDP, UNICIF, UNESCO, UNFPA which are collaborating.

The programme is to run for five years, from 1998 to 2002, then extended upto 2004, covers 139 Blocks spread over nine states - Andhra, Jharkhand, Chhatisgarh, Karnataka, M.P., Maharastra, Orissa, Rajasthan and U.P. The project outlay is Rs. 103 crores 13 lakhs.

Teacher Education

As envisaged in NPE and POA (see Supra) 1986, the centrally sponsored scheme of Restructuring and Reorganisation of Teacher Education was taken up in 1987-88 during the premiership tenure of Rajib Gandhi. The aim is to create a viable institutional infrastructure, academic and Technical resource base for Orientation, training and continuous upgradation of knowledge, competence and pedagogical skills of school teachers, adult and Non-Formal functioneries and teacher educators in the country.

The scheme envisaged setting up of District Instruction of Educational Training (DIET) in each district to provide academic and research support to elementary educaiton, teachers and Non-Formal education, Adult education instructors. It also envisaged upgradation of selected Secondary Teachers Education Institutions into colleges of secondary Education (CTE) and Institutions of Advanced Studies in Education (IASE). It was also envisaged to organise Pre-service and in-service training for Secondary teachers, also resource support services in Secondary Schools.

About 492 DIETs, 86 CTEs, 38 IASEs have been sanctioned in various states and Union Terriotors (UT). Financial assistance has been extended for strengthening of 20 State Councils of Educational Research and Training (SCERTs). More than 23 lakhs teachers were given orientation training under special orientation progrmme (SOPT) for school teachers in the use of Operation BlackBoard material and implementation of Minimum Level of Learning (MLL) with focus on language, Mathematics, and Environmental Studies.

National Council For Teachers' Education (NCTE)

The National Council for Teachers Education (NCTE) was established by an Act of Parliament in August 1995, when Narsima Rao was the Prime Minister.

This provides for achieving

(i) Planned and Co-ordinated development of teacher educaiton system.

(ii) Regulation and proper maintenance of norms and standards of teacher educaiton in the country

Ncte is fully financed by the Central Govt. As on 2003, 2726 teacher educaiton institution were recognised by Ncte.

Naitonal Bal Bhawan

National Bal Bhawan, formerly Bal Bhavan Society, was established in 1956 when Jawharlal Nehru was the Prime Minister (15 August 1947 to 27 May 1964 - 18 years). It is a project aimed at enhancing creativity amongst children in the age group 5-16 years, specially from the weaker sections of the society. The children can persue their activities of choice at the Balvaban such as creative arts, perfoming arts, environment, astronomy, photography, integrated activities, physical activities, science related activities etc. The Balvaban aims at all round growth of a child in a free and happy atmosphere and helps the child to develop scientific temper.

National Population Education Project

This project was launched in 1980 when Indira Gandhi was the Prime Minister [14 January 1980 to 31 October 1984]. The view was to institutionalise population educaiton in the school education system. This is an externally aided project which is fully funded by United Nations Population Fund. This project is also being implemented in Higher and Adult education sector. The fourth cycle of the project was completed in December 2002. It was decided that from 2003, Central Govt. would fund the project.

Environmental Orientation to school education

The National Policy of Education 1986, adopted during the Premiership of Rajib Gandhi (October 1984 to December 1989), provides that the protection of environment is a value which must form an integral part of educaiton at all stages. The mind and intellect of the student must be sensitised to the hazards inherent in nature upsetting the ecological balance. This project is to inculcate awareness and respect for conservation of environment.

Improvement of Science in Schools

The NPE, 1986, envisaged to improve quality of science education and to inculcate scientific temper through education. In 1987-88 "Improvement of science Educaiton in schools" was initiated. Under this scheme financial assistance is provided to states and UTs and voluntary agencies. Science Kits are to be provided to students of Upper Primary schools by states and UTs. Voluntary organisations have to conduct experimental and innovative programmes. Improvement of science laboratories in the schools and training of science and Mathematics teachers are also included in this scheme.

One of the important components of this scheme is participation of Indian students at school level in the Internaitonal Science Olympiads - International Mathematical Olympiad (Since 1989), Internaitonal Physics Olympiad (Since 1998), International Chemistry Olympiad (Since 1999) and International Biology Olympiad (Since 2000).

During 2002-2003, 14 voluntary Organisations were provided financial assistance to the extent of Rs. 139.34 lakhs for undertaking innovative and experimental projects in the field of science education.

Indian delegations to the above science Olympiads won during 2002 -

4 Gold Medals,

9 Silver Medals,

6 Bronze Medals.

Boarding and Hostel Facilities for Girls Students

Under this scheme financial assistance is being given to eligible voluntary organisations to improve the enrolement of adolescent girls belonging to rural areas and weaker section. Preference is given to hostels located in educationally backward districts, particularly those inhabited by SC/ST and educationally backward minorities.

The following types of grants are given under the scheme -

(i)   Rs. 10,000 per annum per student boarder (girl) for food, lodge, salary of cook, warden etc.

(ii)   A one-time grant at the rate of Rs. 3000 per girl boarder for purchase of beds, utensils, books basic equipments etc.

(iii)   Assistance for maintenance and reimbersement of rent upto 75 percent of expenditure.

Navodaya Vidyalaya

The NPE, 1986, envisaged setting up of model schools one in each district of the country. Accordingly a scheme was formulated under which it was decided to set up co-educational residential schools (Now called Jawahar Navodaya Vidyalaya). Navodaya Vidyalayas are fully residential co-educaitonal institutions providing educaiton upto senior secondary stage. The scheme which started with only 2 schools on experimental basis in 1985-86, has now grown to 491 schools in 34 states and Union Territories with more than 1.43 lakhs students. About 30 thousands students are admitted every year.

Kendriya Vidyalaya Sangathan

On the recommendations of the Second Pay Commission, the Central Govt. approved the scheme of Kendriya Vidyalaya in 1962. Initially, 20 regimental schools were taken over as Central School in 1965.

To cater to the needs of the children of Central Govt. employees who are transferable, including Defence Personnel and Para-Military forces, an autonomous Body called Kendriya Vidyalaya Sangsthan was established in 1965. At present there are 899 Kendriya Vidyalaya in the Country of which one in Kathmandu and one in Moscow. All Kendriya Vidyalayas follow Uniform syllabus.

Secondary Education

To assist and advise the centre and the states in the matter of school education. The National Council of Educational Research and Training (NCERT) was set up in 1961, with headquarters at New Delhi.

The NCERT provides academic and technical support for qualitative improvement of school eduation through its constituent units, namely Naitonal Institute of Education (NIE), Delhi ; Central Institute of Educational Technology (CIET), Delhi ; Pandit Sundarlal Sharma Central Institute of Vocational Education (PSSCIVE), Bhopal ; Regional Institute of Education (RIE) at Ajmer, Bhopal, Bhubaneswar, Mysore and and Shillong. The council

(i)   Aids, promotes and coordinates

(ii)   Conducts research in school education and teacher education

(iii)   Organises, pre-service and in-service training of teachers

(iv)   Develops and experiments with improved eduaitonal techniques, practices and innovations

(v)   Collects compiles, processes and disseminates educational informative

(vi)   Assists in developing qualitative improvements of school education

(vii)   Collaborates with international organisations

(viii) Prints and distributes textual materials

Recently Ncert has also set up a National Research Centre for Value Education (NRCVE).

It has so many other such educational activities.

National Talent Research Scheme

Though the name and title is fixed - National Talent Research Scheme, in 1977, it was a scheme started by NCERT in 1963. Its aim is to identify brilliant students of Class X for the Union Territory of Delhi. It has been extended throughout the country in 1964 with a total number of scholarships of 350 and now the number of scholarships are 1000 of which 150 for SC and 75 for ST categories.

The selection of scholarship is done in two stages - The first selection is done by the states and Union Territories through a written examination in November every year. A stipulated number of students are recommended to Ncert for second level selection which involves both written and interview.

The written examination is invariably held in May and the interview in July-August every year.

University and Higher Educations

In the period under review (2002-03) there are 306 University level institutions in India -

18 Central Universities

186 State Universities,

5 established under State Act,

84 Deemed Universites,

13 Institutions of national importance.

Of these, 38 institutions provide education in agriculture including forestry, dairy, fishery, veterinary, 21 in medicine including Ayurveda, 44 in Engineering and Technology, 4 in information technology, 4 in legal studies.

The number of Open universities are nine, that of women universities five.

The total enrolement of students in Universities and colleges is 88 lakhs, while the number of teachers is more than 4 lakhs upto 2002.

University Grants Commisison

The UGC was set up by an Act of Parliament in 1956, to take, in consultation with Universities or other bodies concerued, all such steps as it may think fit for promotion and coordination of University education and for the determination and maintenance of standards of teaching, examination, and research in Universities. So, the UGC serves as coordinating body between the Union and the State Govts. and Institutions of higher learning. It also acts as an adviser in matters relating to Higher learning, to States and the Union.

The Commisison consists of the Chairman, Vice-Chairman and 10 members appointed by the Central Govt. It has its Regional Offices at Hyderabad, Pune, Bhopal, Kolkata, Guwahati and Bangalore. The office located at Ghaziabad, located earlier, has now merged with the UGC Head Office at New Delhi and renamed as Northern Region College Bureau.

To fulfill its object the UGC can enquire into financial needs of the Universities, allocate and disburse grants to Universities and colleges.

Autonomous Research Organisations :

The following autonomous Research Organisations were set up at different times for specific purposes.

(1) **The Indian Council of Historical Research (ICHR)** was set up in 1972. It operates research projects, finances research projects by individual scholars, award fellowship and undertakes publications and translation works. Head Office New Delhi.

(2) **The Indian Council of Philosophical Research (ICPR)** set up in 1977. It reviews the progress, sponsors or assists projects and programmes of research in philosophy and gives financial assistance to institutions and individuals to conduct research in philosophy and other allied discipline. Offices are at New Delhi and Lucknow.

(3) **The Indian Institute of Advanced Studies (IIAS)**, set up in 1965. It is in Simla. It is a residential Centre of advanced research on Humanities. Social Sciences and Natural Sciences. It is a community of scholars engaged in exploring new frontiers of knowledge aimed at conceptual development and offering inter disciplinary perspective on questions of contemporary relevance.

(4) **The Indian Council of Social Science Research (ICSSR)**, New Delhi, is an autonomous body for promoting and co-ordinating social science research. Its main functions are to review the progress of social science research, give advice on research activities in government or outside, sponsors research programmes and, give grant to institutions and individuals for research in social sciences.

(5) **The National Council of Rural Institutes (NCRI)**, set up in 1995 as an autonomous organisation fully funded by the central Govt. to promote rural higher education on the lines of Gandhiji's ideas on education, consolidate net work and develop educational institutions and voluntary agencies in accordance with Gandhian Philosophy of education and promote research as a tool of social and rural development.

Open University

The Indira Gandhi National Open University (IGNOU) was established in 1985 when her son Rajib Gandhi was the Prime Minister of India. This establishment of a new type of educational institution is responsible for the introduction and promotion of Open University and distance education system in the educational pattern of India.

The major objectives of the University include :-

(1) Widening access to higher education to larger segments of the population.

(2) Organising programmes of continuing education

(3) Initiating special programmes of higher edcuation for specific target groups like women and people living in the backward rigions and hilly regions.

At present (2002-03) there are ten such open universities in the country, namely, B. R. Ambedkar Open University, Hydrabad (Andhra). Kota Open University, Kota (Rajsthan) Nalanda Open University, Nalanda (Bihar), Yasabanto Rao Chavan Maharastra Open University, Nasik (Maharastra), Madhya Pradesh Bhoj Open University, Bopal (Mdhya Pradesh) Ambedkar Open University, Ahmedbad (Gujrat), Karnataka State University, Mysore (Karnataka), Netaji Subhas Bose Open University, Kolkata (West Bengal), Rajrishi Tandon Open University, Allahabad (U.P.). Tamilnadu State Open University (T.N.).

There are 104 correspondence course institutions, imparting education through the distance mode in the conventional system.

On January 26, 2003 the IGNOU launched another Satellite Channel for technical education. This is known as EKALAVYA Channel. It is a mile stone in the growth and development of distance education in the country.

Education of SC and ST

After independence, the Govt. of India have taken a number of steps to strengthen the educational base of the scheduled castes and Scheduled Tribes. Yet these communities still have a long way to cover to come up to the level of the other communities in the field of educational development.

Persuant of the NPE, 1986 and POA i.e. Programme of Action, Special Provisions have been incorporated in the exising schemes of the Departments of Elementary Education and literacy, secondary and Higher Secondary Education : Relaxed norms for opening of Primary and middle schools.

District Primary Education Programme (DPEP) provides infrastructure facilities and special interventions for the education of girls, SC, ST, Disabled etc.

It is notable that in Shiksha Karmi Schools, 74 percent are from SCs, STs and OBCs. Reservation of seats for SC & ST in Central Govt. institutions of higher educaiton including IIT, IIM, Regional Engineering Colleges, Central Universities, Kendriya Vidyalaya and Navodaya Vidyalaya are arranged and provided. There is also relaxation in the minimum qualifying cut off stages for admissiion in Universities, Colleges and Technical institutions apart from reservation. The UGC established SC/ST cells in 109 universities to ensure proper implementation of the reservation Policy.

The UGC provides relaxation of 5 PC (i.e. from 55 percent to 50 percent) at the Master's level for appointment as Lecturer for SC/ST candidates. The commisison has also reduced the minimum percentage of marks required for appearing at the NET examination.

Many other relaxations and facilities are provided including the field of awarding scholarships, for SC and ST students.

Minority Education

The National Policy of Education (NPE) 1986, updated in 1992, envisages paying greater attention to the education of the educationally backward minorities in the interest of equity and social justice.

In persuance of the revised programme of Action POA 1992, two new centrally sponsored schemes were launched in 1993 - 94. Those are (i) scheme of Area - intensive programme for educationally backward minorities. (ii) Scheme of financial assistance for modernisation of Madrasah Education.

Technical Education

In order to improve the quality of Technical Education being imparted in 17 Regional Engineering Colleges (REC) and to grade them to the level of IITs, these institutions have been made fully funded institutions under the Central Govt. from April 2003. These RECs were renamed as National Institutes of Technology with Deemed to be University status and professional management structure. The academic practices were made similar to IITs. These institutes offer education in Engineering and Technology at under graduate and post graduate level with a total intake capacity of about 6000 pupils.

Adult Education

The National Literacy Mission (NLM) was set up in 1988. Its aim is to attain a sustainable threshold level of 75 percent literacy by 2007 by imparting functional literacy to non-literates in the age group 15-35 years, which is the productive and reproductive age group and constitute a major segment of the work force.

1. The Total Literacy Campaign (TLC) is the principal strategy of NLM for eradication of illiteracy. These campaigns are area - specific, time-bound, participatve, cost effective and outcome oriented. These are implemented through Zilla Saksharata Samities (districts level literacy committee) as independent and autonomous bodies, having due representation of all sections of the society.

Apart from imparting functional literacy, the TLC also disseminates a 'busket' of other socially relevant messages such as enrolement and retention of children in schools, immunisation, propagation of small family norms, women's equality and empowerment, peace and communal harmony etc.

2. Non Govt. Organisations (NGO) The Naitonal Literacy Mission (NLM) fully recognises the vast potential of NGOs in furthering the objectives and has taken measures to strengthen its partnership with NGOs and has assigned them an active promotional role in the literacy movement.

The State Resource Centres (SRCs) managed by NGOs provide academic and technical resource supports in the form of training material preparation, extension activities, innovative projects, research studies and evaluation etc. Upto 2003 there were 25 SRCs.

3. Female Literacy As per Census 2001, 30 districts in U.P., Bihar and Orissa are identified where the female literacy is below 30 percent. These districts have sizeable population of women from weaker section and the minorities.

In U.P. nearly 100 NGOs were involved in an accelerated programme of female literacy. Approximately, 20 lakhs women are undergoing literacy classes in 1.25 lakhs centres.

In Bihar, the lieracy programme has focused on involvement of women volunteers including a sizeable number from minorities. Roughly 30 lakhs women are undergoing literacy classes in about 2.5 lakh centres in 15 districts.

In Orissa approximately 8 lakhs women are being made literate in 7 low-female literacy districts.

4. Jana Shiksha Sansthan The objective of Jana Shiksha Sansthan (J.S.S.) is educational, vocational and occupational development of the socio economically backward and educationally disadvantaged groups of Urban / Rural population. Particularly neo-literates, semi-literates, SCs,

STs, women and girls, slum dwellers, migrant workers etc. During the period under review there are 122 JSS in the country.

Directorate of Adult Education

The Central Directorate of Adult Education (CDAE) also provides academic and technical resource support to NLM. It has also been playing an important role in the development of net-work of resource support particularly production of media materials and harnessing of all kinds of media for furtherance of the objective of National Literacy Mission (NLM).

Achievement :

(i)   The literacy rate in 1991 was 52.21 percent as per census report. In 2001 it has increased to 65.38 percent [In 2011 census the literacy percent is recorded as 74.4 percent].

(ii)   As on 31 March 2001, 102.29 million persons made literate

(iii) The rate of growth is more in rural areas than in Urban areas

(iv)   The gap between male female literacy rate has decreased

(v)   Female literacy has increased from the last census - from 39.3 to 54.16 percent.

(vi)   Out of the total 600 districts of the Country 587 districts were covered by NLM under literacy programme.

Scholarships

The Department of Secondary and Higher Secondary Educaiton funds scholarship / Fellowship programmes for Indian students for school and higher education. These programmes are administered through State Governments and Union Territories. They include the National Scholarship Scheme for Post-matric studies, a scheme of scholarships to help students of non-Hindi speaking states studying Hindi and schoarships to enable talented rural students to continue secondary education.

The Govt. provides scholarships to Indian scholars for post-Graduate Research, Post Doctoral Studies abroad on the basis of offers received from foreign Govts. under the various Cultural / Educational Exchange Programmes. The details of offers and other conditions are given wide publicity in leading newpapers while inviting applications for scholarships. The amount and other facilities provided by foreign Govts. varieus from country to country and time to time.

During the year 2002-2003, 105 scholarships were awared under various Cultural programmes / Educational Exchange Programmes.

Name of the Country	No. of Scholarship awarded
1. Belgium	3
2. China	14
3. Czech	2
4. Canada	4
5. Germany	9
6. Ireland	4
7. Italy	21
8. Isreal	5
9. Japan	20
10. Mexico	2
11. Norway	2
12. Syria	2
13. U.K.	17

Promotion of Languages

Language being most important medium of Communication and Education the National Policy of Education (NPE) and Programme of Action (POA) gave a good importance to this aspect. The promotion and development of Hindi and other languages listed in the constitution of India, have received due attention.

Hindi

In order to assist non-Hindi speaking States and Union Territories, to effectively implement the three languages formula, support for provision of facilities for teaching of Hindi, appointment of Hindi teachers in schools under Centrally sponsored scheme etc. financial assistance are given. Even voluntary Organisatios are financed to hold Hindi teaching classes.

An academic course for Hindi teaching to foreigners is being conducted by Kendriya Hindi Sansthan. The Central Hindi Directorate runs programmes relating to purchase and publication of books and its distribution to non-Hindi speaking States and Indian Missions.

The Commission for Scientific and Technical Terminology, New Delhi, parepares and publishes definitional dictionaries and terminology in various discipline.

Modern Indian Languages

Financial assistance is given to voluntary organisations and individuals to bring out publications like encyclopedias, dictionaries, books of knowledge, original writings on linguistic, literacy, indological, social anthropological and cultural themes, cricitcal editions of old manuscripts etc. for the development of modern Indian languages. States are given special help for the production of University level books in regional languages.

Since 1996, The National Council for Promotion of Urdu Languages has been functioning as an autonomous body. The Council (NCPUL) also works for Arabic and Persian languages. The NCPUL is working on developing an advance software for Urdu. The NCPUL has established 54 centres for computarised calligraphy training.

The Govt. also provides facilities for studies of all Indian languages. For this, the Central Institute of Indian languages (CIIL), Mysore, conducts research on the areas of language analysis, language pedagogy, language technology and language use.

In the Tenth Five year Plan two major scheme relating to minorities have been clubbed together to form the Area Intensive and Madrasah Modernisation Programme in a United Programme i.e. Area Intensive Programme for Educationally Backward Minorities and the Scheme of Financial Assistance for the Modernisation of Madrasah Education.

English and Foreign Languages

The Central Institute of English and Foreign Languages, Hyderabad, a fully funded autonomous organisation interalia, conducts training programmes for school teachers, develop teaching materials, implements, monitors the scheme of English Language Teaching Institutes and provides financial assistance for publication, purchase of books in the English language and for holding seminars, conferences, workshops etc and to bring about substantial improvement in the standards of teaching and learning English.

Sanskrit Division

The Govt. has formulated various schemes / programmes for development of Sanskrit Education in pursuance of NPE. These schemes/ programmes are being implemented through the following agencies.

    (i)   Central Plan Scheme of Development of Sanskrit Education

    (ii) Three Deemed Sanskrit Universities

        (a) Rashtriya Sanskrit Sansthan, New Delhi.

        (b) Sri Lal Bahadur Sastri Rashtriya Sanskrit Vidyapeetha, New Delhi and Rashtriya Sanskrit Vidyapeetha, Tirupati.

(c) Maharshi Sandipani Rashtriya Veda Vidya Pratisthan, Ujjain
Besides, there is one Modernisation of Madrasah Education.
These schemes include financial assistance to State Govts. and voluntary Sanskrit Organisations, their development into Sanskrit Mahavidyalayas, incentive to retired scholars as Sashtra Chudamoni Pandits, Publication of original writings of contemporary writers, editing and publication of rare manuscripts and catalogues of manuscripts, reprinting of important out of print Sanskrit texts, promotion of oral Vedic tradition, vocational training to the products of Sanskrit Pathasalas, national Award to eminent Sanskrit, Pali, Prakrit, Arabic and Persian Schoalrs and preparation/publication of Sanskrit dictionaries.

The Department of Secondary and Higher Secondary Education also conducts an All-India Vedic Convention through Maharsi Sandipani Rashtriya Veda Vidya Pratisthan, Ujjain, where scholars in different Sakhas of the Vedas from all over India are invited with a view to identify rare Veda Shakhas and its respositories and devising ways and means for preservng the oral tradition.

The scheme for Modernisation of Madrasas is being implemented since 1993-94.

Book Promotion

The Naitonal Book Trust (NBT) is an autonomous Organiation under the Ministry of Human Resource Development (HRD). It was established in 1957. The activities of the NBT are : (i) Publication, (ii) Promotion of books and reading, (iii) Promotion of Indian books abroad, (iv) Assistance to authors and publishers, (v) Promotion of children's literature. It organises World Book Fair in New Delhi in every alternative year. This is the largest Book Fair in Asia and Africa. The NBT observes 14-20 November every year as National Book Week.

Unesco, the International Publishers' Association, and a number of books -related international Agencies found India to be the most suitable country to be declared as the World Book Capital (WBC) and hence, New Delhi, the capital of India, was honoured as World Book Capital in 2003-04.

ISBN : International Standard Book Number (ISBN) system was introduced in India in 1985. It is related to HRD, Govt. of India. ISBN is a unique International Publishers Identifier Number meant for monographic publicatons, which is also known as short machine readable identification number that makes separate and easy to access.

Copy right : Administering the copy right Act, 1957, one of the several legislations in India in the area of Intellectual Property Rights (IPR), is the responsibility of the Union Ministry of Human Resource Development (HRD), Department of Secondary and High Education. The Act of 1957 was ammended in 1994, taking into account the technological developments. It was brought into force on 10th May 1995. The Act was further amended in 1999, which came into force on 15 January 2000.

As per provision of Sec. 11 of Copy Right Act 1957, the Govt. of India have constituted a Board to be called the Copyright Board. This Board is a quasi-judicial body consisting of a chairman and not less than two or more than 14 members. The Chairman and other members of the Board are appointed for a term of five years. The Board also was reconstituted for a term of 5 years with effect from 22 February 2001.

The Board hears cases regarding rectification of Copy right registration disputes in respect of assisgnment of copyright and granting of licenses in works withheld from public.

Intellectural Property Education
Research and Public Outreach (Iperpo)

During the Ninth Plan Period (1997-2002), two plan schemes, namely (a) Scheme for Financial Assistance on Intellectual Property Rights studies and (b) Scheme of organising seminars and workshops on copyright matters were introduced for implementation in August 1998.

Both the schemes were merged into a single scheme - "Scheme of Intellectual Property Education, Research and Public Outreach (IPERPO) together with another plan scheme, namely Financial Assistance on WTO studies, in the Tenth Plan (2002-07).

Through these schemes, several universities, Educational Institutions and NGOs in the field are provided assistance every year to conduct research, seminars, hold conferences, establishe IPR chairs and Depositories.

The Indian Copy right Act, 1957, provides penalties for the offences committed under the Copy right Act and empowers the police to take necessary action. The actual enforcement of the Law is the concern of the State Govts.

Co-operation with Wipo

World Intellectual Property Organisation (WIPO) is a specialised agency of the United Nations, which deals with copyright and other Intellectual property rights and plays an important role in its deliberation. India is a member of WIPO and pays an annual contribution of Rs. 40 lakhs, subject to foreign exchange rate fluctuation.

Elementary Education Progress of Enrolement L.P. (in lakhs)

Period	Middle Level Class VI-VIII 11 - 14 years	Primary Level Class I-V 6 - 11 years
1950-51	31	192
1960-61	67	350
1968-69	125	544
1979-80	193	716
1989-90	322	973
1999-2000	421	1136
2000-2001	342	925
2001-2002	426	1098

Source : HRD Govt. of India

Plan Expenditure on Education

1.	1st	Plan	1951-56	151	Crores
2.	2nd	Plan	1956-61	273	Crores
3.	3rd	Plan	1961-66	589	Crores
			1966-69	323	Crores
4.	4th	Plan	1969-74	747.4	Crores
5.	5th	Plan	1974-79	1143.5	Crores
6.	6th	Plan	1980-85	2618.7	Crores
7.	7th	Plan	1985-90	7632.9	Crores
			1990-92	4727	Crores
9.	8th	Plan	1992-1997	21800.1	Crores
10.	9th	Plan	1997-2002	22096	Crores
11.	10th	Plan	2001-07	43825	Crores

Source : Ministry of HRD

TABLE : PLAN EXPENDITURE ON DIFFERENT SECTORS OF EDUCATION

Sector	First Plan Expdt. 1951-56	Second Plan Expdt. 1956-61	Third Plan Expdt. 1961-66	Plan Holiday Expdt. 1966-69	Fourth Plan Expdt. 1969-74	Fifth Plan Expdt. 1974-79	Sixth Plan Expdt. 1980-85	Seventh Plan Expdt. 1985-90	1990-92 Expdt.	Eighth Plan Outlay 1992-97	Ninth Plan Outlay (1997-2002) (Central Sector)	Ninth Plan Expdty. (1997-02)	Tenth Plan Outlay (2002-2007) (Central Sector)
1	2	3	4	5	6	7	8	9	10	11	12	13	14
Elementary Education	58 (870)	35 (950)	34 (2010)	24 (750)	50 (3743)	52 (5913)	32 (8414)	37 (28494)	37 (17290)	48 (103940)	66 (163696)	65.7 (145233)	65.6 (278500)
Secondary Education	5 (80)	19 (510)	18 (1030)	16 (530)	@	@	20 (5344)	24 (18315)	22 (10530)	24 (52311)	10 (26035)	10.5 (23227)	9.9 (43250)
Adult Education					2 (126)	2 (248)	6 (1533)	6 (4696)	9 (4160)	5 (11421)	3 (6304)	2.4 (5204)	2.9 (12500)
Higher Education	8 (120)	18 (480)	15 (870)	24 (770)	25 (1883)	28 (3188)	21 (5604)	16 (12011)	12 (5880)	10 (20944)	10 (25000)	10.3 (22709)	9.5 (41765)
Others	15 (230)	10 (300)	12 (730)	11 (370)	13 (936)	9 (1071)	11 (2729)	3 (1980)	2 (1180)	3 (7398)	2 (4314)	1.6 (3492)	1.4 (6235)
Technical Education	14 (210)	18 (490)	21 (1250)	25 (810)	10 (786)	9 (1015)	10 (2563)	14 (10833)	17 (8230)	10 (21987)	9 (23735)	9.5 (1095)	10.7 (47000)
Total	100 (1510)	100 (2730)	100 (5890)	100 (3230)	100 (7474)	100 (11435)	100 (26187)	100 (76329)	100 (47270)	100 (218001)	100 (249084)	100 (220960)	100 (438250)

Source: Five Year Plan Documents, Planning Commission and Analysis of Budget Expenditure, Ministry of HRD

Note: 1.Figures in parenthesis in millions of rupees

2.Figures in Col. 2 to Col. 13 includes the share of States/UTs.

@ Included under Elementary Education

Universities in India upto 2017

	Central universities [4]	State universities[5] [note 1]	Deemed universities [12]	Private universities [14]	Total
Andhra Pradesh (list)	0	20	5	0	25
Arunachal Pradesh (list)	1	0	1	7	9
Assam (list)	2	12	0	5	19
Bihar (list)	3	15	1	2	21
Chandigarh (list)	0	1	1	0	2
Chhattisgarh (list)	1	13	0	9	23
Delhi (list)	5	7	10	0	22
Goa (list)	0	1	0	0	1
Gujarat (list)	1	28	2	31	62
Haryana (list)	1	14	6	20	41
Himachal Pradesh (list)	1	4	0	17	22
Jammu and Kashmir (list)	2	9	1	0	12
Jharkhand (list)	1	8	1	8	18
Karnataka (list)	1	26	14	14	55
Kerala (list)	1	13	3	0	17
Madhya Pradesh (list)	2	22	1	24	49
Maharashtra (list)	1	22	21	10	54
Manipur (list)	2	1	0	1	4
Meghalaya (list)	1	0	0	8	9
Mizoram (list)	1	0	0	1	2
Nagaland (list)	1	0	0	3	4
Odisha (list)	1	16	2	4	23
Puducherry (list)	1	0	1	0	2
Punjab (list)	1	9	2	15	27
Rajasthan (list)	1	21	8	46	76
Sikkim (list)	1	0	0	5	6
Tamil Nadu (list)	2	22	28	0	52
Telangana (list)	3	16	2	0	21
Tripura (list)	1	1	0	1	3
Uttar Pradesh (list)	6	29	9	29	73
Uttarakhand (list)	1	11	3	13	28
West Bengal (list)	1	26	1	9	37
Total	47	367	123	282	819

Epilogue

India's projection in the outside world in various fields, temporal as well as spiritual, since the dawn of creation, has been possible through its eduation system followed in ancient period upto 1000 A.D.

The diffusion of India's cultural immensity over the vast expanses of Asia and other countries and continents is a glorious epic of human achievement in the domain of thought and its expresson in space and time.

The story of the spread of Buddhism since the time of Asoka, about the middle of the 3rd Country B.C. is well known. Far less known is the fact that Hinduism i.e. the puranic form of Brahmanical religion, was also spread in all parts of Asia, and abundant traces of Hinduism and other aspects of Indian culture associated with it still remain in various regions of the continent.

It would perhaps be a news to many that there was an Indian colony in the region of the Upper Euphrates river, to the West of lake Van, as early as the 2nd Century B.C. and the temples of Hindu gods, like Krishna, erected there, were destroyed by the Christian monk St. Gregory early in the 4th Century A.D., after defeating the Indians who stoutly resisted the iconoclastic fury of the Christians. It was Swami Vivekananda who revived the old missionary spirit of Hinduism towards the close of 19th Century A.D.

India had its cultural contact with such remote countries as Siberia, Korea and Phillipines, Tibet (Central Asia, China, Japan, Burma, Indo-China and of these Japan, Burma, Indo-China and Indonesia formed very powerful strongholds of Indian culture. Nearer home Afganishtan, Ceylone and Nepal and their relation with India is fairly known.

The influence of India's Culture and education have contributed to many countries of the World.

The history of India which the school and college syllabi present to our young generation in schools and colleges and compel to understand and memoriese for the examinations, in many cases a bunch of distortions and far behind Truth which is the very basis of History. 'Supressio veri and suggestio falsi' [Supress the truth and suggest the false] is in most cases has been followed.

Consequently, an Indian student seldom feels a pride in their Nation and country.

The much sloganised 'National Education System' is not yet found out. Neither the National political leaders nor the Academicians have yet been able to prescribe - what is National Education system. They are not unanimous on the concept of 'National'.

Now, by 'Education' we mean Degrees and Diplomas to be invested for earning livelihood, and earning money and accumulation of wealth. A citizen seldom thinks that discharging of his duties has a national importance and impact. Education has not evoked in him the much needed sense of responsibility to the nation and as he does not feel any national pride and as he has no sense of National responsibility, he is prone to corruption. The corruption has spread from Panchayat to P.M.O. (Prime Minister's office). Corruption percolated.

But what may be the result or effect of education we have noted in the remarks of some foreigners who visited this country and studied about this country, in part one of this book under the sub-heading 'Result of education'.

The national policy of Education taken up in 1986, may be geographically national but it has no grain of national ethos or national philosophy.

But it is Education and Education only that can create a national pride and can build up a Nation. The history is the subject which inculcates and evokes National Pride and National Responsbility.

It has already been stated in the Prologue of this book that there is hardly any country in the World which can boast of a history of Education of Four thousand years.

[Reference should be made of the book - India's Contribution to World Thought and Culture, published in 1970 by Vivekananda Rock Memorial Committee, led by Eknath Ranade, from 12 Pillaiyar Koil Street, Triplicane, Madras-5].

Appendix

Short Notes

There are Certain expressions regarding Certain Ceremonials and rituals. Those expressions are in Sanskrit language derived from Vedic language. But we, literate or not, often use these expressions as 'Words'. These short notes are only clarification of the significance of those oft-used 'words'.

In this chapter there are short notes on the ancient universities of our land Bharat.

There are valuable information on Vedic literature and the Art of writing, also a special note on Spread of Bharatiya Learning in China.

Contents

1. Virat Purusha
2. Yajna
3. Dwija
4. Upanayana
5. Gotra
6. Agnihotra
7. Vedic Literature
8. The Vedangas
9. Art of writing in Bharata
10. Seats of Learning in Ancient Bharat

    A   Takshasila
    B   Nalanda
    C   Vallavi
    D   Vikramsila
    E   Jagaddal
    F   Kanchi
    G   Benaras
    H   Kanauj
    I   Nadia
    J   Paithan

K   Mithila
L   Ujjain
M   Tanjore
N   Kalyana
O   Odantapuri

11. Spread of Bharatiya Learning to China

1. Virat Purusha

The concept of Virat Purusha is a fundamental concept in Sanatan Hindu Dharma and practice. The concept originated in the Vedas. The Purusha Sukta is a hymn in the RikVeda (x90). It is interpreted that this Sukta lays down the doctrine of self-sacrifice as constituting the true worship of the Divine - and the device of Yajna evolved to give a concrete shape to this doctrine. The creator sacrificed himself to create (x, 81, 5). He offers up the whole universe as an oblation to himself.

The creation originiates with the Desire of Brahma. The Universe is periodically dissolved, dissolved in Him and He recreates it. He desired to be many and many were created.

This indicates three stages in creation (i) His Will, (ii) the process of 'being' and (iii) the manifestation - Prana, Prakriti and Prakriya. These three stages in creation are indicated in the three constituted elements of the word 'Yajna' viz. (1) Ya - implied implicit, (2) Jana = manifestion of what is implicit (3) As - the growth itself - the manifested state. Thus the Vedic Philosophy of creation is that 'We are all evolved by His Will, out of His Will, we are emancipated or merged in Him after growth or expansion" (R. K. Mookerjee's book, P - 9).

The World is named Jagat which is evolving, moving, it is not something static or stationery. This Will is being worked out by different agencies like the Sun, the Moon, Fire, Storm, Cloud, Rain and the like. These are conceived as His Manifestions and worshipped as Adhi-Devatas.

It is pointed out by professor A. B. Keith, "in the Purusha hymn of the Rigveda occurs the conception of the creation of the universe from the Purusha". This Purusha is Prajapati - lord of creation.

Through Yajna men worship the creator.

2. Yajna

Yajna is the most significant factor in Vedic culture. According to Sayana (14th Century A.D.) though worship or Yajna is offered by individuals to different deities, all such worship is fundamentally the worship of the One Supreme God. Though Indra and other deities are invoked in this or that Yajna, it must be understood that it is the Supreme God who exists in the form of those deities. (i, 164, 46 R.V.)

Yajna is sacrifice. All the Yajnas are modelled on the primodial Yajna of the Virata Purusha. The Divine Yajna shows creation in its three process - beginning (Sristhi), Evolution (Sthiti) and Dissolution and Emancipation (Pralaya) (R. V. X, 81). The human Yajnas were so modelled as to symbolise and signify this mystery and meaning of creation.

Though based on the basic idea of self-sacrifice as in the case of Virata Purusha or Creator, man's sacrifice cannnot be that of creator's. Instead of offering himself as sactifice, he thought of symbolic sacrifice. An animal is seized for sacrifice on behalf of the sacrificer - he who holds the Yajna.

But Vedic religion did not accept this bloody sacrifices of animals which is known as Pasu-Yaga. In Chhandogya Upanisad (iii 6) it is very clearly stated that - Gods who do not eat or drink should not be offered meat and blood tainted with violence.

Pasu-Yaga was replaed by Isthiyaga where purodasa is sacrificed. Purudasa is cake of Brihi or Yava, i.e. rice or barley.

There are Varieties of Yajna and the names are according to matter or material of sacrifice.

(1) Soma-Yajna-where the juice of the Soma plant is sacrificed. A greater pominance is given to it in RigVeda. In viii, 48 of the RigVeda Soma is addressed as Madhu (honey) or Amrita - a coveted drink for immortality.

(2) Dravya Yajna - where material objects are offered as oblations.

(3) Tapa Yajna - where all desires are offered as oblation.

(4) Yoga-Yajna - where Senses are sacrificed.

(5) Swaddhaya - Yajna - in the form of study of the Veda and presuit of knowledge by Brahmacharya.

The different kinds of Yajnas depended on the different stages of spiritual progress of Yajmana concerned. It is said that the highest form of Yajna is prescribed in Bhagvad Gita in Chap-IV Jnana Yoga, Sloka - 24.

Brahmarpanam Brahma-havih Brahmagnau Brahmna hutam.

Brahmaiva tena gantavyam Brahmakarma Samadhina.

To lead a life as a Brahma-Karma - an offering of all its fruits to Brahma in total absence of Desires.

In the RigVeda, the more important Yajnas are those in honour of two particular Gods - Agni and Soma.

3. Dwija

The word 'Dwija' literally means twice born (Diwi = two, Ja = birth). The ceremony of Upanayana (initiation) was a solemn and sacred one indicating the teacher's (Guru's) absorbtion of the pupil. It was very significant ritual which took three days, during which, as explained in the Atharva Veda, the Guru (teacher) held the pupil within him to impart to him a new birth (or the second birth). And the pupil emerged as a Dwija.

His first birth he owes to his parents, who gave him only his body - a mere physical birth. His second birth is spiritual which unfolds his mind and soul. Here the important most role of the Guru (Teacher) is also signaled.

In the Chanddogya Upanisad the supreme need of a teacher is explained through a metaphor (vi, 14). A man who is left blind fold cannot decide his way to his home and requires one who will take of the bandage of his eye and show him the direction of his home, then and then only he can go back to his home. A blind-fold man goes astray to the east or north or south. The teacher shows his pupil the way or right direction by unfolding the bandage of his pupil's eyes.

The individual treatment was all the more essential where the supreme purpose of education was the attainment of highest knowledge i.e. Para Vidya as distinguished from Apara Vidya which is a body of contingent truths, half-truth and falacies.

The distinction between grades of knowledge is very well described in the Chanddogya Upanisad (vii-1, conversation between Narada and Sanat Kumara).

The teacher (Guru) was the walking library and source of knowledge to be tapped directly by the pupil.

Ancient schools were largely located far away from the din and bustle, in Sylvan retreats. The teacher's home was the school. The school was thus a natural formation and not an antificially created institution. As Rabindranath points out - A most wonderful thing we notice in India is that here the forest, not the town, is the fountain of all its civilization. It is the forest (Aranya) that has nurtured the two great ages of India - Vedic and Buddhist.

[For detals : The cultural Heritage of India Vol-2, P-640 onwards, Pub.: The Ramkrishna Mission Institute of Culture, Gol Park, Kolkata - 29].

4. Upanayana

The earliest reference of Upanayana may be traced in the Atharva Veda. There is mystic hymn on Brahmacharin and Upanayana [XI, 5 A.V., P-384 A.V. - Pub - Haraf].

In the Satapath Brahmana, there is reference [For details S. K. Das's book P-655, 66]. There is reference also to a lad going to a teacher with firewood in his hand and asking him to become his pupil.

In the Satapatha Brahmana there is an account of the Upanayana ceremony of a Brahmana student who brings firewood (Samidh) and alms for his teacher. This offering of sacrificial fire to a teacher became the regular way by which a youth sought to be recognised as his pupil and implied a desire to pertake in his domestic sacrifice and to accept the duty of helping to maintain it. [This has reference to Kausitaki, Chhanddogya and Mundaka UpaniSadas].

S. K. Das in his book refers to Satapatha Brahmana (X 6, 5, 4, 2, 6, 15) where it is mentioned that Prajapati - the creator and Brahmana students are guarding their teacher (Guru), his house and cattle lest he should be taken away from them. This book contains an account of the Upanayana ceremony of a Brahmana student. He is made to say his teacher, 'I have come for Brahmacharya (studentship), let me be a Bramachari (student) - according to Brhadaranyaka Upanisad with the words 'Upaimyaham Vabantam'. In Manduka Upanisad it is referred to 'Vidhibat' (1, 1, 3, P-247, Upanisad Vol.-1 Haraf).

Before receiving as his pupil, the teacher makes enquiry into his name, his birth and family. In Chhandogya Upanisad there is such a conversation between Satyakam Jabala and Gautama. Goutama told him - Bring firewood (Samidh), I shall do your upanayana - 'Saumya Samidham Aahara, upa twa nesye', (IV, 4, 4, P-119, Vol-1, Haraf). It may be assumed that uncertainity of Parentage was not a bar to the teacher's acceptance of a pupil. The duties pertaining to the new life of a pupil were to put fuel into fire, to cleanse with water, to do service and not to sleep at day hours. He was to be as firm as a stone which meant that the pupil had to overcome the temptatations inside and outside. The teacher touches the chest of the student with his fingers upwards and says - thy heart shall dwell in my heart, my mind thou shall follow with all thy heart, may Brihaspati join thee to me. To me only thou shall adhere. In me thy thoughts shall dwell. Upon me thy veneration shall be bent. When I speak thou shall be silent. May I be dear to thee ; let us dwell here in breath and life." Then the teacher bestows him the blessings "The bliss in which the Fire, the Sun, the Moon and the Waters go their way, even in that, bliss go thou that way thou hast become the pupil of Breath. May Indra, Saraswati and the Aswins bestow intelligence on thee." For himself the teacher prays that he may through his pupil, "become rich with holy lusture." the food to be taken by the pupil was to make him strong, longlived and covered with splendour. [Ref. ; Sankhyana IV, 4, 2, as quoted in S. K. Das's book P-67].

In course of time sacred thread - 'Yajnopabita', came to be used for the performance of Upanayana ritual and sacrifice. It may be noted that the followers of Abesta also uses such a cord at the worship of Fire.

In the Satapatha Brahmana there are references regarding wearing of 'Sacrificial Cord' or Yajnopobita. In Kausitaki Upanisad (II 4, 2, P-537, Upanisad Vol-1, Haraf) there is reference of Yojnopobita where Kausitaki adores the Sun.

The Spiritual significance of the Upanayana Ceremony is indicated in Satapatha Brahmana.

In Samkhy Samhita, in Vyasa Samhita it is said that the Brahmanas, the Kshatriyas and the Vaisyas are three twice-born (Dwija) castes. The second birth is symbolised by the wearing of the Sacred thread - Yojnapobita. The preceptor who imparts the Gayatri Mantra should be regarded as his father and the Mantra itself should be looked upon as fulfilling the office of his mother.

So great was the importance of Upanayana that one who had not had his Upanayana in due time was considered upapataka and Bratya. Such a Bratya should be avoided and Manu advises not to take any help from a Bratya even in distress Manu Samhita (II 40). Manu has also prescribed the period or age of Upanayana (II 38-39).

Men and gods with fuel in their hands are submitting to the conditions of pupliage. Chhandogya and Kausitaki Upanisads relate story of pupilage of Indra and Aruni respectively. In the Brihadaranyaka Upanisad, in Prasana Upanisada Garga, Sukesa, Satyakama, Sauryayanin, Kausalya, Vaidarbhi with fuel in their hands approach Pippalad for pupilage.

There are stories in Brihadoranyaka and other Upanisadas that it was possible for a man to receive instruction from his father or from other teachers. But a father often favoured a famous teacher for his son.

It is very interesting and significant to note that Baudhayana alone, among the law givers, admits the Sudra, Rathakara to the ceremony of Upanayana. He says, 'Let him initiate a Brahmana in spring, a Kashatriya in Summer, a Vaisya in Autumn, a Rathakara in the Rainy season, or all of them in spring. The ancient Vedic ritual in certain cases admitted Sudras, particulary Rathakaras (carpenters), to participate in the Srauta rites. Baudhayana defines Rathakara as the off spring of a Vaisya male and Sudra female. The Taittariya Brahmana mentions certain Mantras which are to be recited by Rathakaras. [Ref. R. K. Mukherjee's book P-174 for details]

Age : The ages of Upanayana are fixed according to the different capacities and aptitudes for learning in the pupil and the studies of their choice determining the periods required for their completion. It is also to be noted that the maximum limit of age of Upanayana is also fixed on the basis of the same considerations. The age of 16 is not too high for a Brahmana who has completed his preliminary training of Vedic studies.

The normal age of Upanayana is 8 for a Brahmana, 11 for a Kshatriya and 12 for Vaisya. But these normal age limits are different where the Upanayana is performed with a particular aim as stated by Goutama. Manu sets the age at 8, 9 and 11 as aforesaid but he also suggests age between 8-16 for the Brahmanas, 11-22 for Kshatriya and 12-24 in case of Vaisya [Manu Samhita, II, 36, 38]. The number of years is to be calculated from conception.

As said above, the season of Upanayana was spring for the Brahmana, sumner for the Kshatriya and Autumn for the Vaisya. Spring in Bharat is the season of peace and plenty, Summer is the time when tropical sun is at the height of its power and glory and autumn is the season of harvest.

Upanayana : What it means : It is not the introduction of the pupil to the teacher by his father or any other relation. The texts imply that it is the introduction of the pupil to Brahmacharya by the teacher himself.

The term Upanayana (Upatni) literally means introduction of the pupil. But it is not introduction to a teacher, it is introduction to Brahmacharya. The pupil 'upaiti' that is, enters upon Brahmacharya or enters with the teacher and he who has thus entered into studentship is designated 'upeta'. In this sense, 'Upayana' is the word which is usually termed 'Upanayana'.

Saucheya says to Uddalaka Arui 'I will enter as a student with the reverend one - Ypayami bhazabantam.' Aruni replies 'come, enter' and he initiated him.

In later text - Viromitrodays, the Upanayana is described as a ceremony by which a Dwija is brought into contact with Guru, Vrata, Veda, Yama, Niyama and the Devatas.

Satapatha Brahmana says that a teacher who has initiated a Brahmana as a student, should abstain from sexual intercourse because a student who enters upon Brahmacharya becomes as it were a garbha (Pregnancy).

The ceremony of Upanayana takes three days during which the teacher holds within him the pupil to impart to him a new birth and regenerated life. It is his second birth - the spiritual birth. It unfolds his mind and soul. *'Acharyah Upanayamano brahmacharinam Krinute garbhamanta = Acharya antah Vidya-Sarirasya madhye garbham Krinute'.* The teacher recreates the pupil in a new body of learning.

After his Upanayana, he emerges as a Brahmacharin, a new and changed person both externally and internally. He lives according to prescribed regulations. He wears a girdle of Kushagrass, the skin of black antilope, his hairs long. He carries fuel for Agni both morning and evening. He is also distinguished by some inner attributes and disciplines. These are (1) Srama - self restraint, (2) Tapasa - Practice of Penance, (3) Diksha Consecration to a life of prescribed discipline. Thus the Brahmacharin is an example of that discipline and detachment which have created and sustained the universe. [For details R. K. Mookerjee's book P-67-68].

Dress : The first step in Upanayana is to impose upon the pupil certain external marks of differentiation.

(1) The Brahmacharim is to wear Ajina as upper garment. Ajina is the skin of antelope.

(2) His lower garment will be made of materials like (i) Sana (hemp), (ii) Kshauma - fibre of Atasi plant, (iii) Chira, darva - Kusa grass, (iv) Kutapa - wool derived from mountain goat, (v) Karpasa, Cotton - it must be manufactured in the house of the pupil for the purposes of ceremony.

According to Manu, Brahmana should use Sana (hemp), the Kshatriya of Kshauma and the Vaisya of Avika goat's wool. Brahmana's wearing should be white, that of Kshatriya yellow, that of Vaisya Kauseya. The Brahmachari is also to be equipped with a Danda or Staff of wood - the woods are to be of either Bilwa or Palasa or Vata or Khadira or Pilawa or Udambara or Plaksha or Nyagrodha or Vetasa or Aswattha, failing these any wood fit for use in sacrifice. The length of the Danda will be head length for Brahmana, upto forehead for Kshatriya, upto nose for Vaisya.

Yajnopavita : It is three sets of three threads each. Those nine threads are consecrated to nine deities Omkara, Agni, Naga, Soma, Pitri, Prajapati, Vayu, Surya and all ties together. He who does not know the significance of the Upavita will have all the religious ceremonies fruitless.

Admomition : The ceremmony concludes with the following charge laid upon the Brahmacharin : A Brahmmacharin are thou ! Drink water. Do the service, Do not sleep in the day-time, Devoted to the teacher, Study Veda. Sankhayana adds : Put on fuel.

The Brahmachari starts his career taking to Savitri Vrata as a part of the Upanayana Ceremony. Brahmacharya literally means attendance to Brahma or Veda. The study of the Veda opens with Savitri.

The Brahmana student is to be taught Gayatri which belongs to Viswamitra (Rig Veda iii, 62, 10). The Kshatriya is to be taught Trishtubh which is a verse ascribed to Hiranyastupa (Rv. i. 35, 9). the Vaisya is to be taught Jagati which is a verse ascribed to Vamadeva (Rv iv, 4, 5)

Medhajanana : After three days observance of Savitri Vrata, the Ceremony of Upanayana is ended by the performance of the Medhajanana rite, whereby the gods are involved for the development of Brahmachari's mental power.

Food : The student is allowed to eat pungent and saline food and vegetables. Many forbids the taking of honey, meat, substances used for flavouring food and substances turned acid.

The hour of eating is the fourth, sixth or eighth hour of the day. He shall eat in silence, contended and without greed.

Duties : According to Apastamba the duties consist in acts pleasing to the spiritual teacher, the observance of rules conducive to his own welfare and industry in studying.

One of the standing duties was to go for begging twice a day. He should not beg to low caste people.

The next important duty was, the pupil has to fetch firewood out of the forest without damaging the tree and before sunset. Along with it was tending fire twice daily. Besides, he has to fetch water in a vessel for the use of the teacher twice daily. Plucking and fetching of flower also his duty.

He has to rise from bed before his teacher and before sunrise. Penances are prescribed for the sin of sleeping when the sun rises, sets or the teacher is awake. While bathing he is not to sport in the water. The swim must be motionless or plunge in to water like a stick. His next duty is to perform his morning devotions. (Sandhya or muttering of Savitri) with very much concentration, out side the village, in a standing posture and in silence. The prayer is to start when the stars are visible and to end when the sun rises.

The evening prayer is to begin when the sun still stands above the horizon until the stars appear.

Restrictions : He must avoid luxuries, perfumes, garlands, anointing his body, applying collyrium to his eys, use of shoes, umbrella, parasol, carriage and sleep in the day-time. He must avoid singing, playing musical instruments, dancing to which he must not look even. He must not go to assemblies, nor to crowds assembled at festivals.

[For details P. 174 - onwards R. K. Mukherjee's book].

5. Gotra : Gotra/Kula means a family depending on a real or imaginary community of blood. It may exist among all the three castes. The Charana, confined to Brahmins only, depends not on community of blood but on sacred texts and thus ideal fellowships held together by ties more sacred than the ties of blood signified by Gotra. Members of different Gotras might belong to the same Charana.

The names of the Gotras were liable to confusion in later times when their number became too large. Gotra refers to genealogical line. All Brahmin families are supposed to have descended from seven Rishis - Bhrigu, Angiras, Viswamitra, Vasistha, Kasyapa, Atri and Agastya, but the real ancestors are the following eight - Jamadagni, Gautama, Bharadwaja, Viswamitra, Vasistha, Atri, Kasyapa, Agastya. The eight gotras descending from these eight Rishis are again subdivided into forty-nine Gotras, these 49 again subdivided in to a still larger number of families. A Brahmin, who keeps a sacrificial fire, is obliged by law to know to which of the 49 Gotras, his family belongs. He must invoke the ancestors who founded the Gotra. This invocation of the ancestors came to be known as Pravara. Each of the forty nine Gotras claims one or two or three or five ancestors and the names of these ancestors constitute the distinctive character of each Gotra. [List of these are to be found in the Kalpa Sutra works] So Gotra may be defined as a system of relations based upon community of ancestors.

The Vedic mantras, religious traditions, and sacrificial customs which came to be associated with the name of a particular Rishi beame the property of the Gotra in later times. Thus a knowledge of ancestors descened from generation to generation and helped to impart a certain degree of stability or definiteness of the genealogical relations of various families.

The Gotra became more and more indicative of the blood relationship while the 'charana' indicated a spiritual relationship.

[For details : R. K. Mukherjee's book P-83, 242-243].

6. Agnihotra : Yajnas were performed for the worship of God in the form of deities like Agni, Indra, Soma, Varuna and the like. Each of these deities was associated with a particualr aspect of formative force of the formless Absolute - Virat Purusha.

Agni represents the Energy operating in the whole universe. He is the closest approximation of the Formless creator. Agni has received more attention in the RigVeda. He is worshipped as the cause of Light and Heat, of Cloud and Rani of Food and Knowledge.

Thus Agni is at the root of our life, knowledge and bliss. Therefore Agni becomes our house-hold deity worshipped in every hearth and home- by the Yajna called Agnihotra. The house holder offers Him his best as oblation. The offer may be 'Sraddha' instead of material object - the Mantra is - I offer my reverence as Sacrifice' - Aham Sraddham juhoni.

This continuous performance of Agnihotra in a family connotes its perpetuation along with the family fire which is inherited and transmitted.

7. Vedic Literature: The Vedic Literature consists of the Four Vedas and a good number of auxiliary works. Each of the four Vedas is divided into (i) Samhita Portion containing the original texts of the Vedas and (ii) Brahmana Portion containing the interpretation of the contents of the original text. This later is again divided into (a) Brahmanas proper, dealing with interpretation of rituals, (b) the Aranyakas, dealing with the worship and contemplation and (c) the Upanisads dealing with philosophical questions. All these constitute 'Sruti'.

The Vedangas are works needed for understanding Vedic texts. They are six - (i) Siksa (Phonetics), (2) Kalpa (ritual), (3) Vyakarana (grammar), (4) Nirukta (etymology), (5) Chhandas (metre) and (6) Jyotish (astronomy).

Kalpa is subdivided into (a) Srauta Sutras, (b) Grhya Sutras and (c) Dharma Sutras. Srauta Sutra deals with sacrificial rites, Grahya Santra deals with domestic rituals and Dharma Sutra deals with social rules.

The Pratisakhyas which contains Grammar, phonetics and metre the Anukramanis (indices) and the Carana Vyuhas (branches of the Vedas) also must be brought under Vedangas, though they cannot be placed under any of the six recognised Vedangas.

Arrnagements of the Hymus of the RikVeda

The RikVeda Samhita has nearly 10,500 verses, grouped into 1017 hymns, collected in Ten Mandalas of unequal length. These hymns are composed by various Rishis (Poets). The first and the tenth Mandalas are by many authors of different families, each of them contain 191 hymns. The Mondals from second to seventh have complete unity of authorship, II to VI being composed by Grit Samada, Viswamitra, Vamadeva, Atri, Bharadwaja and the Rishis or poets of their families. The entire seventh Mondal is by Vasistha. Kanwya and his family form the predominant group of authors of the eighth Mondala. The whole of the ninth Mondal is made up of hymns addressed to Soma Pavamana. Its poets belong to different families.

The general arrangements thus places the family hymns in the middle, the Soma Pavamana Mondala coming immediately afterwards. Generally thus arrangement is based on an ascending order in the number of hymns. If there is any deviation, there is an explanation. The third Mondala by Viswamitra is longer than the fourth Mondala by Bamadeva, it is placed before the later as it contains the famous Gayatri Mantra.

The internal arrangement within a Mondala places the father's hymns first, the Son's hymns follow. But in the fith Mondala, Sukta 52 and the following, composed by Syarasva, preceed the Suktas 63 and 64 composed by his father Arcananas. Here the order is reversed, as the son had composed for more hymns than his father. Except in the 8th and 9th Mondalas, everywhere hymns to Agni come first, then those to Indra, followed by those addressed to other deities.

[Ref. : The Cultural Heritage of India Vol-1 P-199-200, Pub. - The Ramakrishna Mission Institute of Culture, Kolkata.]

8. The Vedangas: The entire body of the Vedic works composed in the style of the Sutras is according to Indian traditional view divided into Six branches called Vedangas i.e. member of the Veda. In Mundaka Upanishad the names of these six subjects are first mentioned (i, 1, 5) [P-248, Vol-2 of Upanisad Pub. by Haraf A-126 college St. Market, Kolkata - 73]

The six are : Siksha, Chhandas, Vyakarana, Nirukta, Kalpa and Jyotisha

(i) Siksha : By Sayana (supposed to be in 14th Century A.D.) Siksha is defined as the Science of the pronunciation of letters, accents and the like. In the Taittiriya Aranyaka (Seventh book), some of the headings are - on Letters, on Accents, on Quantity, on the Organas of pronunciation, On delivery, On Euphonic Laws. So its study was an important branch of study which was necessary for proper understanding of the Sacred texts, specially its philosophical part. Pratisakhya is the name of an independent Scientific treaties. It is a collection of phonetic rules peculiar to a Sakha of a Veda. It gave a start to that scientific study of language which reached its perfection in the grammatical master piece of Panini.

(ii) Chhandas : The second Vedanga is Chhandas or Metre to which there are many scattered references in the Brahmanas. But the Shankhyana Srauta Sutra, the Rig Vedic Pratisakhya and the Nidan Sutra are attempts to arrange the archaic metres systematically.

(iii) Vyakarana : The foundation of Vyakarana was already laid down in 'Padapathas; which distinguishes parts of compounds, prefixes of Verbs and Suffixes etc. in a word, four parts of speech. Yaska (700 B.C.) did a lot on this and Panini developed it.

(iv) The fourth Vedanga is Nirukta or etymology as represented in the work of Yaska. It is a sort of an etymological lexieography of Vedic terms. Nirukta is in reality a commentary on Nighantu a collection of Vedic words and synonyms. The Nirukta together with Pratisakhya and Panini's grammar supplies important information on the growth of grammatical science in Bharat. Yaska had before him five such collections of which the first three contain synonyms, fourth a list of specially difficult Vedic words and the fifth a classification of the various divine personages who figure in the Veda.

(v) The fifth Vedanga is the Kalpa. The Kalpa sutras are based entirely on the Brahmanas. The Sutras were composed as a kind of grammar of the Vedic Ceremonials. There were Kalpa Sutras for the different classes of Priests - Hotri, Udgatri and Adhwarju.

(vi) The last of the Vedanga is called Jyotisha or Astronomy. The growth of this subject was due to religious requirements. The knowledge of the heavenly bodies was necessary to fix the days and hours of the Vedic Sacrifices. The Vedic hymns point to observation of the moon as the measure of time. [RV - viii, 3, 20 and other Vedic hymns where phases of the moon is noted.]

There were also minor subjects of study developed during this period. The Sutras had their supplements called 'Parisishtas'. 'Prayoga' - manual which describe the course of each sacrifice and the functions of different priests, 'Paddhatis' - or guides, 'Karkas' - versified accounts of the Sutras and Anukramanis' or Vedic Indices giving lists of hymns, the authors, the metres and the deities and the name of the Samhita where they occur.

Traditional History of Bharatvarsha

Chronology has always been a knotty point in both the political and cultural history of ancient India. Generally the Puranas, Vedic Texts and epics are relied on. But in some cases Purana and epic differ in genealogical account. For example, Ramayana genealogy of the solar dynasty runs counter to the Puranic genealogies.

Again, definite texts of Puranas are not available. The Puranas have been vitiated by exaggerations, mythological details, religious bias. Inspite of the defects, the Puranas cannot be treated as wholly unreliable. In the Vayu Purana it is laid down that there were 'Sutas' whose special duty was to preserve the genealogies of Gods, Sages, glorious Kings and greatmen. These accounts probably formed the basis of the Original Puranas. [Suta-Vayu Puran 1,31-32 as quoted in HCIP, Vol.-1, Page 271].

The Puranas in their present form can hardly be placed earlier than the Gupta period (4th Century A.D.) But those, related events of very earlier times. But the account of the Sutas may be the basis.

Pargiter holds that the original Puranas were composed more or less about the same time when the Vedic texts received their final form.

[A note on Pergitar : Pergitar Frederick Eden (1852-1927) an English, had his education in Oxford University. In 1875 Indian Civil Service I.C.S. - Service in Bengal for 31 years - 1885 under Secretary, 1887 Dist. Session Judge 1904 Judge Calcutta High Court. 1906 retired back to England. While a student, learnt Sanskrit which helped him to be a scholar in Indian ancient history. During his years in India and after retirement his scholastic interest in Puranas of India turned him to be an Indologist. In 1905-06 he was Fellow of Calcutta University, was Secretary of the Asiatic Society in 1884-85 and President in 1905-06. 1916 President of Royal Asiatic Society. Showed Scholarship in Indian Purans, Epics, History, Geography, wrote hundreds of articles on these subjects. Translated into English Markandeya Purana. In 1913 he published - Purana Texts of the Dynasties of the Kali Age. He made a comparative study of the Chronology and genealogy described in Puranas. In 1922 was published his look Indian Historial Tradition. He made a distinct mark in deciphering Brahmi and Kharosthi Lipi]

In any case, there is hardly any doubt that the Puranas embody many genuine historical traditions and genealogies.

A comparative study of the Puranas and Vedic texts shows that the Puranas, though reduced to writing at a comparatively late period, embody earliest traditional history. When we find Puranic accounts corroborated by the Vedic evidence, it is legitimate to take their testimony as valid, even in matters where the Rig Veda is silent.

Mahavarata describes a war between the Kurus and Pandavas. This is known as Bharata war. It is the cultural landmark in Indian traditional Hisotory. Vedic texts no where mention this Bharata war. But that does not disprove the historicity of this war. Pargiter in his book Ancient Indian Historical Tradition (AIHT, PP 283-284) observes that Bharata war was a political affair, so it naturally did not interest the Brahmanas. The kernel of the story of Mahabharata takes us back to the period between 1500 and 1000 B.C. The Aswalayana Grihyasatra (111 4.4) refers to Bharata and Mahabharata and Sankhayana Srauta Sutra (XV, 16) refers to the disastrous war of the Kauravas. Panini (5th entury B.C.) observes that the heroes of the Bharata War are objects of worship. All these clearly point to the historicity of Mahabharata.

Here, it is better to mention that almost all the powers of different reigions of the then Bharat participated in this war. The Pandavas' supporters were Panchalas, Matsya, Chedi, Kurusha, Western Magadha, Kasi and South-Western Yadavas. To the Kaurava's side was the whole of Eastern India (Anga, Banga, Kalinga), the whole of North-West, Kosala, Vatsa and Surasena in the Madhyadesa, Mahismati, Avanti and Salya in the west. In short, the Madhyadesa and Gujrat stood for Pandavas and the rest viz, east, north west and western India opposed them. (HCIP, Vol. I PP-306-308).

According to Aihole Inscriptions of Pulakeshin II (7th Century A.D.) the Bharata War took place in 3102 B.C. This is the starting period of Kaliyuga according to Astronomical tradition [Epigraphica Indica PP 11-12, quoted in HCIP, Vol. I, P-272]. Another school of Hindu astronomers represented by Barahamihira, Vriddhagarga and Kalhans, places this war 653 years after the Kaliyuga era i.e. 2449 B.C. (3102-653). Astronomical reference in Mahabharat itself (Nakshatras and Planets), yield various divergent results (Brihat Samhita, Rajtarangini).

Pargiter places the Bharata war in 950 B.C. considering the puranic tradition (number of kings and dynasties those flourished between king Adhisima Krishna, great grandson of Janmejaya, and the Coronation of Mahapadma Nanda (382 B.C.) Janmejoy was in 91st generation down to Manu Vaivaswata. If each generation is taken to be 18 yrs, and Manu's that of 3100 B.C., the period of Janmejoya stands (3100-18X91) some where near 1462 B.C. Janmejoy's great grand son Adhisima Krishna comes somewhere near 1392 B.C. Between Adhisimakrishna and Mahapadma Nanda 1392 B.C. to 302 B.C, the period is roughly 1008. So Pergiter fixes the year 950 B.C.

Pargiter's date is contradicted by holding that between the birth of Parikhsit and Coronation of Mahapadmananda, there elapsed 1015 or 1050 yrs. This brings the date of Bharata war to 1397 B.C. or 1432 B.C. 1400 B.C. as the date of Bharata was is corroborated by a consideration of the Vansabali list of teachers. So we may take 1400 B.C. as the provisional date of Bharata war.

The period of Manu Vaivaswata may be plaed in 3110 B.C. taking into consideration the genealogies prepared on the basis of traditional account. Manu was 95 generation before the Bharata was i.e. 1400 + 95 x 18 = 3110 B.C. (One generation is taken as 18 yrs.)

Again the beginning of the hypothetical Kali Yuga has been taken to be 3102 B.C. Curiously enough that 3110 B.C. and 3102 B.C. match the idea of the period of Manu Vaivaswata and Bharata war.

In the Satapatha Brahmana and in other accounts there is a reference of a Great Flood during the period of this Manu, at which he was the saviour of humanity.

The flood of Mesopatemia is held to have occurred in 3100 B.C.

The year 3102 B.C. represents the age of Manu and the Great Flood. Manu was the first traditional King in India. Yayati who figures in the Rigveda flourished 5 generations i.e. 90 years after Manu i.e. 3090 B.C. Mandhatri after 20 generation from Manu i.e. 3100-20x18 = 2740 B.C. Thus according to this formula Viswamitra, Jamadagni, Parasuram, Harishchandra can be plaed between 2550-2500 B.C. Sagara of Ayodhya and Dushyanta and Bharata of Hastinapur flounirished between 2300-2350 B.C. Ramchandra flourished 65 generations after Manu. So it may be 3100-65x18 = 1930 B.C. The famous Dasarajna war occured 3 or 4 generations after Ramchandra, which may be 1900 B.C.

Pre-Flood Tradition

As in Sumer and Egypt, in India also there is a list of pre-flood dynasties. But these accounts have a mixture of myths and legends.

It begins with the mythical king Manu Swayambhuba - said to be son of Brahma. He had two sons Priyabrata and Uthanapada and three daughters. These three daughters are themes of so many legends connecting Gods, Sages, Sacrificas etc. Swayambhuba Manu was also known as Viraj. He was the Lord of the first Manu cycle.

Vayu Purana mentions Ananda as Brahma (Supreme ruler). He was the predecessor of Swayambhuba. He (Ananda) is said to have established

Varnas, formulated their duties and also established the institution of marriage. But those fell into abeyance in a short time and were revived by Manu Swayambhuba. Manu's capital lay in the bank of Sarawati. The second Manu - Manu Swarochisa was the son of his daughter Akuti. Priyabrata is said to be the first of the Kshatriyas. His three sons Uttama, Tamasa and Raivata renounced the World in childhood to perform penance. They became 3rd, 4th and 5th Manus in the next Manwantaras.

Utthanapada, the second son of Swyambhuba had three sons - Dhruba, Kirtivat and Uttama. Dhruba's son - Prachinagarbha Chakshusha was the sixth Manu. His grandson Vena was a very wicked and tyrant king. There was a general rebellion against him and he was deposed and killed. His son Prithu was the first consecrated king, from whom the earth received the name Prithwi. He levelled the earth, clearing it of ups and downs encouraged cultivation, cattle breeding, commerce and building of cities and villages. Fifth in descent of Prithwi was Dakshya. Dakshya's daughter's grandson was Manu Vaivaswata who saved the humanity from the great Flood.

Manu Vaivaswata 3100 B.C.

The great Flood was not an event in Bharata only. Common flood legends suggest that the same event has been described in Indian, Hebrew and Babylonian accounts.

The year 3100/3102 B.C. represents the age of Manu, the first traditional king in India. Yayati, who is in 5th descent from Manu and figures also in Rigveda, thus flourished 90 years after Manu i.e. 3100-90 = 3010 B.C. Mandhatri after 20th generations i.e. 3100-360 = 2740 B.C. The period of Viswamitra, Jamadagni, Parasuram and Harishchandra, thus calculated, comes to roughly between 2550-2500 B.C. Sagara of Ayodhya and Dushyanta and Bharata may be placed roughly between 2350-2300 B.C. Ramachandra flourished 65 generations after Manu and so the period comes to (3100-65x18) 1930-1950 B.C. The famous Dasarajna War took place in 1900 B.C. [Ref. A.D. Pusalkar Asst. Director and Head of the Dept. of Sanskrit, Bharatiya Vidyabhuban in the History and Culture of the Indian People Vol.-I, PP-271-320]

The earliest and the shortest Indian account of the flood is found in Satapatha Brahmana, also embellished versions in Mahabharata and the Puranas (Matsya). The story is like this : Manu was washing hands in the morning. A small fish came in to his hand and requested protection from big fishes. It gradually grew up and Manu finally (from Jar, Jar to pond) left it in the sea. The fish warned Manu about the flood and promised to help him. It also advised Manu to prepare a ship and enter into when the flood came. Manu did accordingly. The flood began to rise and Manu entered the ship. The fish then swam upto him and passed siwftly to the northern region. Manu was directed to ascend the mountain, fastening ship to a tree and disembark after the water had subsided. Accordingly, Manu gradually descended, and hence the slope of the northern mountain is called Manoravataranam' or Manu's descent. Manu Vaivaswata is said to be the originator of human race and all the dynasties mentioned in the Puranas, sprang from him. He framed rules and laws of Government (constitution, so to say] and collected one sixth of the produce of the land as a tax to meet administrative expenses.

Manu had ten sons. The eldest had a dual personality as the male Ila and female Ila. His other nine sons were - Ikshwaku, Nabhaga, Dhrista, Saryati, Narishyanta, Pramsu, Nabhanedishtha, Karusha and Prishadhra. Of these nine, four are important. Ikshwaku - capital Ayodhya and his son Vikukshi formed the solar dynesty (Aikshwaka). From Drhrista came a Kshatriya dynasty ruled over Balika (Punjab), Saryati, the founder of the Saryats, lived in Anarta (Gujrat). There is confusion about Narishyanta. Some suggest that the Sakas to be his descendants. Nothing is known about Pramshu. Nabhaga settled in North Bihar - Vaisali dynasty originated. From Karusha came the Karushas - a race of determined fighters. Prishadhra was excluded from any share of the earth because he killed his Guru's cow.

From Ila, as the female, who married Budha, was born Pururavas the originator of the Lunar Dynasty (Aila Dynasty). From the Ailas sprang the dynasties of Kanyakubjas, Yadavas, Haihays, Andhakas, Vrishais, Turvasu, Druhyus, Anavas, Panchalas, Chedis, Barhadrathas etc.

Ila transformed into Kimpurusha named Sudyumna. His three sons Utkala, Gaya and Vinatsya.

The Yayati Period
[B.C. 3000 - 2750 - 250 yrs]
Lunar Dynasty

Pururavas Aila, Ila's son through Budha was the progenitor of the celebrated Lunar Dynasty. The kingdom was Pratisthana (near Allahabad - Prayag). Being intoxicated by power he declared war on the Brahmanas. The Sages in revolt killed him and installed his eldest son Ayu on the throne. Pururavas were the contemporaries of Ikshaku of the Solar Dynasty. Amavasu was the second son of Pururavas. Ailas extended their territory to a long extent. That was divided between Ayu and Amavasu. Ayu continued in Pratisthna Amavasuta whose share fell in the northern territoris founded the Kanyakubja dynastry.

Ayu had five sons. Of them Nahusa the eldest, ruled with his capital in Pratisthana. The second Khshatra-Vridha established himself at Kasi. Nahusa was a famous king, a great conqueror, the first man to establish a theatre on earth.

His son and successor Yayati is mentioned as a Samrat. He extended his kingdom far and wide. Mahavarata and Puranas give a detailed account.

Yayati had two wives - Debyani and Sarmistta. Deyani was the daughter of the great Usanas rishi and Sarmistha was the daughter of Vrisaparban of the Asuras.

Debyani bore two sons - Yadu and Turvasu, Sarmistha bore three - Anu, Druhyu and Puru.

Yayati devided his kingdom among his five sons, placing the youngest Puru in the main line. Lunar line came to be known was Puruvamsa. Puru was succeeded by his son - Janmejoya.

From the divergence of the Puranas regarding distribution of the territories of Yayati, Pargiter suggests that Yadu was given the territories towards the South-West embracing the country watered by Charmanvati (Chambal), Vetrabati (Betwna, Suktimuti (Ken), Turvasu got the South-east territory (round Rewa). To Druhyu was assigned the West, Country west of the Yamuna and north of the Chambal. Anu was assigned the north - the portion of the Ganga-Jamuna doab.

The Kanyakubja and Kasi-subsections of the Lumar dunasty had no remarkable achievement. Yadu-the eldest son of Yayati founded the Yadava dynasty - the first of the Lunars, came to prominence. Of the Yadu's sons only Kroshtri and Sahasrajit are to be mentioned.

Chitrarath about 12th in descent of Yadu was contemporary of the Paurava King Matinara. Gouri the daughter of Matinara was married to Yubanswa II of the Solar dynasty of Ayodhya. Again, Yubanaswaen's Son Mandhatri married Bindumati - grand daughter of Chitraratha (Sasabindu was his son and Bindumati was Sasabindu's daughter). Thus the Yadavas branched off to Yadavas and Haihayas.

Solar Dynasty : Ikshwaku was the eldest son of Manu Vaivaswata. He was given Ayodhya. He had 100 sons of whom Vikukshi was the eldest. Besides, two of his sons Nimi and Danda were also famous. Nimi founded the Videha line and Danda in Dandakaranya territories. Paranjoy on

Kukustha was the son of Vikukshi, Yuvanaswa was 5th in descent from Kukustha. Yuvanaswa's son was Kuvalaswa was known as Dhundumara for his fight with the aboriginals or Asuras of Rajputana. His eighth descendant was Yuvanaswa II, also known as Saudyumni. His son was Mandhatri, said to be nursed by Indra with nectar exhaled from his thumb.

The Vidhehas sprang from Nimi. The capital was Mithila, named after his son Mithi.

Brahman families : In the traditional history of India, the Brahmanas play very important roles. The Brahmana families claim decent from eight mythical rishis who are said to be the mind-born sons of Brahmma. The eight are : Bhrigu, Angiras, Marichi, Atri, Vasistha, Pulastya, Pulaha and Kratu. The last three did not produce true Brahmana Stocks. Kratu had no wife. But some accounts say that he was married and his progeny were known as Valakhilya. Pulastya was the progenitor of Rakshasas, Vanaras, Kinnaras and Yakshas. Pulaha was the progenitor of Kimpurusha, Pisacha, goblins, lions, tigers and other animals. Of the rest five, Bhargavas, Vasistha and probably Angirasa are earliest. The Atris and Kasyapas (Marichi) originated later.

Chyavana and Sukra are the earliest Bhrigus. Sukra was connected with Danavas as their Guru and was the rival of Brihaspati, the Guru of the Devas. Sukra's daughter Debyani married Yayati and bore him Yadu and Turvasu. Vasisthas have been connected with the Kings of Ayodhya. Prabhakara is said to be the descendant of Atri. From Pravakara, the Atreya Gosthi originated through his ten sons.

Jamadagni and Viswamitra emerged at a later period.

The Mandhatri period 2750-2550 = 200 years

Solar dynasty - Mandhatri was the son of Yuvanaswa II and Gouri. He is considerably eulogised in the puranas. He conquered the earth in one day etc. He was succeeded by Purukutsa - his eldest son. His other two sons were Ambarisha and Muchukunda.

Purukutsa continued the conquest of his father. Muchukunda, the third son of Mandhatri was a famous king. He built and fortified a town on the Narmada between Paripatra and Pikha mountains. Haihaya King Mahismount subsequently conquered that town and named Mahismati.

Lunar Dynasty : The Anavas grew in power. King Mahamanasa, seventh in descent from Anu, extended sway of Anavas towards the east of Punjab and the bifurcation of Anavas under his two sons - Usinor and Titikshu shows the extent of his conquest.

Usinor established a kingdom on the eastern border of Punjab, which was divided among his five sons.

Titikshu moved eastward and crossing Vedaha and Vaisali, founded a kingdom in Bihar - which later developed into the five kingdoms - Anga, Vanga, Kalinga, Pundra and Suhmha.

The Drhyus were cornered into the north-western portion of Punjab. It came to be known as Gandhara.

The Parasuram period 2550-2350 be 200 years

This period of 200 years comprising about 12 generations, till the rise of Sagara of Solar dynasty in Ayodhya, was dominated by Haihayas and Bhrigus in turn.

The Bhrigu-Vamsa dwelt in Anarta (Gujrat). The men of this Vamsa are called Bhargavas. The western India was dominated by the Haihayas after the Sarayatas. The Bhrigus became associated with the Haihayas. The Bhargavas were the priests of the Haihayas. The King Kartyavirja bestowed great wealth on the Bhargavas. His successors ill-treated and used violence against the Bhargavas. They fled to Kanyakubja in Mudhyadesha for safety.

The chief among the Bhrigus was Richika, son of Urva, a famous rishi skilled in archery. To wreck vengence on the Haihays, the Bhargavas collected arms and sought martial alliance with the Kshatriya families. Richika wanted to marry satyabati - the daughter of King Gadhi, of Kanyakubja, Gadhi did not approve. So to avoid Richika, he demanded an impossible price that of Richika could provide thousand black-eared horses, Satyabati would be married to Richika. Richika fulfilled the condition and married Satyabati. Jamadagni was the son of Richika and Satyabati. Jamadagni was skilled in archery. He made alliance with the ruling family of Ayodhya by marrying Renuka, daughter of a junior King Renu. Jamadagni was not a militant rishi.

The Haihaya King Kartyabirja once came to Jamadagni's hermitage. Jamadagni treated him with royal hospitality through the help of his Kamdhenu (wish-giving cow) Kartya birya demanded Kamdhenu as a gift. Jamadagri refused. Kartavivya applied force. He destroyed the hermitage and carried away the cow.

Of the four of five sons born to Jamadagni, Rama was the younger. He always carried a Parasu (battle axe) with him and so known as Parasurama to differentiate with Dasarathi Rama. The Puranas represent Parasurama as an incarnation of Vishnu. The slaughter of the Kshatriyas twenty-one times, and ridding the earth of Kshatriyas is said to be the Principal feat of Parasurama.

The Bhrigu-Haihayas conflict started when Kartavirya took away Kamdhenu from Jamadagni. Rama was not present then. When he heard that his father was molestad and Kamdhenu was forcibly taken away, he slaughtered Karta-birya. For this act of sin, his father advised him to go on pilgrimage. Taking the advantage of Rama's absence, Kartyabirya's sons slew Jamadagni when he was indeep meditation. This enraged Rama to extreme and he declared a vendetta, not only against the Haihayas, but also against the Kshatiryas in general. It is said that Rama filled several lakes near Kurukshutra with the blood of Kshatriya. He is said to have rid the earth twenty-one times of the Kshatriyas. As a result many Kshatriyas fled to mountains, many hid themselves among the women-folk.

Riksavan, of the Pauravas, Sarvakarma of Ayodhya, Brihadratha of Magadh, Chittraratha of Anga and Vatsa of Kasi are said to have escaped Ram's slaughter (Mahavarata).

It may so happen that Rama organised a confederacy of various Kingdoms and faught against the Haihayas who in the meantime had become unpopular for their raids and atrocities. And that political history is eulogised in the Puranas and Muhabharata in favour of Parasurama and the story of ridding earth of Kshatriya, for twenty-one times had evolved.

Finally to rid himself of the sin, he donated the whole earth to Kasyapa who banished him from the earth. Rama then wrested from the sea the West Coast and colonised it. The whole of the West Coast from Bhrigukachhas (Broachu) down to Cape Comorin retains association with Parasurama.

Thus, Parasurama is several times prior to Rama of Ramayana and the heroes of the Mahabharata. But his name is always associated with the period of Ramayana and Mahabharata. To solve this anachronisms, a theory was promulgated at a later date, that Parasuram was Chiranjiva (immortal).

The Haihayas : After the death of Purukutsa, the Kingdom of Ayodhya lost prominence. The Haihaya branch of the Yadavas extended to North India. Arjuna or Kartavirya Arjuna became famous. The thousand arms ascribed to Arjuna was possibly his fleet of thousand ships. He led his victories campaign from Narmada to as far north as the Himalayas. He is said to have conquered the whole earth. He was cursed by Agasta, as he had burnt his hermitage in Himalaya. Barring his conflict with Jamadagna and Vasistha, Arjuna was always praised.

Mr. Kirandikar's observation : Bhrigus were great navigators who controlled the maritime trade between India and the Western world and occupied the coastal line on the Arabian Sea. They amassed great wealth through their trade with the foreign countries. The Haihaya King Arjuna did not wish that the Bhrigus, who were agents of the foreigners should thrive at the cost of the people. This was the origin of the conflict. Arjuna wanted to capture the trade under the Bharatiyas, Bhrigus were Self-seekers. Arjuna sought the help of the Atris who were equally expert in ship-building. The Atris built for Arjuna a fleet of thousand ships or a ship with thousand oars. Accordingly Arjuna was named Srahasrabahu or Srahasradhara. Arjuna's effort to getting back the control of the sea trade was opposed by Parasuram who organised a team defeated by Arjuna. In this strife Arjuna was killed by Parasurama and Haihaya power declined. The annihilation of Kshatriyas twenty one times refers to destruction of the population of the Narmada region a number of times to wipe out the memory of the popular king Arjuna. Thus Parasuram kept the sea-trade in the hands of the South, the Dravidians against the of the North-Arjunas.

Arjuna's one son Jayadhwaja reigned in Avanti, another son in Mathura, another in Saurastra. Jayadhwaja's son Talajangha had many sons. Vitihotra was the most powerful among them. According to Puranas the Haihays formed five groups - Vitihotras, Saryatas, Bhojas, Avantis and Kundikaras. (Matsya and Vayua). They carried their raids against the Kingdoms of Madhyadesha, Kanyakubja, Kosala and Kasi. The Haihays had to meet the reverse later on. Vitihotra had to take refuge with a Bhargava Sage. After this, the Haihaya dynasty came to an end, the king became a Brahmana.

Earlier, the Haihayas attacked Ayodhya which was weakened after the death of Mandhatri and Purukutsa. Bahu (or Asita according to Ramayana), the king of Ayodhya had to leave the throne. He took shelter in the hermitage of Aurva Bhargabha. He died there. His queen gave birth to a son in the forest, who was named Sagara. He was educated by Aurva.

This Sagara was the greatest King of the solar dynasty during the period. He recovered his lost Kingdom with the help of the Bhagavas.

Other Lunar Dynasties : The Yadavas, the Anavas, the Kanyakubja.

Contemporary to Sagara of Ayodhya was Vidarbha of the Yadavas. He sought peace with Ayodhya and gave her daughter Kesini in marriage with the latter. King Vidarbha retired to the Deccan, leaving the whole of north India, accepting the Suzerainty of Sagara. After the death of Sagara, the three sons of Vidarbha extended the north India and established separate line.

The Anavas Kingdom in the east founded by Titikshu, extended by Bali a contemporary of Sagara, Bali Subvidided his kingdom to his five sons - Anga, Vanga, Kalinga, Pundra and Suhmna. These five sons were begotten by the sage Dirghatamas on queen Sudeshna at Bali's request.

The capital of Anga was Malini, four miles west of Bhagalpur. Anga comprised to modern districts of Bhagalpur and Munghyr. Vang is further east comprising Dacca and Chitagunge. Pundra was north-Bengal. Suhmna comprised Burdwan division and Kalinga in the sea-coast of Orissa. (for Lumar dynasty).

Kanyakubja

After few generations of Jahnu came Kausika. From Kausika-Gadhi who is described as an incarnation of Indra. Gadhi's daughter Satyabati was given in marriage to Vrigusage Richika Aurva. Through Richika's favour Gadhi had a son Viswamitra or Viswaratta - who is a prominent figure in the ancient legends. There are legends of controvery between Vasistha and Viswanitra relating to Kamadhenu (Sacred cow), Trisanku, Harishchandra. Viswamitra admitted the superior power of Brahminism in Vasistha. He renounced the kingdom and set out to attain Brahminism. He was successful. Even Vasistha acknowledged him.

The name of Viswamitra, like Parasuram, appears in different ages. He appears in connection with Rama of Ayodhya, father of Sakuntala who gave birth to celebrated emperior Bharata, as the wife of Dushyanta the Pururava.

It appears that the Puranas combine the various accounts of various Viswamitras and roll those into one.

Viswamitra, the Kanyakubja King, was related to Jamadgni and Parasurama. It is likely that the Kanyakubja Kingdom helped the confederacy raised by Parasuram against the Haihayas.

Kasi : Divodas's son or his grandson Pratardana extended his sway and annexed the country around Kausambi. It was named Vatsa country. Vatsa's son Alarka regained the capital of Varanasi from the Rakshasas who occupied it long ago. Alarka had a long and prosperous region.

Solar Dynasty Ayodhya : After Mandhatri, Purukutsa and Trasadasyu, Ayodhya had lost its name. Again it flourished during the period of Satyabrata Trisanku and Harishchandra. Sixth in descent of Harishchandra was Bahu. Sagara was his son who was born in the hermitage of Aurva and was taught by him - Sagara learnt Agneyastra from him.

Sagara made an expedition against the Haihays. After destroying them Sagara challenged the Sakas, Yavanas, Kambojas. He would have completely crushed them. But his Priest Vasistha intervened. Sagara then left them off after imposing on them certain signs of symbolical defeat and disgrace. The sakas were made to shave only half of their heads, Kambojas to have their heads completely shaved, Paradas were forbidden to shave or trim their hair of their heads, Pahlaves to shave their beard. Thus they were rendered unfit for Vedic Ceremonials (Vayu purana)

Sagara subjected all contemporary powers and was the emperor of the whole of the north, Videha was the only exception.

Sagara's son Asamanjas was cruel and was discarded. His son Amsumant became the King.

Vaisali : Karandhama, King of Vaisali defeated the powers which sieged him. He rescued his son Avikshit from the King of Vidisa. He dealt a severe blow to the Haihayas. Daughter of Vidisa King, Visala was married to Abhikshit. Their son Marutta is said to be one of the sixteen universal monarchs of antiquity. Marutta deserves credit for ending the Haihaya aggression permanently in the east.

Brahman Families : The Bhrigus or Bhargavas dominated the whole period (2150-2350 B.C.). Richika, Jamadagni, Parasurama, Agni, Aurva were the prominent Bharagavas.

Ayasya is the first Angiras mentioned in traditional history. He officiated in the sacrificial ceremony of offering Sunasepa as a victim in the reign of Harishchandra of Ayodhya. The Angirasas were connected with the Vaisali kings as their hereditary priest. Usija Angirasa was the priset of Karandhama and Avikshit. Two of the sons of Usija Angirasa officiated for Marutta. Dirghatamas was the son of Uchathya i.e. grandson of Usija Angirasa. Diragahatamas was born blind. He was expelled for his misdeed and set adrift in the Ganges. King Bali of the Anavas rescued him. At Bali's desire, he begot five sons on Bali's queen. Dirghatamas later got back his sight.

Dattar Atreya was the only prominent figure among the Atris. Devraja Agasta was the priest of the Ayodhya Kings. His descendants officiated for the Sakas, Yavanas etc. Apava Vasistha was in the Himalaya. His hermitage was burnt by Arjuna - the Haihayas.

Kasyapa officiated as priest at the sacrifice of Rama Jamadagnya. Kasyapa got the whole earth as donation (stated earlier).

The only historical figure of the Agastyas was the Agastya who married Lopamudra and was a contemporary of Alarka grandson of Pratardana of Kasi [For details see History and culture of the Indian People P-271-242, Vol-1].

The Ramchandra Period (2350 BC - 1950 BC = 400 years).

The Kritayuga, according to Puranas, ended with the wars of Parasurama and Sagara. The old kingdoms of the Pauravas, Kanya Kubjas, Druhyus and Anavas gradually disappeared. The Yadavas receded to Deccan. Haihayas were completely routed The eastern kingdoms of Vaisali, Videha, Ayodhya, Kasi and the Anavas of Bengal continued to exist during the next period 2350-1950 B.C. that we discuss now.

Solar Dynasty : After King Sagara's death, his grandson Amsumant succeeded. Amsumant's second successor was Bhagiratha - a legendary figure. He is reputed to have brought down the sacred river Ganges (Bhagirathi) from heavens, inorder to liberate his ancestors cursed by Kapilamuni. Probably Bhagiratha was the originator of the worship of the Ganges. Bhagiratha was succeeded by Ambarish and Ambarish's third generation next, was Rituparna who succeeded. Sudasa, son of Rituparna succeeded. Sudasa has been identified with Sudas referred to in the Vedas. He was one of the famous Dasarajnas of the time. [But there is no support of identy of Sudas and that of Vedic Sudas.] Sudasa's son Mitrasahu was the next in the throne. He is known as Kalmashpada. There is legend on Kalamashpada. The King Kalmashpada is said to have served human flesh to his preceptor Vasistha, through mistake. Vasistha cursed him. But on realising that the King was not at fault, the sage limited the duration of the curse to 12 years. Kalmashpada, in return, was going to curse his preceptor. The queen intervened. So the mantra-charmed water, which the King was about to throw to Vasistha in retaliation, was dropped on his feet. As a result his feet turned stone - so he is named Kalmashpada. Had he thrown the Mautra-charned water on earth, the earth would have been barren. After Kalmaspada resumed his natural state, on account of a curse, he had to raise an issue from his wife by a Niyoga with Vasistha. Asmaka was the son of this union. Asmaka's son was Mahuka (Narikavacta).

It appears that there was a bifurcation of the Ayodhya line for some six or seven generations after Kalmashpada. The two lines, however, were united under a single monarchy under Khatvanga - known as Dilip II. He was a Samrat and a Chakravartin. He was a devotee of Vishnu. His son was Raghu. The Ikshwaku dynasty came to be known as be Raghuvamsa on account of this celebrated Raghu. He conquered the whole earth and performed the

Viswajit Yajna. Being an ideal monarch. Raghu has been called the first King of Ayodhya.

Raghu was succeeded by his son Aja. Aja and his consort Indumati (Vidarva Princess) had their son Dasarata. Dasaratha had a daughter Santa by name who was given to Anga King Lomapada in adoption. Santa was married to Rishya Sringa. Dasaratha was a valiant and all conquering King. He led his victorious campaign throughout the length and breadth of North India.

The Yadava contemporary of Dasaratha was Madhu who had consolidated the Yadavas. The region south from Jumna upto Gujrat and beyond the Vindya and Satpura mountains was under the Yadavas with emperor Madhu as the Lead.

Though Dasaratha had a number of queens, Kausalya, Kaikeyi and Sumitra were the principals. Being without a heir, Dasaratha performed Putra-Kamesthi (rite for securing male issue) Yajna on the advice of Vasistha, under the guidance of Rishyasringa. Four sons were born unto him. Rama of Kausalya, Bharata of Kaikeyi, Lakshman and Satrughna of Sumitra. Rama and Lakshmana were trained by Viswamira in archery. They vanquised the Rakshasas that disturbed him. Viswamitra took them to Mithila. Rama there was maried to Sita.

Though there are interpolations and fabulous legends, the text can be made to yeild historical facts. The story of Rama is particularly important as it brings South India to our view for the first time.

When Dasaratha was taking preparation to instal Rama on the throne, a palace intrigue set in. Dasaratha married Kaikeyi on the stipulation that the son born of her was to succeed Dasaratha. Rama was son to Kausalya. As a result of the palace -intrigue, Rama was banished to Dandaka forest (Dandakaranya). Lakshmana and Sita accompanied Rama. Rama first went to Prayaga and thence to Bhopal region, crossed the Narmada, proceeded to South. To the South of the Godavari, he reached Janasthan, said to be a colony of the Rakshasas having intercourse with Ceylone. Rakshasas ill-treated the rishis and Munis. Rama killed a number of Rakshasas. In revenge, the King of Rakshasa of Kingdom Cyclone, Ravana carried away Sita to Ceylone. Rama proceeded further South to Pampa and Rishyamuk. Here he made friendship with Sugriba who was expelled by his brother King Vali. With the help of the Vanar army Rama invaded Ceylone, killed Ravana, made Bivishana the brother of Ravana, the king of Ceylone and returned to Ayodhya.

Bharata, during the period was the regent of the Kingdom. Rama now reigned prosperously for many years. The governance was so popular that Rama's Rule (Ram Rajatya) is still a popular proverb.

Ayodhya sinks into insignifance. None of the sons of Rama (Lava and Kusa), Bharata (Taksha and Puskara - Takshasila and Purkaravati), Lakshman (Angada and Chitraketu) and Satrughna (Subahu) could make a show in the lands given to them. Kusa who succeeded Rama, also could not show any brilliance. During the time the chief role was played by Pauravas and Yadavas.

Videha : Siradhwaja, the father of Sita, was one of the celebrated Janakas. King Sudhanya of Sankishya Kingdom wanted to marry Sita. Siradhwaja killed Sudhanya in a fierce battle and installed his brother Kusadhwaja on the throne of Sankishya, Siradhwaja's daugthers Sita and Urmila were married to Rama and Lakshmana respectively. Kushadhwaja's daugthers Mandavi and Srutakirti respectively were married to Bharata and Satrughna.

Vaisali : Marutta's son Narishyanta was a great donor. He performed a grand yajna. His son was Dama - a great warrior. He won his queen in a Swayamvara. His son Trinabindu married Alambhusha. Their son was Visala and daughter - Ilavila. Ilavila was given marriage to Pulastya. Visala founded the Kingdom and the capital was ? Vaisali (used in anticipation). The last name in the list is Pramiti or Sumati - who was a contemmporary of Dasaratha.

The Lunar Dynasty : Dushyanto, the famous Paurava hero flourished few generations after Sagara of Ayodhya. Turvasu king Marutta adopted Dushyanta as his heir as he had no son. So the Turvasu line merged with the Paurava line. Dushyanta married the daughter of Viswamitra who was brought up in the hermitage of Kanwa of Kasyapa family. Her name was Sakuntala. Bharata was their off spring.

Bharata was a great conqueror and thereby Samrat. His territory stretched from the Saraswati river to the Ganges. The Paurava dynasty came to be called Bharatas after the time of Bharata. Probably during his reign the capital was shifted to Hastinapur from Pratisthana. Hastin was the successor of Bharata.

According to some accounts, Bharata gave his name to our country, which was henceforth called Bharatvarsha.

Bharata was disappointed in his sons and killed them. By the grace of Maruts, Bharadwaja the son of Brihaspati, was given him as his heir.

Bharadwaja's son Vitatha succeeded Bharata. Hastin the fifth successor from Bharata, had two sons - Ajamidha and Dwimidha. They extended the Paurava Kingdom. Ajamidha continued the mainline at Hastinapur and Dwimidha established the Dwimidha dynasty in the modern Bareily.

Ajamidha had three sons - Riksha, Nila and Brihadvasu. After Ajamidha's death the main Paurava line was divided among his three sons. Riksha succeeded at Hastinapura. Nila and Brihadvasu founded North Panchala and South Panchala dynasties. [N. Panchala comprised the modern Rohilkhand (U.P.), S. Panchala, which incorporate the old Kanyakubja, consisted of the district of modern Agra and Kanpur.]

The name Panchala was derived from the 'five' (Pancha) sons of Bhrimyaswa, the sixth successor of Ajamidha. The Panchala was thus a branch of the Bharatas.

The Panchala kingdom was divided among the five sons of Bhrimyaswa. Mudgala the eldest, founded an important branch. His grandson Vadhryaswa, extended the Kingdom and his son Divodasa further augmented it. Divodasa and his descendant Somadatta Sudasa is referred in Vedas in reference to the famous battle of ten kings. [Rama is in 65the descendant of Manu Vaivaswata i.e. 3100B.C. 3100-65x18 - 1930 B.C. Somadatta Divodasa whose name appears in the Vedas was almost 63rd descendant of Manu i.e. 3100-18x63 = 3100-1134 = 1966 B.C.]

Yadavas : Kratha-Bhima continued the main Yadava line of Vidarva. His brother Kaisika was the progenitor of the Chedis. The most important King of Vidarva was Bhimaratha. His daughter was the famous Damayanti who was married to the Nishadhaking Nala. Yadavas later divided into many principalities. Madhu who came 10 generation after Bhimaratha consolidated the Yadavas. Madhu's son Lavana was killed by Satrughna (Rama's brother). He installed his son Subahu in Mathura. Bhima Satvata (son of Satvata) who was Madhu's sixth successor ousted Subahu from Mathura.

Eastern Anavas : Very little is known of the particulars of the Kings of this dynasty. We know of Lomapada of this dynasty who was a great archer. He was contemporary of Dasaratha of Ayodhya. Lomapada was childless and adopted Santa - the daughter of Dasaratha. It is already noted that Santa was married to Rishyasringa. This Rishyasringa perfomed the Putra-Kamesthi Yajna of Dasaratha as a result of which Rama and his brothers were born. The Same Rishyasringa performed the same Yajna for Lomapada. As a result a son was born unto Lomapada. His name was Chaturanga.

Kasi : Ritudhyaja or Vatsa had a son (born out of Madalasa) named Alarka. He becamme the King, drove away the Rakshasas from Benaras and reestablished his capital there. He relinquished his Kingdom to his brother. The name of his son was Sannati.

Brahmana Families : Among the Bhargavas during this period appears Valimki of the Ramayana who was called Prachetasa.

The Krishna Period 1950 - 1400 B.C. = 550 years

The Dwapara Age began after the destruction of Rakshasas (Ravana) and coronation of Rama. This Age ended with the Bharata war (Mahabharat) in which Krishna took the major role. During this period only Panchalas, Pauravas and Yadavas figure prominently. It was Hastinapur, not Ayodhya, was the central scene.

Panchalas : During the reign of Sudasa North Panchala came to prominence. Paurava king (Sambaran) was defeated. Sahadeva succeeded Sudasa and Somaka succeeded Sahadeva. Sambaran recovered his Kingdom. King Ugrayudha of Dwimidhas dynasty, killed north Panchala King - His grandson Prishata took shelter in South Panchal. Ugrayudha attacked South Panchal and was killed by Bhishma who restored Prishita in his Kingdom. Drupada succeeded his father Prishita in north Panchala. Drona - who once was insulted by Drupada, defeated Drupada with aid of his desciples Pandu and Kuru. Out of two Panchalas, Drona kept north Panchala for himself and gave south Panchala to Drupada. Drupada seeking vengence on Drona, performed a Penance in order to get a son who would avenge Drona. Dhristyadumna was born as a result, Drupada's daughter was married to Pandavas. This Panchala played a very important role in Bharata war. Drona was in favour of the Kauravas and Dhristyadumna in favour of the Pandavas.

Pauravas : Sambarana had recovered his Kingdom through Vasistha's help. He had by Tapati a son named Kuru. Kuru raised the Paurava Kingdomm to eminence. He was celebrated for his righteous rule and Kurukshetra was regarded as a religious place. There is some confusion regarding immidiate successors of Kuru. According to Pargitar's book Ancient Indian Historical Tradition, Kuru had three sons

Pratipa is the King in the main line. [Janmejoy's branch lost sovereingnty. He injured the sage Gargya's son and was cursed. Through a horse-sacrifice absolved him of the sin, he could not recover.]

[The line of Sudhanya was bifurcated into Chedi and Magadha branches founded by his further successor Vasu.]

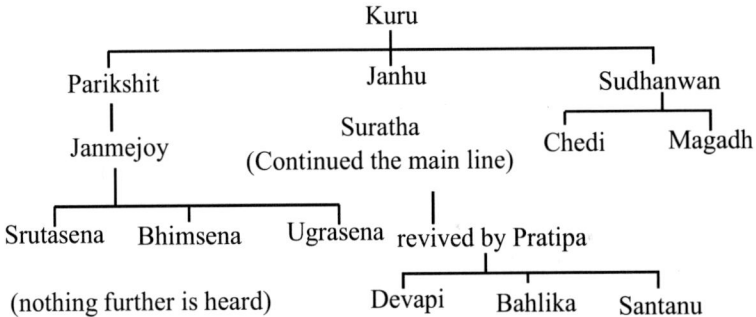

Pratipa was a famous ruler. He had three sons - Devapi, Bahlika and Santanu. Devapi was a leper and Bahlika resigned in favour of Santanu, who thus succeeded to Pratipa.

Santanu married Ganga and Vishma or Debabrata was born. That his father Santanu could marry Satyabati, Debabrata vowed to remain celebate all his life, that Satyabati's sons might rule.

To Santanu and Satyabati were born Chitrangada and Vichitrabirya. Chitrangada was killed in a fight against Gandhavas. So Vichitrabirya succeeded the throne. But he died young. The queen through Niyoga (Levirata) had two sons from Vyasa. They were Dhritarastra and Pandu. Dhitarastra being blind was not entitled to throne. Pandu was crowned as King of Hastinapur of the Pauravas. Bhimsa looked after the affairs of the state. Dhritarastra was married to Gandhari and had hundred sons. Pandu married Kunti the daughter of King Kuntibhoj. He also married Madri the sister of Salya - the Bahika King.

The kingdom held by the main Paurava line decliend till the time of Pratipa. He was a famous ruler. He had three sons - Devapi, Bahlika and Santanu. Devapi was a leper so unfit, Bahlika resigned in favour of Santanu - who succeeded Pratipa.

Santanu married Ganga and Debabrata, famous in the name of Bhishma was born unto them. He vowed to remain celebate all his life and renounced the throne in favour of his younger brothers born out of Santanu and Satyabati. Chitrangada and Vichitravirya were sons of Santanu - Satyabati.

Chitrangada was killed in a battle with Gandhavas. Vichitravirya becamme the successor but he died young. Through Niyoga (Levirate) system two sons from Vyasa were born unto the queen. They were Dhritarastra (born blind) and Pandu. Pandu became the King of Hastinapur in the main line of the Paruvavas.

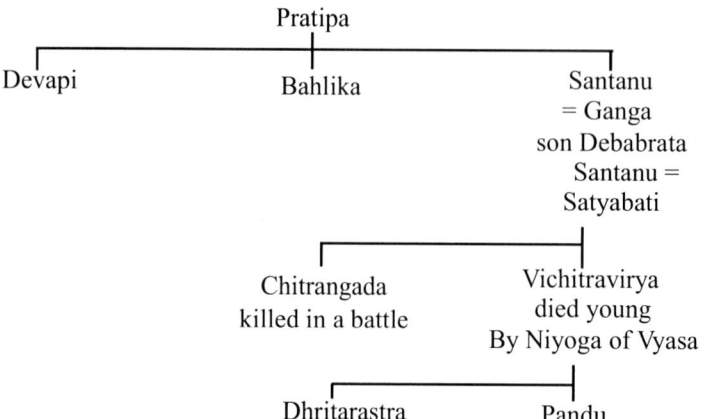

Pratipa

Devapi   Bahlika   Santanu
                                 = Ganga
                                 son Debabrata
                                 Santanu =
                                 Satyabati

Chitrangada   Vichitravirya
killed in a battle   died young
                         By Niyoga of Vyasa

Dhritarastra   Pandu

Dhritarastra married Gandhari of Gandhar and had hundred sons and one daughter. Pandu married Kunti - the daughter of Kuntibhoja. Her other name was Pritha. Pandu's second wife was Madri - sister of the Bahika King Salya. Kunti had three and Madri had two sons - who were called Pandavas. Yudhisthir, Bhimma and Arjuna - the sons of Kunti or Pritha - are said to be the sons begotten through Yamma, Bayu and Indra and Nakula Sahadeva twins of Madri are said to be begotten by Aswins. Madri burnt herself in the funeral pyre of Pandu - who was cursed by a sage and was living in a hermitage with his wives. The Pandus were born in that hermitage. Kunti then returned to Hastinapur with five sons.

Dhritarastra was ruling during the absence of Pandu. Now, he appointed Yudhisthira as the crown prince as he was the eldest. Though the sons of both Dhritarastra and Pandu were Kaurava (Kuru Dynasty), the term now restricted to the sons of Dhritarastra and so the sons of Pandu were named Pandavas [After the Kurukshetra war - this distinction was abolished and the Pandavas were called Kauravas]

Let us remember that Kuru had three sons of whom Sudhanwan was the third. Vasu was his fourth successor. He was a conqueror and established a dynasty. His capital - Suktimati lay near the river the Suktimati (the Ken). Vasu was a Samrat and Chakravartin. He had five sons to whom he divided his territory. Magadha came to the share of the eldest son - Brihadratha. Magadha under Brihadratha became a prominent place in the traditional history. Jarasandha - of his dynasty rose to great promminence. He extended territory upto Mathura where the Yadava King Kamsha ruled. Kamsa was the son-in-law of Jarasandha. Kamsa was very much unpopular for his tyrany. Ultimately Krishna killed him. At this Jarasandha was enraged.

Ugrasena father of Kamsa was placed on the Mathura throne by Krishna. Jarasandha attacked Muthura and defeated the Yadavas and the Bhojas there. The Yadavas ultimately migrated to Dwaraka under Krishna. Jarasandha was killed by Bhima - the Pandava. Jarasandha's son Sahadeva became an ally of the Pandavas.

Yadavas : The period dealt with is named Krishna Period (1950-1400 B.C) because of the importance of Krishna. He originated from the Yadavas. Though thousands of legends and myths are associated with the name, Krishna was essentially a historical figure. He had developed in him all the qualities - physical, intellectual, mental, psychic and spiritual in their best-bloomed form. This being very much impossible for any man, God-hood is added to his name.

The Yadava Kingdom was ruled by Bhima Satya. He divided it among his four sons - Bhajamana, Devabridha, Andhaka and Vrishni. Bhajaman's discendants made no mark. Devabridha's discendants were the Bhojas in a country near Mount Abu. Andhaka reigned in Mathura. He had four sons of whom Kukura formed the main dynasty down to Manisa. Andhaka's another son, also named Bhajamana, ruled some where near Mathura. Kritavarma, son of Hridika was in the line of Bhajamana. Kritavarma helped the Kauravas in the war. He was one of the three of Kauravas side who survived. Vrishni had four sons. Anamitra was the eldest and the youngest was also Anamitra. From eldest Anamitra or Sunitra was born Nighna. He had two sons - Prasena and Satrajit. He was the father of Satyabhama whom Krishna married. Devamidhusa was one in this line. He married an Ikshwaku Princess (Pauravas) named Asmaki. He had a son named Sura. From Sura and his queen a bhoja princess ten sons and five daughters were born. Basudeva was his eldest son. Pritha was one of his daughters. Pritha was adopted by King Kuntibhoja and came to be known as Kunti. She was married to Pandu (Paurava). Vasudeva married seven daughters of King Devaka. Of the seven one was Devaki, Balarama and Krishna were the sons of Vasudeva and Devaki. Vasudeva had a daughter Suvadra whom Arjuna married. Abhimanyu was the son of Arjuna and Suvadra Abhimanyu's son was Parikshit.

Of the Kukuras, Ahuka married a Kasi priness. He had two sons - Ugrasena and Devaka. Ugrasena had four sons and five daughters. Kamsa was his eldest son who sent Ugrasena to jail and ascended the throne of Mathura. Killing Kamsa, Krishna reinstated Ugrasena. Devaka had four sons and seven daughters. Devaki was one of his daughters who was married to Vasudeva. Balaram and Krishna were their sons. Suvadra was married to

Arjuna. Their son was Abhimanyu who died in the Bharata war., His wife Uttara gave birth to Parikshit.

Devaki was cousin to Kamsa who had usurped the throne. Relying on a prediction he killed seven children of Vasudev and Devaki. The prediction was that the eighth issue of Devaki - Vasudev would slay Kamsa.

Krishna was born in the prison of Kamsa in Mathura. Immidiately after his birth he was removed from Prison to Gokula on the other side of Jumna river. With the aid of guards who too were dissatisfied with Kamsa's tyrany. Krishna was brought up in the Gokula as the child of Nanda and Yosoda. As a child, Krishna appears to have been endowed with extraordinary gifts. Various incidents connected with Krishna are described in the Puranas and other texts. The incidents are presented in the garb of myths and miracles, but there may be a real basis. Krishna subjugated Kaliya - the chief of the Naga tribe and ordered him to leave the place with his tribe. Krishna's extra-ordinary expolits and adventure earned him popularity. After killing Kamsa, Balarama and Krishna went to Kasi for education. But they had to return soon as Jarasandha invaded Mathura to avenge the death of Kamsa. Kamsa was Jarasandha's son-in-law. This Jarasandha was killed by the Pandava Bhima later. Krishna, in the Mahabharata epic, appears for the first time at the Swayamvara occasion of Draupadi. He was friend, philosopher and guide of the Pandavas. His sister Subhadra was married to Arjuna.

In fact, it was mainly due to the important part played by Krishna that the Pandavas won the great war. And all except three of the Kauravas were killed.

Krishna returned to Dwaraka after Yudhisthira was installed on the throne of Hastinapura. He had revived the still born child of widow Uttara, later known as Parikshit. The Pandavas and Krishna met last at the Aswamedh Yajna of Yudhisthira.

Almost all the Yadava males were destroyed in a fratricidal struggle among the Yadavas. Krishna retired to the forest. Before that Krishna had sent messenger to Hastinapura inviting Arjuna to come to Dwaraka to look after the women and children whom Krishna had advised to accompany Arjuna. Arjuna came to Dwaraka, installed Vajra the only surviving grandson of Krishna on the throne of Mathura, he took with him the remnants of the Yadu family. While in deep moditation, Krishna was hit by the arrow of a hunter who mistook him for a deer.

Thus passed away one of the grandest figures of ancient Bharat.

Eastern Anavas : Anga came to be ruled by Karna under the suzerainty of Jarasandha the King of Magadha. He was a faithful ally of the Kauaravas. Duryodhana crowned him the King of Anga - when Karna was ridiculed publicly for his low birth. But practically he was the eldest son of Kunti begotten through SunGod while she was maiden. Karna was abandoned by Kunti and was brought up by a Suta. Karna died in the Bharata war, not because he was beaten, nor on account of being inferrior to anybody, but he was the victim of his own greatness. He is a unique hero who should be admired for his magnanimity, valour, skill and truthfulness. His eldest son was Vrishbahana. Along with his five brothers Vrishabahana was killed in the Bharata war.

The solar dynasty : After Rama's time, Ayodhya plays no remarkable role in the traditional history. Rama's son Kusa became the ruler of South Kosala. His capital was Kusasthali. He extended the Vedic culture in the Vindya region and married a Naga Princess. The next important figure was Hiranyanabha. He was a desciple of Jaimini and learnt Yoga. The last king of the solar dynasty was Brihadbala of the Pre-Bharata-war period. He fought for the Kauravas and was killed by Abnhimanyu.

In the Bharat war between Kauravas and Pandavas, the Pandavas supporters were - Panchala, Matsya, Chedi, Karusha, Western Magadha, Kasi and South-western Yadavas. Under the Kauravas came practically the whole of Eastern India, the whole of North-West Kosala, Vatsa, Surasena in the Madhyadesha and Mahismatti, Avanti, Salva in the west. Broadly speaking, Madhyadesh and Gujrata stood for Pandavas and the rest stood for the Kauravas.

Krishna was the non-combatant adviser of the Pandavas and Balarama remained neutral.

Yudhisthira became King of the Kurus and rulled at Hastinapur. The hundred sons of Dhritarashtra were killed in the war. Yudhisthira performed a horse sacrifice (Aswamedh Yajna) as was advised by Vyasa in order to perge himself of all sins. Dhritarashtra retired with Gandhari, retired to forest and a few years after, was consumed in a forest conflagration. Arjuna had come back from Dwaraka with Survivers of Yadavas and Krishna's grandson, Vajra was placed as the head of the Yadavas.

Yudhishthira and his brothers retired to forest placing Parikshit, the grandson of Arjuna, on the throne. The accession of Parikshit marks the beginning of the Kaliyuga as the Dwapara ended with the end of Bharat war (1400 B.C.)

The dynasties of the Kaliyuga begin with the accession of Parikshit. [Some begin their accounts of the Kali Age after AdhisimaKrishna. He was fourth in descent from Parikshita].

Bharata war was an epoch-marking event in the annuals of the country. The non-mention of Bharata war in the later vedic literature does not necessarily disprove its historicity. It was entirely a political issue and hence naturally did not interest the authors of the Brahmanas. The very significance of the term Pandavas, as distinct from Kauravas, was forgotten soon after the war, and the term Kauravas only survived.

Puru Dynasty at Hastinapur

[Riksha (2) was 64th in descent from Manu Baibaswata (3100 B.C.) Sambaran was the 69th and Kuru was in 71st descent. Pratip was 87th descent. The Puru dynasty at Hastinapur started from King Hasti 51st in descent from Manu i.e. 2182 BC.

Baibaswat Manu (3100 B.C.) was of Ayodhya and it was Solar Dyanasty. Contemporary was Chandra (Lunar Dynasty)

Pururaba was 3rd in descent from Chandra
Ayu
Nahusha
Yayati = Sarmistha, Yayati - Devjani
Puru
Janmejoy (1) 8th
Hasti (51st) Hastinapur
Dushanta (43rd)
Bharat
Bitatha Varadwaj (46th)
Adopted
Hasti (50th)
Aamih
Rikshya (1) (53rd)
Rikhsya (2) (64th)
Sambaran (69th)
Kuru (71st)
Parikshit (1)
Janmejoy (2) (73rd)
Dilip (86th)
Pratip (87th)

Santanu (89th)
Vichitravirja (91st)
Pandu (93rd)
Yudhisthira (94th)
Parikshit (2) (96th)
Janmejoy (3) (97th)

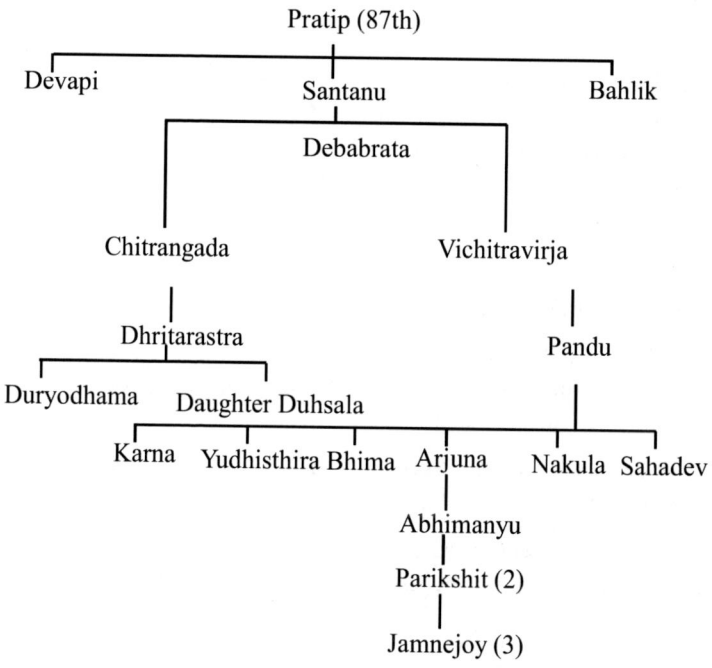

Ref. : F.E. Pargiter - Ancient Indian Historical Tradition and Debiprasad Sengupta - Puran Prasanga.

Yayati (6th descendat from Manu 3100 B.C.)

Yayati Sharmistha   Devjani - Yayati
Puru
Janmejoya (8th)
Prachimban
Samyati
Ahamjati
Raudraswa
Ritesu
Matinar

Tangsu   Jaya   Mahavirya   Nara
Vim
Dushyanta
Sakuntala
Bharat
Bitatha Vardwaj
(adopted son)
Vumanyu
Suhotra
Brihat   Kshetra
Hasti
(Founded Hastinapur)
Ajmirah
Rikhsya (1)
(53rd from Manu)

The list of Dynasty is from the book Puran Prasanga (Beng) by Sri Debiprasad Sengupta.

[Ref. : Puran Prasanga - Debiprasad Sengupta, Pub. : Somnath Dutta, 60, Pratuatola Lane, Kolkata - 700 009.]

Among scholars there exists differences of opinion regarding the value of the Vedic Texts and the Puranas in regard to the historical data.

Scholars like Keith are sceptical about the historical value of the Puranas and one doubtful about the historicity of events. They mainly rely on Rigvedic evidence.

Scholars like Pargiter give more weight to the Puranas as historical element. To their opinion, despite a good deal of what is untrustworthy in them, they above contain something continuous historical narrative. They say, it is absured to suppose the elaborate genealogies were all figments of imaginations and falsehood.

There are others who hold that vedic tradition is Brahminical and that Puranas of Kshatriya tradition. This theory is not acceptable on the ground that the said two traditions were not watertight compartments. There are glorifications of Brahmanas in Kshtriya tradition and glorifications of Kshatriyas in Brahmnic traditions. It is to be remembered that the Puranas take pride in styling themselves as 'Fifth Veda'.

It may be observed that there is no irreconciliable contradiction or conflict between the Vedic Texts and the Puranas. Kings, who are mentioned in the Vedic texts but not mentioned in the Puranas, were possibly princes and chieftains of smaller dynasties. The proper procedure should be to take into account both the testimonies of vedic texts and puranas and to try to bring harmony into apparently conflicting texts.

There are some important persons whose names appear both in the vedic literature and the Puranas. But the relation-ship of those persons with other, does not corroborate in the Vedic or Puranic descriptions. Yayati, Nahusha, Turvasu, Yadu, Anu, Druhyu and Puru are described in a way but in the Vedic literature the description is otherwise. The names of Divodas and Sudas, Mitrayu, Maitreya, Soma, Srinjoya, Chyavana, Sudash or Somadutta are there. But there is no consistency.

The identity of Janmejoya Parikshit mentioned in the Vedic texts and in the Puranas and Mahabharata appears to be a problem.

Some scholars are of opinion that the Vedic texts and the Puranas are neither independent nor contradictory. The traditional history as mentioned in the Puranas are not imaginations. Those have their basis in facts. And those when supported or corroborated by Vedic texts, it stands unimpeachable.

Such traditional history has its value and is a necessary preliminary step for discovery of genuine history. No student of Indian history should ignore the legendary element in the Puranas and epics.

Such traditional history has its value and is a necessary preliminary step for discovery of genuine history. No student of Indian history should ignore the legendary element in the Puranas and epics.

Lunar Dynasty

Pururavas Aila, Ila's son through Budha was the progeni of Lunar Dynasty. Pururavas was killed by the Sages. He was contemporary Ikshwaku of the Solar Dynasty.

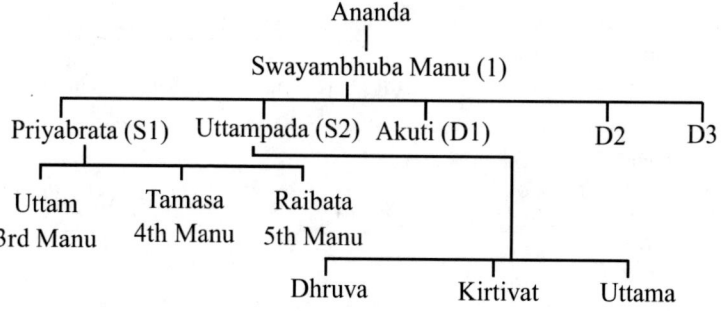

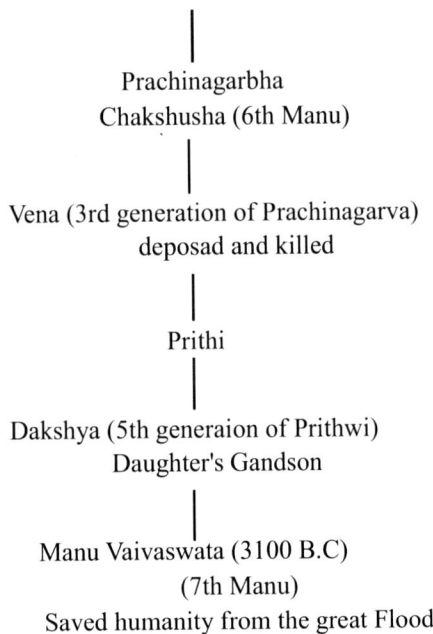

Prachinagarbha
Chakshusha (6th Manu)

Vena (3rd generation of Prachinagarva)
deposad and killed

Prithi

Dakshya (5th generaion of Prithwi)
Daughter's Gandson

Manu Vaivaswata (3100 B.C)
(7th Manu)
Saved humanity from the great Flood

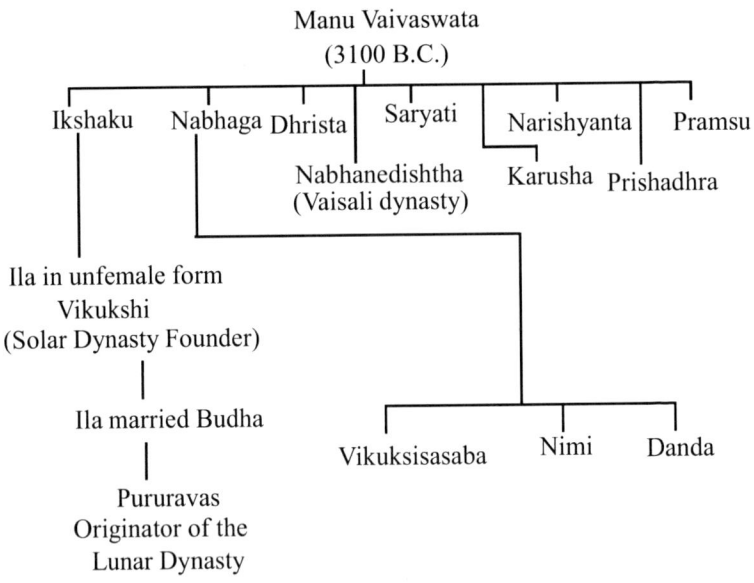

Manu Vaivaswata
(3100 B.C.)

Ikshaku   Nabhaga Dhrista   Saryati   Narishyanta   Pramsu

Nabhanedishtha   Karusha Prishadhra
(Vaisali dynasty)

Ila in unfemale form
Vikukshi
(Solar Dynasty Founder)

Ila married Budha

Pururavas
Originator of the
Lunar Dynasty

Vikuksisasaba   Nimi   Danda

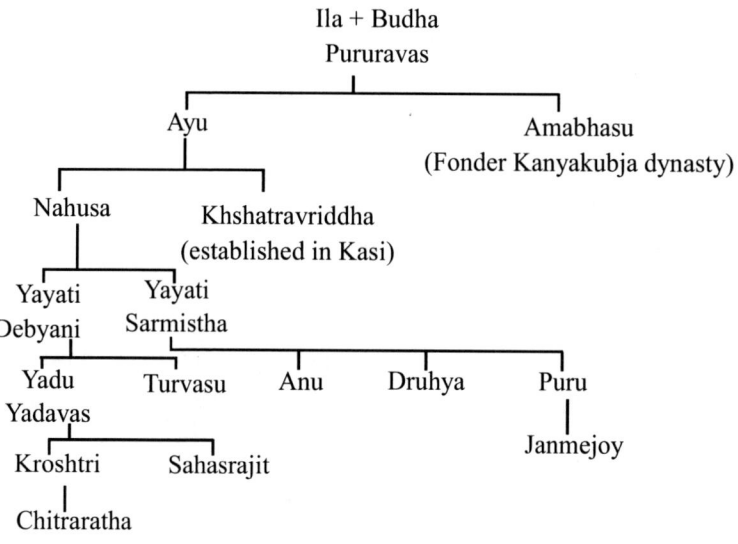

Ila + Budha
Pururavas

Ayu — Amabhasu (Fonder Kanyakubja dynasty)

Nahusa — Khshatravriddha (established in Kasi)

Yayati Debyani — Yayati Sarmistha

Yadu Yadavas — Turvasu — Anu — Druhya — Puru

Kroshtri — Sahasrajit

Janmejoy

Chitraratha

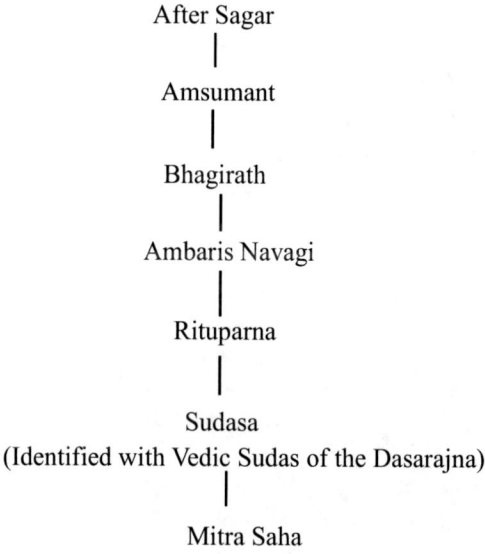

After Sagar
|
Amsumant
|
Bhagirath
|
Ambaris Navagi
|
Rituparna
|
Sudasa
(Identified with Vedic Sudas of the Dasarajna)
|
Mitra Saha

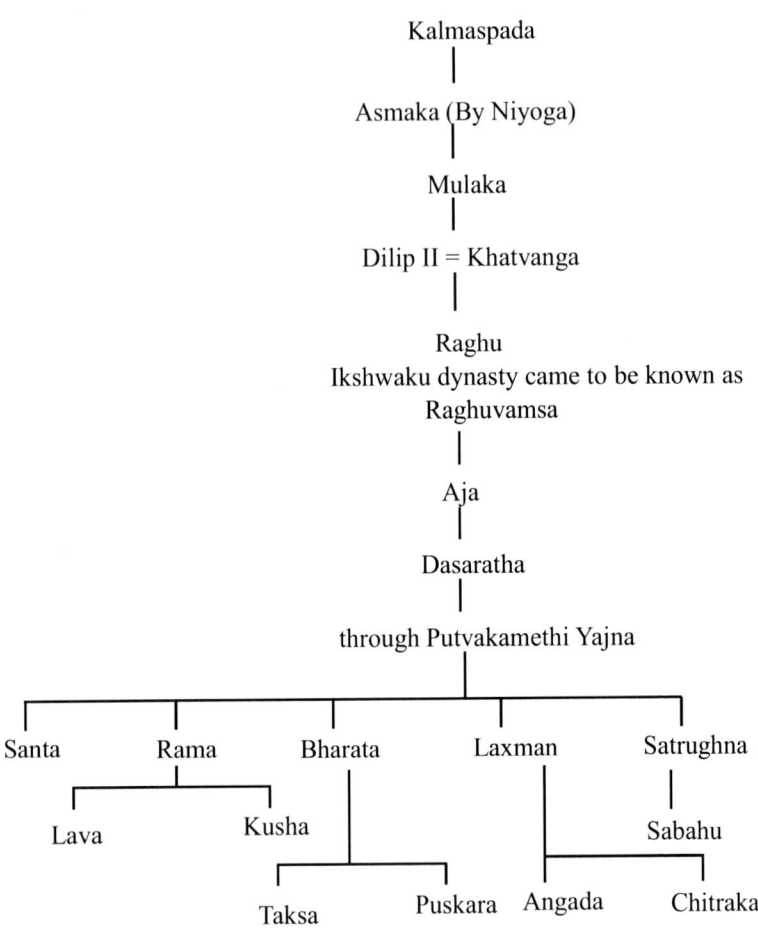

Kalmaspada

Asmaka (By Niyoga)

Mulaka

Dilip II = Khatvanga

Raghu
Ikshwaku dynasty came to be known as
Raghuvamsa

Aja

Dasaratha

through Putvakamethi Yajna

Santa   Rama   Bharata   Laxman   Satrughna

Lava   Kusha   Sabahu

Taksa   Puskara   Angada   Chitraka

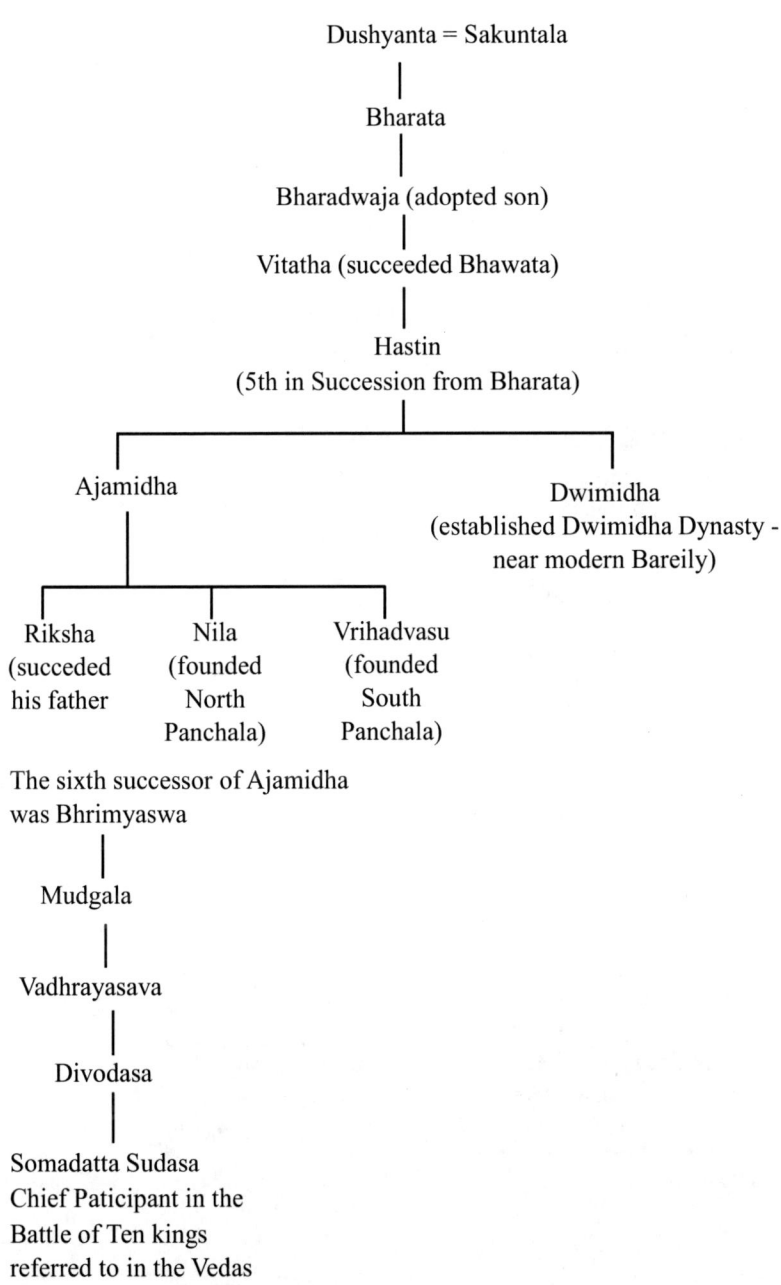

Dushyanta = Sakuntala

Bharata

Bharadwaja (adopted son)

Vitatha (succeeded Bhawata)

Hastin
(5th in Succession from Bharata)

Ajamidha

Dwimidha
(established Dwimidha Dynasty -
near modern Bareily)

Riksha
(succeded
his father

Nila
(founded
North
Panchala)

Vrihadvasu
(founded
South
Panchala)

The sixth successor of Ajamidha
was Bhrimyaswa

Mudgala

Vadhrayasava

Divodasa

Somadatta Sudasa
Chief Paticipant in the
Battle of Ten kings
referred to in the Vedas
(appears to be contemporary of Aja)

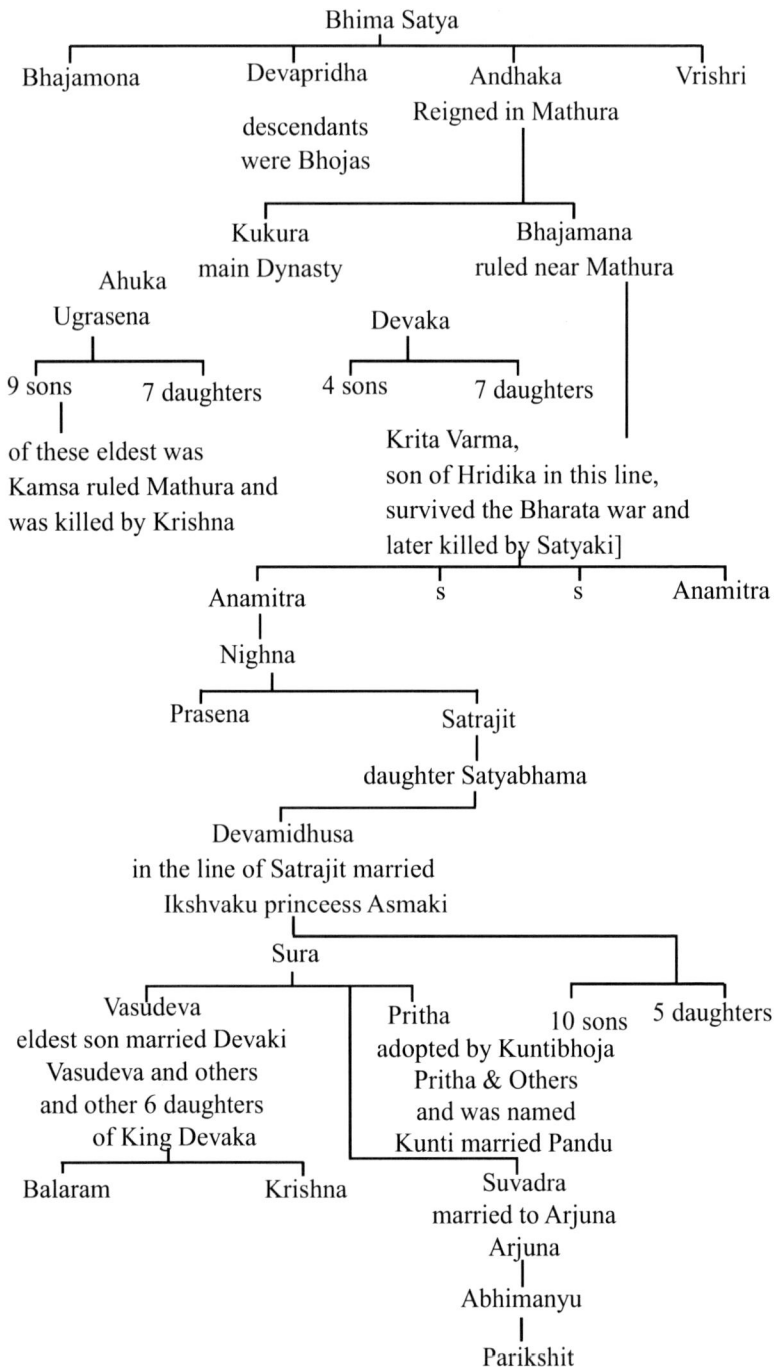

Bhima Satya

Bhajamona   Devapridha   Andhaka   Vrishri

descendants   Reigned in Mathura
were Bhojas

Kukura   Bhajamana
main Dynasty   ruled near Mathura

Ahuka

Ugrasena   Devaka

9 sons   7 daughters   4 sons   7 daughters

of these eldest was   Krita Varma,
Kamsa ruled Mathura and   son of Hridika in this line,
was killed by Krishna   survived the Bharata war and
later killed by Satyaki]

Anamitra   s   s   Anamitra

Nighna

Prasena   Satrajit

daughter Satyabhama

Devamidhusa
in the line of Satrajit married
Ikshvaku princeess Asmaki

Sura

Vasudeva   Pritha   10 sons   5 daughters
eldest son married Devaki   adopted by Kuntibhoja
Vasudeva and others   Pritha & Others
and other 6 daughters   and was named
of King Devaka   Kunti married Pandu

Balaram   Krishna   Suvadra
married to Arjuna

Arjuna

Abhimanyu

Parikshit

Solar Dynasty (2350 - 1950 B.C.)

Art of Writing in Bharata

There is no doubt that instructions were orally imparted. It is a very debatable point whether the art of writing was known at all in this age, the Vedic age. It is a well-known fact that no actual specimen of alphabets have been discovered in India which can be very definitely dated before the 4th century BC (Sisunaga dynastry, Nanda dynastry, Dairius II, Alexander,Reign of Chandra Gupta upto Bindusara).Consequently most of scholars are of opinion that art of writing was unknown in ancient India. Buhler sought to prove that the Indian merchants learnt this art in Westren Asia and introduced it in their country sometime before 8th Century B.C (before Buddha whose year of birth is said to be 623 BC i,e 7th century.)

But the discovery of the numerous seals at Mohenjodaro with pictographic writing, has put an altogether new complexion on the whole question .It is now believed by many that the Indus script formed the parent source from which the oldest Brahmi alphabets have been derived. Some are even of opinion that when the Rigveda was finally arranged in its present form it was written in a script which formed an intermediate stage between the Indus script and Ashokan alphabets. [the latest settlement of Mohenjodaro has been attributed to 2750 BC it may be 3500 BC also and Ashok's reign is 273-236 BC).

If we have to accept the old theory of Buhler, we have to presume that the vast Vedic literature was composed and preserved by oral transmission alone - a stupendous feat of memory which appears to be miraculous. On the other hand, if we believe that these voluminous text were in writing, we are faced with the problem of writing materials, of which we know nothing.

The oldest alphabet, known as Brahmi, is employed in the majority of the records of Ashok (273-236 BC) and from it have been derived the various scripts used today all over India. The Aramaic was introduced in Punjab by its Achaemenian conquerers. From it was derived Kharosthi alphabet written from right to left (like Arabic, Farsi and Urdu). It was confined to North-West Bharat and thence was carried to Central Asia, but it went out of use after 3rd or 4th Century AD.

There are evidences to show that the teaching in the Vedic period and even in Buddhist system was oral and the study of manuscripts was not encouraged, if not condemned. It has been suggested that the art of writing was introduced late in Bharat in the intellectual development, and that too after they had already brought to perfection another and a very excellent method i.e. learning by heart. Being accustomed to preserve massive literature by stupendous feats of memory, they would not realise the use or necessity of writing it down. There are more than one who indicate that the Brahmins, so to say, the custodians withheld the sacred text (mantras) from the people and retained teaching to the exclusion if Books. They emphasized the role of teacher in an educational system which sought both knowledge and character to develop in a pupil. So they insisted on not books but teachers should be the main source of instruction. [This has reference to an essay written by Radhakumud Mookherjee in the 2nd Vol of the History and culture of the Indian People P 584-85 and the essay written by V. M. Apte in the 1st Vol. of the same book P-394]

Radhakumud Mookerjee writes in his own book - Ancient Indian Education Brahmanical and Buddhist that Rigvedic Education as its first step comprised the transmission of the sacred text by the teacher to his pupil by means of regulated recitation and prescribed pronunciation which the pupil had to listen to as Sruti and commit to memory. Sayana (commentary Introduction to Rigveda) quotes that "the text of the Veda is to be learnt by the method of learning it from the lips of the teacher and not from manuscript. [The reference to Manuscript confirms the existence of written book - author.] Because this education was thus primarily a matter of hearing and memorising like croaking of frogs (Rigveda Frog hymn VII-103), it has been assumed that the art of writing had not evolved. [The sardar Parhuya system in the Pathsalas of Bengal may be interpreted as residuary of that Vedic systemm of frog croaking - author].

It has been believed that the Sruti or Veda should appeal to the ear and not to the eye and was not to be reduced to writing. But even if such learning had passed from ear to ear directly under a system of oral tradition and banned the transmission through writing, it does not follow that a knowledge of writing or alphabets for the use even for secular purpose was not achieved then.

Radha Kumud Mookerjee has opined that Vedic Sanskrit has grown out of the spoken tongue. In support of his deduction he has cited several Riks from different sections of the Rigveda. He has referred to Yaska's Nirukta also. He has written that at Yajna-Assemby each Rishi brought forward his individual contribution to speech and then these were collected and codified. Then this standardised speech was suitable for being imparted to pupils and was thus propagated through the whole country. Sayana writes "The Veda expounds the truth about Gods, Dharma and Param Brahma. He who does not recite the Veda but utters only Secular speech full of slander, falsehood and strife, can not have access to true knowledge."

Spread of Bharatiya Learning to China upto 11th Century A.D.

The gradual growth of greater India was the work of the Indian Schools and Scholars. It is a romance of the history of Bharata, and a unique achievement in the annuals of mankind.

While the Islam and Christian are spreading over the World with the might of their Sword and trade, Bharat invaded the countries with power of education and knowledge.

Besides the Universities mentioned above, there were in Northern India Peshwar, Mathura and Sarnath famous School of Sculpture. Mathura was famous for its study of Astronomy. Cunningham observes, "Everywhere in the North West I find that the old Buddhist statues are made of Sikri Sandstone from which it would appear that Mathura must have been a great manufactory for the supply of Buddhist sculptures in Northern India."

In South India Karavir, Giri and Vijoynagara were also famous Seats of Learning.

The scholars who were the products of these Universities, distinguished themselves by their works in foreign countries like China, Tibet, Srilanka and the islands of the Indian Archipelago. The work of these assiduous, self-sacrificing scholars that Bharatiya Learning and Culture Spread in foreign lands - as to build up a greater Bharat beyond the boundaries of India proper. It is one of the greatest achievements in Bharat's long history.

The Buddhist Civilization of China was the work of Bharatiya Scholars which continued for several centuries. They made China and Tibet their adopted home to carry on their missionary enterprise.

The Chinise emperor Mingti (58-75 AD) interested himself in Buddhism had sent to India an embassy of eighteen persons to study its doctrines. They returned with Buddhist holy books, statues and two Hindu monks. The two were Kasyapa Matanga and Dharmaratna.

These two Bharatiya Scholars were Pioneers who opened up a vast field of work in China. The following are the most prominent Bharatiya scholars who worked in China in the fist three centuries AD. They are :

(1) Samgrabarman

(2) Dharma Satya

(3) Dharma Kala

(4) Mahabala

(5) Vighna

(6) Dharmapaala

(7) Kalasivi (255 AD)

(8) Kalaruchi (281 AD)

(9) Lokaraksha and others

Among these Bharatiya monks working in China were some Tibetans who settled in Bharat whence they came to China. One of them - Khanku was the son of a Prime Minister. These scholars built monasteries. translated books in Chinise and spread the philosophy of Buddhism.

The next geneation of Bharatiya scholars who gave impetus to chinese Buddhism are :

(1) Dharma Raksha (381 AD)

(2) Goutama Sangha Deva

(3) Buddha Bhadra

(4) Samgabhuti

(5) Dharmapriya

(6) Kumarajiva

(7) Vimalaksha

(8) Punyatrata and others

Dharma Raksha mastering Chinese in a short time, translated 111 works into Chinese. Kumarajiva was born in a family of hereditary minister of an Indian state. He was taken to China as a prisoner, simply because the emperor needed his service. By working for twelve years he translated into Chinese one hundred Sanskrit works. Kumarajiva in his works was assisted by Vimalaksha (his Guru), Buddha bhadra and Punyatrata. It was in 5th Century A.D.

In these days Kashmira was the strong-hold of Buddhist Learning and Religion. Kashmira supplied erudite Bharatiya scholars to China to work for the cause of Chinese Buddhism. Among these, the following names may be mentioned.

(1) Buddhayasas

(2) Dharmayasas

(3) Dharmakshema

(4) Buddhajiva

(5) Dharmamitra

Of these the most renowned was Dharmakshema. He translated into Chinese many important works between 414-421 A.D. including Buddhacharita by Aswaghosa.

Gunavarman who was of a royal family was the most distinguised scholar of Kashmira. At an early age he was known as master of Tripitaka and became a monk at the age of 20. He declined the honour of Kingship at 30, and proceeded to Ceylone (Srilanka) and then to Java. It was left to Gunavarmana to spread Buddism in Java. From Java he was invited to China and arrived at Nanking in 431AD where the emperor received him personally and became his disciple. Gunavarmana worked on organisation more. He died in China at the age of 67.

About the end of the 5th Century Gunabhadra came to China to dedicate himself to the cause of Buddhism. He was a Brahmana of Central India and was famous for his erudition in Mahayana. In 8 years he translated into Chinese as many as 78 works. He died at 75 in 468 A.D.

The next century (500-600 AD) saw a continued influex into China of Bharatiya scholars, such as ;

(1) Dharmaruchi

(2) Ratnamati

(3) Bodhiruchi

(4) Buddhasanta

(5) Goutama Prajnaruchi

(6) Upasunya

(7) Vimokshasena and others

Of these Dharmaruchi was from South India. He translated three works into Chinese. Buddha Santa translated ten works in fifteen years (524-539 AD) Bodhiruchi became an accomplished Chinese scholar and translated more than thirty works in twenty seven years (508-535 AD)

Goutama Prajnaruchi was from Benaras who translated eighteen works in three years (538-541).

Upasunya was a prince of Ujjain who renounced Kingship and turned a monk.

In 557 A.D. China was visited by a learned mission of four scholars from Bharata.

Gautama Dharmajnana, son of Goutama Prajnaruchi of Benaras, won the distinction of being appointed as a Governor of a District in 577 AD. Later he was called to the capital where he translated a work in 589 AD.

The seventh century saw only six Bharatiya Monk coming to China. But three chinese monks - Hiuen Tsang, Wang Hiuen-Tse and I-Tsing came to Bharat and returned to China laden with Bharatiya learning.

In the eighth century, the notable monk was Amoghavajra. He was a Brahmin monk of Northern India. He came to China accompanying his Guru - Vajrabodhi in 719 A.D. His Guru died in 732 A.D. Amoghavajra came to India in 741 A.D. He travelled all over India and Srilanka and returned to China in 746 A.D. with many manuscripts. The emperor conferred upon him the title - Prajna - moksha.

The movement of Bharatiya schoalrs to China decliend after Amoghavajra. The ninth Century is almost a blank. In tenth century only three Bharatiya monks had gone to China.

The visit of a few more Bharatiya Scholars in the eleventh Century brings to a close of a glorious chapter of Indian history recording how the cultural contact between Bharata and China had continued for long 1000 years and established Buddhism in China.

In 1004 A.D. Dharmavaksha of Magadha and Maitreyi Bhadra in 1110 A.D. came to China. The Chinese sources refer to Silabhadra, Sraddhapala and Jnanasri. Jnanasri went to China in 1053 A.D. and translated Tathagata-Jhana-Mudra-Sutra.

The political disturbances following the Muslim invaders into India interfered with the peaceful movements of scholars between China and Bharat along the land routes.

It is very much clear that Bharatiya scholars played a far more active prominent role than the Chinese scholars including eminent Fa-Hien, Hiuen-Tsang, I-Tsing in introducing Bharatiya thought to China.

This is a story of sacrifice for the cause of Learning and Religion which has no parallel elsewhere. It was the same self sacrifice of Bharatiya scholars that found for itself another vast field of work in Tibet.

[Ref. : For further details - Radha Kumud Mookerjee's - Ancient Indian Education]

Seats of Learning in Bharat
A. Taxila or Takshasila
1000 BC - 500 AD

A famous city of ancient Bharat in Takshasila. According to Rammayana, King Bharata founded this city and enthroned his son Taksha.

Taxila was named after the name of Taksha (Takshasila). King Janmejoy (referred to in Mahavarata) held his Sarpa Yajna in the place. In the Jataka, Taxila is mentioned in so many contexts.

This town is now more than 12 sq.m. of ruins to the North West of Rawalpindi (33⁰45' North and 72⁰49' East). According to Sir John Marshall, the site embraces three separate cities, namely Bir Mound to the South which was in occupation from 1500 B.C. to the close of Maurya domination about 180 B.C. Secondly the city known as Sir Kap further North, which is believed to have been founded by the Greek invaders in the 1st half of the 2nd Century B.C. and Parthians until about 70 A.D and third, the city of Sirsukh, still further North, to which Kusanas transferred their capital from Sirkap. Thus within 5 Centuries, Taxila became subject to five different empires - the Macedonian, the Mauryans, the Bactrians, the Parthians and the Kushans. It must have inherited much of the culture and of the arts peculiar to each.

In the Ramayana (Uttara Kanda) it is referred that Law (Vyabahara Vidya) was a specialised subject at Taxila. The Mahabharata also refers it as a remarkable seat of Learning. One of the teachers Dhaumya had three very ideal students - Upamanyu, Aruni and Veda. We know a story of Aruni who threw his body to the breach of the water course. Aruni was from Panchala. From a Pali Source (Dhammapada - ttha Katha) we learn that a student from Benaras went to Taxila to learn Silpas and he had 500 classmates. Pasendi, the King of Kosala was educated at Taxila. Jivaka the renowned physician at the court of Bimbisara (reigned from 544-493 BC) was educated in Medicine and Surgery at Taxila. Reference of Takshasila in the Ramayana and the Mahavarata proves it to be an ancient city. But it was not a Seat of Learning then.

Jivaka studied medicine at Taxila under a World renowned Physician for the prescribed period of 7 years. But before he was given license to practise medicine, he had to undergo an ordeal. His teacher gave him a spade and ordered to seek round Taxila a Yojana on every side (NSEW), to find out a plant of non-medicinal nature. After a good deal of botanical investigation, Jivaka did not find any such plant and so reported to his teacher. The teacher was satisfied and gave Jivaka a little money and permission to practise as a physician. He was from Saketa. His first earning came from his successful treatment of a rich setthi's wife who had a chronic disease of the head which no physician could cure. Jivaka had taken a handful of glhee boiled it with various drugs and administered that to the patient through her nose. She was cured and Jivaka earned a fee of 16 thousand Kahapanas together with a present of a coach, horses and 2 servants. These earnings Jivaka tendered to his Patron Prince Abhaya (Son of Bimbisar). Jivaka, after birth was thrown to dustbin where from Abhoya collected him and patronised althrough. Jivaka was the son of a prostitute named Salabati at Rajgir. Jivaka next treated emperor Bimbisara and cured him of a fistula. His third important case came from Benaras where a merchant's son had a strangulation of the intestine caused by a gymnastic feat. It was a surgical case. He cut through the skin of the belly, drew the twisted intestine out and showed them to his wife, then disentangling the twisted intestine, he put them back into their right position and stiched the skin together. He was cured and his father paid a fee of 16 thousand Kahapanas. King Pradyot of Ujjain was his next patient. He was suffering from jaundice. Jivaka cured him. Lord Buddha was his another important patient who was suffering from constipation. Jivaka cured him by making him smell three medicated lotuses, bathe in warm water and live on liquid food for some days.

The Jataka stories tell a lot of Taxila as a University. The great grammarian Panini and Chanakya are said to have had their education at Taxila. In the Adiparba of Mahabharata it is told that men of Taxila were unrivalled in discussions on matters of learning. Greek invader Alexander and his men were astonished at their asceticism and strange doctrines. At the time of Asoka, Taxila was one of the greatest and most splendid cities of the East and enjoyed special reputation as the headquarters of Hindu learning. Sons of Upperclass people, Chiefs, brahmanas and merchants flocked to Taxila in order to study Indian Arts and Sciences, specially medicine. At the time of HieunTsang (600-664 A.D.) the brahmanas of this town (Taxila) were well-grounded in their literary work and were of high renown for their talents, well-informed of things and of a vigorous memory.

The fame of Taxila as a Seat of Learning was mainly due to that of its teachers. And it was the presence of Scholars of such acknowledged excellence and wide spread reputation that caused a steady movement of qualified students drawn from all classes of society towards Taxila from far off Benaras, Rajgir, Mithila and other places. The students used to go to Taxila to complete their educaiton and not to begin it. So Taxila was a seat of higher education. The age limit of admission was curiously enough the same as is prescribed by modern universities.

All castes except Chandalas were admitted and the castes did not confine themselves to their traditional subjects of study. The poorer students who could not pay their tuition fees had to undergo a course of menial service.

But the recognition of the dignity of honest labour secured them a status of equality with aristocratic section. Even a prince was not equipped with enough money to retain for his private use. He entered the institution as a poor one divested of all riches. The poor students who could not pay fees and could not attend day classes for their menial service, found time for study in the nights and the teachers taught them as usual ungrudgingly.

The subjects of study were the three Vedas and eighteen other Vidya (Vijjas). Of these archery was one. Bodhisattwa learnt archery at Taxila (Bhimsen Jataka). Snake charming, religious ceremonies were taught. Law (Vyabahara) was a specialised subject of study. But Taxila was specially reputed for its school of Medicine. It had both theoretical and practical courses.

The institutions were of Heterogenous Composition. Yet there was college of particular community. There is a reference that there was a teacher who taught only the Princes and he had 101 students who all were princes.

For details : The education system of ancient Hindus - S.K.Das (1930) Gyan Publishing House, 23, Ansari Road, Dariyagunj, New Delhi - 110002.

B. Nalanda (425 A.D. - 1205 A.D.)

Nalanda is an oft quoted name as a Citadal of learning. After the archeological exploration carried out at the site, the place has become a very attractive spot to the tourists who definitely visit the spot in their tour of Rajgir. Be it known that of the entire monastic complex, upto now have been unearthed (1) one monastery to the south, (2) the north-west corner of another, the northern monastery (3) the remains of temple building further to the north-east, (4) another monastery to the west of.(1).

Nalanda was mostly a residential Univesity where the total number residents was 10,000. Of these 10,000, 1510 belonged to the teachers rank and the rest were students.

It was an institution of higher studies as can be inferred from the admission system followed there. The institution was noted for its specialisation for aiding in the solution of doubts and training in the arts of disputation and public speaking. Hiuen Tsang (600-664 AD) who was a student there for years, writes that foreign students came to the establishment to put an end to their doubts and then became celebrated. I-Tsing (635-713 AD) refers that students came from Mongolia. Hiuen Tsang refers that students used to come from China, Korea, Tibet and Bokhara.

Nalanda was practically a Research Institute for advanced students and was the highest court of Judges of intellectual worth.

The fame of Nalanda as a centre of learning was mostly due to the fame of teachers. Hiuen Tsang refers to Dharmapala (the predecessor of Sila Bhadra) and Chandrapala, Gunamati, Sthiramati, Prabhamitra, Jnanachandra and Silabhadra, as chancellors of the university. Silabhadra alone had studied and understood the whole number of collections of the Sutras and Shastras. He was unique in learning and character.

History : Nalanda was the name of an ancient village, identified with modern Baragaon, some 16 kilometres north of Rajgir in Bihar. In Buddhist Scriptures it is mentioned as a village near Rajgriha with a Mango Park in Buddha's time. The Jain texts carry the history earlier than Buddhist. It was the place where Mahavira met Gosala and was counted as a Suburb of Rajgriha. Mahavira, is said to have spent 14 rainy seasons. In another reliable source (Sutra Kritanga) it is said that Nalanda had hundreds of houses and there was rich citizen named Lepa who possessed many slaves, cows, buffaloes, sheep, horses, beds, seats, vehicles, gold and silver wares. He offered his hospitality to Buddha and became his disciple. It is said that Nalanda is the birth place of Sariputta whose Chaitya was seen by Asoka (reigned 276-233 B.C.) who added a temple to that Chaitya.

But the place did not become educationally important before the rise of Mahayana Buddhism at the beginning of the Christian era. Nagarjuna (2nd Century AD) spent a large part of his life at Nalanda.

It is interesting to note that the celebrated Buddhist logician Dinnaga (was born towards the end of the 5th Century AD at Kanchi in South India), came on invitation to Nalanda. Here he defeated Brahman Sudurjaya in argument. Dinnaga was a disciple of Vasubandhu. This incident shows that even in the 5th Century A.D. Nalanda was still the seat of Brahmanical learning.

Nala was the name of the place in 4th Century A.D. when Fa-Hien visited it. There was still the tope built upon the burnt ashes of Sariputta. Hiuen Tsang came here in the 7th Century and stayed at Nalanda University, first as a student then a teacher, for 5 years. He records that within the next three centuries (From Fa-Hien's period) Nalanda grew up to be the greatest centre of Buddhist learning. There is, however, a view that Fa-Hien did not visit Nalanda, and that the village Nala, which he visited as the birth place of Sariputta, is called Nalaka or Nalagrama in the Sudarsana Jataka.

Hiuen Tsang prefers the Jataka story that in his former bith as a king of the country, Buddha was insatiable in giving - (in Sanskrit - Na-alam-da) and hence the name - Nalanda.

I-Tsing accepts the tradition that a dragon (named Nalanda) was living in tank of the Mango Park existing to the South of the monastery. I-Tsing was of 8th Century (635-713 A.D.)

It is known from the accounts of Hieun Tsang that the grounds of the monastery was a gift to Buddha by 500 merchants who bought the grounds against 'ten koti of gold coin' (R.K. Mukherjee's Book Page 558 who quotes it from Watters ii P-164)

This original endowment was the precurser of a continuous series of endowments through the centuries by a succession of sovereigns. According to Hiuen Tsang Six Monasteries were built by six kings - Sakraditya, his son Buddhagupta, Tathagatagupta, Baladitya and his son Vajra. The unnamed King of mid-India-may be taken as Harsha who built a Bihara of brass at Nalanda, well round the monastery and a Sangharam. All these he did after defeating Sasanka of Gauda who was said to be an enemey of Buddhism and Harsha.

The University area was marked off by a lofty enclosing wall with one gate which opened into the great college, from which were separated eight other halls. The buildings, all storied ones, were majestic in their site and height with richly adorned towers. [The thickness of the walls 6'6" and even 7'6"].

Besides the gift of Buildings, the University received gifts of land, The lands bestowed upon the monastery by Kings of many generations contained more then 200 villages. The Palas of Bengal were remarkable benefactors to Nalanda. The name of Dharmapala, Devapala occur in the inscriptions and metalic figures. [Pala Dynasty in Bengal 8th Century].

Free Education : Out of the land endowments income, the University provided for all its alumini free of cost their requirements of clothes, food, bedding and medicine. The number of the alumnis in Hiuen Tsang's time was always 10,000. The standard of living varied with the standing of the monks.

The students being abudantly supplied, they could give themselves whole heartedly to their studies and self-culture.

Admission : Nalanda University was noted for its specialisation in the last stages of Higher education - for aiding in the solution of doubts and training in the arts of disputation. The highest degree or distinction of the time was a Fellowship of Nalanda. Nalanda brothers were respected everywhere.

So, the admission to the Institution was a very difficult one. There was entrance test. Only two or three out of ten could succeed. Considering the character of admission, the age of the student must have been very high. The academic life was at a very high level, both on intellectual and moral side. They were all ideal Buddhists.

As many as hundred chairs or pulpits were arranged everyday for the lectures or discourses by so many teachers living there and students attended these discourses without any fail even for a minute.

Range of Studies : The courses of study offered by the Nalanda University covered a wide range almost the entire circle of knowledge then available. They were drawn from different fields of learning, Brahmanical and Buddhist, sacred and secular, philosophical and practical, science and arts.

Hiuen-Tsang himself was a student of Yoga Shastra at the University of Nalanda. Silabhadra was the highest living authority in the subject. After Dharmapala, Silabhadra was the chancellor of this University. Hiuen-Tsang was soon counted as one of the best products of this University for his mastery of Mahayana Buddhism.

Ranking of Monks : The ranking of monks depended on their extensive rather than intensive knowledge. Their rank depended on range of their studies rather than depth. Different grades of the monks carried with them different privilages.

Access to the chancellor was not made cheap or easy. Interview with him was a formal and ceremonial function.

Academic Titles : The titles were indicative of different degrees of status, standing and grade to which each belonged. The highest title was Kulapati for the head of an Institution numbering ten thousand students. The next title was Pandita. It was reserved for the head of the Vihara, then Vidyabhusana. [At the university of Vikramsila AD 800, Pandita title was awarded to a successful graduate].

The rooms to the monks were distributed according to rank. This allocation of rooms was not done by an individual or authority, it was made by the great assembly of Priests Usually this was done at the advent of rainy season.

Time Table : The daily duties at Nalanda were regulated strictly according to time. Time was measured by means of the clepsydra. The day was of eight hours, each of which was indicated by four immersions of the smaller bowl in the larger vessel of water. Each of such immersion was indicated by one stroke of a drum etc.

There was time for meals and for baths. There were ponds in the grounds of Nalanda According to I-Tsing there were more than 10 great pools. A Ghanti (Gong) was sounded to remind the bathing hour. Hundreds with their bathing sheets proceeded to different pools for bath.

I-Tsing also records that the management of the University was very much democratic. Inspite of its size and numbers, the affairs of the University from the annual assignment of rooms to the trial and punishment of offences against the fratermity and expulsion of recalcitrants, were administered on democratic Principles by the entire body of the students. It was so graceful for the seniors to place themselves in the hands of the juniors as regards to the details of their physical life and comforts. Thus the harmony of the establishment was secured by the due combination of the principles of autiocracy and democracy in its management. The principle of autocracy was applied only to the spheres of the intellectual and moral training of the alumni where guidance and direction was indispensible. The harmony of relations among the vast numbers of the teachers and the taught at Nalanda became an established tradition marking the entire course of its history.

Library : It is very very normal that such an Institution must have a well-equipped library. Information on the Nalanda University Library is given in the Tibetan accounts. From that source it is learnt that the Library was situated in a special area given the name Dharmaganja (Mart of Religion). There were three buildings named Ratnasagara (a nine-storied building), Ratnododhi and Ratnaranjaka. After the Turaska raiders incursions in Nalanda, the temples and Chaityas were repaired by a sage named Mudita Bhadra.

[For details : Radha Kumud Mookerjee's Ancient Indian Education P 557-585].

The decline of Nalanda

As to the decline of Nalanda and as to the period of decline there are differences of opinion.

Dr. Kielhorn has calculated on Palaeographic grounds from the Ghosrawan Inscription, that glories of Nalanda vanished from the later half of the 9th Century. In the above said inscription it has referred to the appointment of Viradeva as High Priest of Nalanda by Devapada (835-850 AD). [S. K. Das, P-370].

But there are evidences which go to show that Nalanda was in a florushing condition at least as late as the middle of the 11th Century. (i) During the reign of Mahipala (980-1026 AD) Astasasrika Prajnaparamita was copied at Nalanda which is now preserved in the library at Cambridge. The same manuscript was copied at Nalanda during the period of Mahipala and is now preserved in the library of the Asiatic Society of Bengal. (2) During the reign of Nyayapala (- 1042 AD) Dipankar Srijnana, the head of this Convent went to Tibet at the request of its King. During the reign of Ramapala (- 1084 AD) a manuscript was copied at Nalanda by one Grahana Kunda. All these prove that Nalanda was able to retain its fame as a centre of Learning and culture at least upto the middle of the 11th Century. After Nayapala Nalanda's decadence commenced.

Two causes contributed to Nalanda's decay :

(i) its buildings inspite of repair and reconstruction at times must have become dilapidated. (ii) The rival University at Vikramsila seemed to have monopolised royal patronage.

That Nalanda was destroyed by fire is proved by the Baladitya inscription discovered in 1864 by Captain Marshall among the ruins of Nalanda. This inscription is now preserved in Calcutta Museum and it refers to the rebuilding of a temple after its destruction by fire.

It is already mentioned that the Turaska invaders gave a crushing blow to Nalanda. But it survived these Muhamedan raiders due to magnanimity of the sage Mudita Bhadra.

There is a story that some angry mendicants propitiating the Sun for 12 years performed a fire sacrifice and threw living embers and ashes from the sacrificial pit to avenge their anger. This produced a great conflagration which destroyed among others, the great Library.

[For details of reference : S. K. Das the Education system of the ancient Hindues P-370-372].

C. Valabhi (600 - 1200 A.D.)

Of all the states that arose of the ruins of the Gupta Empire (6th Century AD), the Kingdom of Valabhi proved to be the most durable from (475-775 AD). In Valabhi which was the capital of the Maitraka Kings, a University grew up as a rival to Nalanda. According to Hieun Tsang Valabhi University specialised in Hinayana, as Nalanda in Muhayana - Sect of Buddism.

Fleet and other Scholars identified the Maitrakas with Mihiras and regarded them as Sun worshipping people of foreign origin. Fleet even suggested that Maitrakas belong to the Hunas of which Torman and Mihirgula were famous. But this theory has no basis.

The extent of the Kingdom of Valabhi is also uncertain. The site of the capital city is now represented by Wala or Vala $21^0 52'$ North $71^0 57'$ East in old Bhabnagar State in Eastern Kathiabarh Peninsula. Bhattraka was the governor of Saurastra, it may be presumed that the Kingdom carved out by his successors roughly corresponded to that province.

Valabhi University, like Nalanda was the outcome of Royal benefactions. The first Vihara was founded by Princess Dudda, the daughter of the sister of Dhruva I (515-545 AD). Again in 580 AD King Dharmasena I made a grant in favour of another Vihara called Sri Bappapada which was founded by Acharya Bhadanta Sthiramati.

Hiuen Tsang and I-Tsing on Valabhi

Hiuen Tsang saw at Valabhi some hundred Sangharamas with about 6000 priests. According I-Tsing, Nalanda and Valabhi were the two places in India where scholars used to reside for two to three years to complete their educaiton. Valabhi also attracted students from all parts of India to hold discussions of 'all possible and impossible dectrines.' They achieved fame when their opinions were approved by the Masters of Valabhi. This Monastery was equipped with a library which was considered deserving of royal grant for purchase of books.

Students of Valabhi, like those of Nalanda, after graduation, used to present themselves in the Court of Kings to prove their capacity, to be employed in government service as related by I-Tsing. This shows that Valabhi provided for other studies than purely religious. Secular Vidyas like Dharma, Niti, Varta, Chikitsa Sastras were also taught. This centre of learning specialised Hinayana sect of Buddhism - as Nalanda specialised in Mahayana.

In Kathasaritsagar (xxxii) there is a reference that one Brahman father of gangetic valley (Antarvedi) sent his son to that extent place Valabhi for education. Benaras or Nalanda was comparatively very closer to his place yet he preferred Valabhi.

Unfortunately, we do not possess enough information about Valabhi as a Seat of education in ancient Bharat.

D. Vikramsila (800 - 1203 A.D.)

The monastic University of Vikramsila according to Tibetan Chronicles, was situated in Bihar on a hill on the right bank of the Ganges. But the precise position of the place is not certain. Mr. Cunningham suggested the village Silao near Borgaon. But as the Ganges was never near it, and there was no hill also, so this view cannot be accepted. Mr. Nundo Lal De identified Vikramsila with Patharghata hill - 24 miles to the east of Bhagalpur. Dr. S. C. Vidya Bhusan idenfified the place with Sultangunj. Dr. A. R. Banerjee of Patna College takes it to be Keur, near Holsagunj within a distance of 15 miles from Nalanda. Of these Patharghata seems to be right, for it is on the right bank of the Ganges and has sufficient space for many temples and buildings and a quadrangle accommodating 8000 men. There are also ruins of Buddhist images at Patharghata.

According to tradition the Vihara was named after a Yaksa called Vikrama. As it was founded by Dharmapala the King of Bengal, Bihar and Orissa, Vikramsila was known as the Royal University of Vikramsila.

Dharmapala (785-820 AD) furnished it with four establishments each consisting of 27 monks belonging to the four principal sects of Buddhism. Later on other buildings were added so that it came to have six colleges, a Central Hall called the House of Science and four Satras or free board hostels. There was also a large quadrangle which could accommodate an assembly of 8000 men. There was in this centre the temple with Mahabodhi images. Within the enclosure there were 107 temples, of which 53 were of a private character and 54 ordinary. The monastery was surrounded by a wall, with six gates which opened on its six colleges. In the front wall, on the right of the principal entrance, was painted the likeness of Nagarjuna once the Head of the Nalanda monastery and on the left, the portrait of Atisa, the Head of the Vikramsila Monastery. At the gate outside the wall, there was a dharamsala for strangers who arrived late after the closing of the gate.

[Ref. : S. K. Das's the Education system of the ancient Hindus P-.372-381].

King Dharmapala not only constructed the Vihara after a good design, he also made provision for teaching by appointing 108 teachers and other staff.

The teaching was controlled by a Board of eminent teachers and it is stated that this Board of Vikramsila also administered the affairs of Nalanda. It may so happen that King Dharmapala being the common benefactor, such arrangments were possible. Even exchange of teachers also took place. Atisa Dipankara and Abhayakara taught in both the Universities.

This University had six colleges each with a staff of standard strength. There were six gates opening on the six colleges. The outer wall surrounding the monastery was decorated with artistic works.

The gates of the University were guarded by the most erudite of its scholars called Dwara Panditas so that admission be not cheap and standard lowered. During the reign of Chanaka (955-983 AD), we come across the names of the following eminent logicians acting as the Dwara Pandita - Custodican of the Scholardhip.

(1) Ratnakara Santi - East gate

(2) Vagiswarakirti of Benaras - West Gate

(3) Naropa - North gate

(4) Prajnakaramati - South gate

(5) Ratnavajra of Kashmir - First Central gate

(6) Jnanasrimitra of Gauda - Second gate

The president of the University was always the most learned and religious sage. During 1034-1038 AD Atisa Dipankar Srijnan was the Head.

[Ref : Radha Kumud Mookerjee's book - Ancient Indian Education P. 588].

Syllabus : Unfortunately Vikramasila is not as fortunate as Nalanda in the matter of conservation of its history. The Chinese travellers Hiuen-Tsang and I-Tsing have given us some accounts. Regarding Vikramsila, the Tibetan accounts of some of its famous scholars and teachers provide some information also.

The Buddhist education system as was practised in Buddhist monastery had a pattern, which we can know of while dicussing that topic. Regarding the syllabus of Vikramsila, We can remark that the courses of study here were less comprehensive than Nalanda.

S. K. Das in his book writes that the most important branch of learning here was Tantras. Next to Tantras there were Grammar, Metaphysics and Logic. The fact that Dwara Panditas were eminent logicians goes to prove that Logic was evidently a popular subject.

It will be noticed that the curriculum of the monasteries, in general, excluded technical sciences. It was, therefore, a deteroriation from Taxila where the curriculum was more varied. But there is nothing strange. As the monks were supplied every need gratis, their whole endeavour was given to intellectual and spiritual development.

The history of Vikramasila is written large in the biographies of the great men it produced. Radha Kumud Mookerjee, along with, also writes that scholars of this place were invited in foreign countries, chiefly Tibet, to spread its learning, culture and religion. So the history of Vikramasila may be traced in the Tibetan accounts of some of its famous scholars and teachers - such as

1. Jnanapada
2. Virochana Rakshita
3. Jetari
4. Prajna Karamati - Dwara Pandita
5. Ratnakara - Dwara Pandita
6. Jnanasri Mitra - Dwara Pandita
7. Ratnavajra - Dwara Pandit
8. Vagiswara - Dwara Pandita
9. Dipankar Srijnan - known as Acharya Atisa - the greatest of the Indian scholars who worked as missionary in foreign countries. It is interesting to note that on his first setting foot on Tibetan soil, Atisa was entertained with Tea which was the national drink of Tibet.
10. Viryasimha
11. Abhaykaragupta - a native of Gauda
12. Tathagata Rakshita
13. Ratnakirti
14. Manjusri
15. Dharmakirti
16. Sakya Sri Bhadra
17. Mahapandita Tathagata Raksita who came from a Kayastha family of Orissa, was a Tantracharya of Vikramsila. He composed nine books on Tantra.

Destruction of Vikramasila by Muslims

Tabakat-i-Nasiri is a book on the history of the Ghajni Sultanate. [Ref. : The history of India, as told by its own historians - by H.M. Elliot and John Dowson - Pub. : Low Price Publications A-6 Nimricommercial centre, Near Ashok Bihar Phase-IV Delhi 110052] gives a picture of how this Seat of Learning was deliberately destructed by the Muslims for their inherent disposition of intolerance to other religious beliefs and religions.

It was in 1199 Baktiyar Khilji destroyed the University. As is written in Tabakat-i-Nasiri, the greater number of inhabitants of that place were Brahmans they had their heads shaven (refers to Vikshus) and they were all slain. There were a great number of Books (Library) on the religion of the Brahmanas (Buddhist) there and when all these books came under the observation of the Musalmans, they summoned a number of Hindus that they might give them information respecting the imports of these books, but the whole of the Hindus had been killed. On being acquainted with the contents of the books, it was found that the whole of the fortress and city was a college, and in the Hindu tongue, they call a college Bihar (Vihara). [For details P-306, Vol-II, The History of India as told by its own historians by Elliot and Dewson.].

E. Jagaddal (1203 A.D.)

According to the historical epic Ramcharita, this Seat of learning was founded by King Ramapala (1084-1139) in the 12th Century, on the bank of the Ganges and the Karotoya in the Country of Varenda. Ramapala was the King of Bengal and Magadha. The place is called Ramabati and was equipped with a Vihara - called Jagaddala. The University could work barely for 100 years. The Mahamedan invader Baktiyar swept it away in 1203 A.D. On his way to visit Tibet, SakyasriBhadra visited this place after its destruction.

But within its short life, this University had made substantial contribution to learning through the famous scholars. Among the noted scholars mention may be made of.

(1) Mahapandita Bibhutichandra. He was the author of six books in Sanskrit which he himself translated in Tibetan. Eighteen Sanskrit books written by different authors were translated in Tibetan by Bibhutichandra.

(2) Acharya Danasila for his profound knowledge of both Sanskrit and Tibetan he won titles - Pandita, Mahapandita, Upadhyaya and Acharya. He was born in Kashmir when Mahipala ruled Bengal.

(3) Subhakara is said to have been Guru of Sakyasri Bhadra. He composed in Sanskrit - Siddhaika - vira - Tantratika. This book was translated in Tibetan.

(4) Mokshakaragupta - He was a master of Logic on which he wrote the Sanskrit work 'Tarka-bhasha' which was again translated into Tibetan. He bore the titles of Vikshu and Mahpandita.

F. Kanchi

Kanchi in South India was another great centre of Learning, Hiuen Tsang had conversation with monks from Ceylone on Yoga philosophy here. Dharmapala of Kanchi defeated a hundred Hinayana Sutrakaras in a discussion lasting for seven days. The Jaina Rajabalikatha mentions Samantabhadra as having gone to Kanchipuram a number of times and a Mysore inscription bears this out. South of it there was a large monastery which was a rendezvous of the most eminent men of the country.

[Ref. : S. K. Das, Same book P-388].

G. Benaras

Benaras is one of the oldest Seat of Learning in India. In the Tittira Jataka, we read that World renowned Professor gave instruction in Science to five hundred young Brahmins and afterwards repaired to a forest house on the slopes of the Himalaya to carry on his educational work in that calm sylvan retreat. (S. K. Das P. 385). In the Kosiya Jataka it is stated that in the reign of King Brahmadatta of Benaras, Bodhisattwa being born in a Brahmin family became a renowned teacher at Benaras and used to teach the three Vedas and the 18 Vidyas to the Brahmin boys and Kshatriya princes. (ibid).

In the Jataka period Benaras was, however, largely the creation of the ex-students of Taxila. Benaras was not without its own alumni as educationists. There were several great world-famous teachers who each had 500 students to teach. There were certain subjects in teaching of which Benaras specialised. There is reference of a School of Music which was presided over by the most famous in the subject, in India. It was in Benaras, the Panini (450 BC) wrote his famous Grammar Book, that Yaska (700 BC) wrote his Nirukta, that Kapila evolved his Samkhya Philosophy, and that Goutama wrote his Nyaya Sastra. Here in Benaras Sankaracharya (788 AD) published his new doctrine of Vedanta and convinced the Pandits of its truth. Al Beruni (973-1048) writes that Benaras and Kashmir are the High Schools of Hindu Sciences. According to Al Beruni owing to the plundering exploits of Mamud (Ghazni) Hindu Sciences had retired to distant places like Kashmir, Benaras and other places where Muhamedan hands could not reach then. In the days of Al Beruni, astronomy was specially cultivated at Benaras where Vijoyanandin had composed his astronomical handbook - Karna Tilaka. It appears from Ain-i-Akbari that Benaras continued to be a flourishing Seat of Hindu learning even in the 16th Century.

H. Kanauj

From the reign of Yasovarman (675-710 AD), Kanauj became specially famous for its study of Purva-Mimamsa or the philosophy of the Vedic ritual. Yasovarman was the patron of Bhababhuti 7th Century A.D. whose Guru was the great apostle of Purva Mimamsa - Kumaril Bhatta (7th Century AD) as is evidenced by a colloquy of Bhababhuti's drama - Malati madhava. This together with the story that 5 Brahmins were sent from Kanauj to Bengal to revive Hindu customs there, shows that Kanauj was a centre of Brahminical learning.

[Ref. : S. K. Das, Same book, P-387]

(The period of Bhababhuti cannot be correctly ascertained. He was of Post Kalidas period. It is even doubted whether Bhababhuti was his real name - some say his name was Mandan Misra - Bharatkosh, Vol. 5, P-204).

I. Nadia

Nadia is the popular name of Navadwipa on the Bhagirathi river at its confluence with Jalangi. Once it was a centre of Trade.

When King Lakshman Sena of Gauda made it his capital, Nadia rose to renown (1063-1106 AD). The court of Lakshman Sena was a Centre of Learning (1106-1138). His Prime Minister Halayudha was well-known for his works - Brahmana Sarvaswa, Smriti Sarvaswa, Mimamsha Sarvaswa and Nyaya Sarvaswa. His elder brother was also a learned man who wrote Pasupati-Paddhati on Hindu Rituals.

Jayadeva - the author of Gita Govinda Dhoyi - the author of Pavanaduta, Umapati - who made the language to sprout into luxuriant foliage, built up the reputation of Nadia. Besides there was Sulapani through his work Smritiviveka, dealt the subject of Law.

The invasion of Bakhtiar Khilji put an end to Lakshmana Sena's dynasty and he fled to Vikrampura in East Bengal in 1197 A.D.

During the Muslim rule in India (1198-1857) Nadia rose to be a great Centre of Hindu learning.

Graduates of Mithila were not allowed to take away from its schools any book or notes. They had to leave only with the Diploma. This peculiar rule confined the learning of Mithila within its own limit. Vasudeva Sarvavauma after being educated by his father in Grammar, literature and Jurisprudence went to Mithila to specialise in Law. He was then 25 years old. There he was admitted by the Salaka Pariksha. He was awarded the high title of Sarvabhuma. Vasudeva committed to memory the whole of Tattwa - Chintamoni and the metrical part of Kusumanjali and came back to Nadia. From Mithila he went to Benaras where he studied Vedanta. Then at Nadia he reduced to writing from memory the two works he had learnt at Mithila. He founded his academy of New Logic (Navya - Nyaya) at Nadia.

Reghunath Siromoni was another challenger to Mithila practice. He instituted a chair of Logic in Nadia and broke the monopoly of Mithila in the teaching of that subject.

The Nadia University method of making an appointmemnt to a chair was some what singular. The applicant for the chair must have his own works and possession of dialectical skill to teach. A candidate who could hold his own against his opponents in an open debate at an Assembly of scholars acting as judges, was considered competent for a chair in the University.

Mathuranath (1570 AD), Ramavadra (1680 AD) Gadadhara Bhattacharya (1650 AD) were famous among the logicians.

Gadadhara Bhattacharya is described as "the prince of Indian logicians". The sum total of his own works were named as 'Gadadhari'.

Some of the names of the scholars of later period may be mentioned. They were:

(1) Harirama Tarkasiddhanta (about 1730 AD)

(2) Ramanarayana Tarkapanchanan (about 1760 AD)

(3) 'Buno' Ramnath (so called because he had his school in a wood-vana) about 1770 AD

(4) Krishnakanta Vidyavagisha (about 1780 AD)

(5) Sankara Tarkavagisha (about 1800 AD)

(6) Sivanath Vidyavachaspati (about 1810 AD)

(7) Kasinatha Churamoni (about 1820 AD)

(8) Dandi (about 1830 AD)

(9) Srirama Siromoni author of Padartha-Tattwa.

Along with chair of Logic, there was also a Chair of Smriti which was inaugurated by Raghunandana, the most distinguished jurist of his time in the sixteenth century.

There was also a strong school of Tantrika inaugurated by Krishnananda Agambagisa.

Nadia also boasted of a Chair of Astronomy inaugurated by Ramarudra Vidyanidhi in 1718 AD. He was the author of Jyotisha-Sara-Samgraha.

The duty of the school was to prepare almanacs for the Nawab's court at Mursidabad.

Radha Kumud Mookherjee - has referred to an article published in Calcutta Monthly (January 1791) mentioning some interesting aspects of the Univesity of Nadia.

It states that the University possessed three Chief Centres of Learning - at Navadwipa, at Shantipura and at Gopalpara, patronised by the Maharaja of Nadia. Navadwipa alone counted 1100 students and 150 teachers. In the time of Raja Rudra (1680 AD) the number of students was 4000 and teachers 600. It appears that all these schools were for advanced post graduate studies and the students seeking them spent even 20 years in these schools. They generally got by heart the text they studied. These schools were conducted like seminars. Their method of work was for two teachers to start a debate on an abstruse topic, which the students had to follow and could supplement by their own questions.

The advancement of knowledge by means of learned open debates has been India's indigenous traditional educational method through the ages.

J. Paithan: Under the Satbahanas, Paithan became one of the Chief Seats of Learning in India.

Location : In the 1st Century B.C. two southern powers became predominent in trans-Vindhyan India. These were the Satbahanas of the upper Decan and the Chedis of Kalinga. The power of the Chedis was short lived, but the Satbahana power endured for nearly three centuries. The capital of the Satbahana Kings was at the city of Pratisthan (Ptolemy's Geography), identified with modern Paithan on the Godavari River in the Aurangabad District of Maharastra State. The name of Goutamaputra Satakarni (106-130 AD), one of the Satbahana Kings, is very famous.

Hathigumpha inscriptions, place the Kingdom of the Satabahana Contemporary of Kharvela (2nd half of the 1st Century BC), to the west and not to the South, of Kalinga (the coast country comprising the Puri and the Ganjam Districts and the adjoining area). There is reason to believe that the Southern districts were annexed to the Satbahana empires about the middle of the 2nd Century A.D.

The pre-eminence of Paithan remained so far recognised that even during Muhammedan and Maratha times, complicated cases were settled at Paithan under the Panchayat of the learned men. That Paithan was famous for the cultivation of sciences is evident from Kathasaritsagara where we are told of one Debadatta by name who went to an old preceptor named Mantraswamin in Pratisthan and acquired a perfect knowledge of Sciences.

Besides Paithan, in South India, Karavir, Giri and Vijoynagara were also famous Seats of learning.

[Ref : (i) History and Culture of the Indian People, Vol-2, P-191, (ii) S. K. Das, Same book, Page - 388].

K. Mithila

Mithila was a stronghold of Brahmanical culture. The famous Philosopher King Janaka used to send out periodical invitations to learned Brahmanas to gather at his court for the purposes of Philosophical discussions. Under him Eastern India was vying with North Western India in holding the palm of learning. It was the time of Upanisadas. The time of Janaka cannot be ascertained. But he is referred to in the Epics. In those days the name of Mithila was Videha.

In AD 1097 Nanyadeva of Karnataka dynasty was the King of Mithila and Vijoy Sen was the King of Bengal. King Vijoya defeated King Nanyadeva. But son of Nanyadeva - Gangadeva defeated Vijoy Sen and recovered Mithila. This Karnataka dynasty ruled Mithila upto 1395 A.D. Kameswara dynasty then ruled Mithila upto 1515 A.D. It was followed by another dynasty founded by Maheswara Thakkura in the time of Akbar and this dynasty continued.

Mithila as a Seat of Learning flourished remarkably under this later Kings. During Kameswara dynasty, Jagaddhara wrote commentaries on variety of texts like Gita, Meghduta, Malatimadhava and others.

The next famous scholar was the poet Vidyapati. He has inspired the later Vaisnava writers.

[Vidyapati is difficult to identify as many poets wrote using this name. The Bengali poets and Vaisnavas are referring to him since 16th Century AD].

Mithila made a conspicuous contribution in the realm of scientific subjects. It developed a famous school of Nayaya which flourished from 12th to 15th Century AD., under the great mastership of Logic like Gangesha, Vardhamana, Pakhsadhara and others.

The School of Navya Nyaya was founded by Gangesha and his epoch making work is Tattwa-Chintamoni. He was followed by his son Vardhamana (1250 AD) and Pakshadhara Misra (1275 AD). His pupil and nephew was Vasudeva Misra, another great name was Mahesha Thakkura. His pupil Raghunandandasa Raya, an accomplished logician, went out on an intellectual Digbijoy at the instance of emperor Akbar. Akbar gave him a gift of land in Mithila. But Raghunandan transferred the property to his Guru Mahesa Thakur as Guru-Dakshina. Mahesa became the founder of the Darbhanga Raj family.

Sankara Misra wrote important works on Nyaya, Vaiseshika and Smriti.

Bachaspati Misra flourised about 1450 AD as the Court Officer of Kameswara Kings. He started writing on Smriti but soon drifted to Nyaya and wrote on Nyaya a good number of scholarly books. Nitichintamoni is his book on Ethics.

The literary history of Mithila lasted at least for three centuries 13th, 14th and 15th. By its scholastic activities became as famous a Nalanda of the old and students covering the whole of India used to come for specialised studies on Nyaya.

Mithila instituted a peculiar examination as admission test. It was called Salaka Pariksha. The candidate had to explain that page of a manuscript which was pierced last by a needle run through it.

L. Ujjain

According to Bana, author of Kadambari, "the inhabitants of Ujjain were connoisseurs in all arts, skilled in foreign languages, clever in subtleties of speech, versed in stories of all kinds, accomplished in letters, having a keen delight in the Mahabharata, the Puranas and the Ramayana, familiar with the Brata-Katha, master of the whole circles of arts, lovers of sastras, devoted to light literature". [Kadambari - C. M. Ridding's Eng. Trans. P-212].

Ujjain's fame as a great centre of learning attracted Sankaracharya (8th Century AD) who defeated here in argument a Pasupatacharya. Al-Beruni (10th Cent. AD) relates the story of the Alchemist Vyadi who was a Veritable martyr to the science of Alchemy.

Ujjain was however, famous for the study of Astronomy and it became the meridian from which the Hindus counted the longitude of their places.

[Ref. : S. K. Das - The Education system of Ancient Hindus, P-386].

M. Tanjore

Tanjore of South India was famous for the cultivation of Natyasastra and the sister arts of music and dancing. Rajaraja Chola (985-1014 AD) built music Halls for this purpose and invited and settled in Tanjora female dancers and singers, pipers and drumers. Colleges were also built and learned teachers were appointed who taught literature and Sastras to students.

[Ref. : S. K. Das, Same book, P-387].

(In the famous Brihadeswar Temple premises till now annual music functions are held).

N. Kalyana

Kalyan was an ancient Seat of learning, specially famous for its study of Law and Astronomy. At Kalyan Vijnaneswara composed the famous commentary on the Yajnabalkya Smriti, called Mitaksara which is recognised even to this day as the leading authority in Hindu Law all over India, except Bengal. King Someswara III (1126-1138 AD) himself wrote the Manasollasa a compendium of many sciences and made a solid contribution to the Science of Astronomy by giving the Dhrubankas (Constants to be added).

[Ref. : S. K. Das, P-387, Same book].

O. Odantapuri

Very little is known about this Unviersity. Once there were 1000 monks here. The famous scholar Pravakara who came from Chatarpur of Bengal stayed here.

Some are of opinion that this University existed long before the Pala kings came in to power in Magadha. The Pala Kings expanded the University by endowing it with a good Library of Brahmanical and Buddhist works.

Sri Nihar Ranjan Roy in his book Bangaleer Itihas (Adi Parba) mentions that Odantapur was a Seat of Learning in Bihar Sharif, at a close distance from Nalanda. Tibetan Historian Taranath opines that this centre was founded by Gopala (8th Century) or Devapala (9th Century). Some other View is, it was founded by Dharmapal (775-810) who succeeded Gopala.

The principal of Odantapuri University was designated as Mahasanghikacharya. A Bengali Youth named Chandragarva was a desciple of Shila Rakshita. Chandragarva, later was famous in the name of Dipankar Atisa Srijnan. Dipankar also once the Principal of Odantapuri. Baktiyar did not attack this place as it was at the top of a hill and Bakhtiyar took it to be a fort. The Odantapuri was taken as a model on which the first Tibetan Buddhist Monastary was built in 8th Century AD (749 AD) under King Khri-Spon-deu-Tsan on the advice of his Guru - Shanta Rakshita.

Taxila

Nalanda

Valabhi

Vikramsila

Jagaddal

On Female Education in Bharatvarsha

Whenever and wherever the issue of female education in Bharat, comes to discussion level - casual or serious, we are in the habit of decrying the ancient culture of our land, taking it for granted that the West is very much progressive and the women-folks of the West have been enjoying long since, a venerable position in the society in that culture. This essay is not an attempt to analyse the position of the women folk in the West. This essay is simply an elaboration of the status the women folk enjoyed in this land and why and how that degraded and came to a horribly pitiable state - which we are used to refer in our discussions on the subject, in most cases uninformed.

We often forget or made to forget, we often even do not know and never accept that we do not know that this land of ours has a rich heritage, of long four thousand years of education, which none of the Western Countries do have. In the whole world, excepting our country, there were a few countries with rich heritage. Countries like Greece, Rome, Egypt, Mesopotamia, have antiquity, rich heritage. But there is no continuity of that rich heritage. Now those are read in books and seen in Museum. Ours is a country which has both antiquity and continuity - a matter we may take pride in.

The long years of Semetic Rule (Islam and Christian) have left a very significant influence on us. Five hundred years of Islamic Rule and two hundred years of Christian Rule have made us forget our Hindu Rule of at least for three thousand years.

Pity is, when the Rule changed, the new secular Rulers paid no homage to the antiquity and continuity of Hindu Culture of three thousand years. The new Rulers subdued to the Semetic influence, and accepted by the secular forces unopposed. Either they did not know their Past of rich heritage or they were so busy with the puffs and pleasure of the present that they could not. As a result, always a mean and ridiculous history of the status of women folks of our country is projected by the Semetic forces and accepted by the secular forces unopposed. The new Rulers had not the knowledge and courage to counter that. Consequently, the country of ours which has always shown the right path to humanity, has now been a poor soul following the footsteps of those who roamed in the jungles and ate raw meat when this country of ours reached the level as high as of the thoughts of Upanisadas and produced the greatest human characters - the characters which are unparallel in human history. To conceal the inability to appreciate that level and those characters, we the seculars, name those as 'myths' and try to upkeep and keep up ourselves.

Bacause of this poor and petiable mental standard, we are bound to express that 'Scholars hold widely divergent views about female education in Bharat in ancient times.'

Practically there is no scope of holding 'divergent views' about female education in the vedic period of Bharatvarsa. There are, however, clear indications and instances that even during the ancient period, there were highly educated women, holding an honourable position in house-hold and society.

There were two classes of women students - Brahmabadini or life long students of sacred texts and Sadyodvaha - who persued their studies till their marriage. Panini (5th Century B.C. Some are of opinion that Panini was a man of 7th Century B.C.) refers to the women students of Vedic Sakhas. Katyayana (during the period of Chandra Gupta - 4th Century B.C.), in his Vartika refers to women students who were called Upadhyaya or Upadhyayi as distinguished from Upadhyayanis (wives of teachers). The necessity of Coining a new term - Upadhyaya or Upadhyayanis, shows that the women teachers were large in numbers. Patanjali (2nd Century B.C.) also refers to a special designation for the women scholars who made a special study of Mimamsa Philosophy.

The Buddhist and the Jain texts also refer to women of the Brahmabadini class - who remained unmarried to carry on their studies. Most of the Buddhist nuns, whose songs are in Therigatha, were maidens born in the well-to-do families who renounced the World for the sake of spiritual salvation. The Jain texts refer to Jayanti, daughter of the King of Kausambi, who remained unmarried in order to devote herself to religion and philosophy. She carried on discussion with Mahavira himself on abstruse questions of philosophy and eventually became a nun. The Mahavarata (approx 1450 B.C.) also has portrayed an exulted picture of womanhood.

In addition to higher education, or in place of higher education, women in general received training in the arts of music, dancing, painting etc. In his book Kamasastra, Vatsyayana has detailed the arts practised by women. Many women went in for Military training also. There were female spear-bearers - mentioned by Patanjali. Megasthenes (4th Century B.C.) refers to Amazonian body - guards on attendance of Chandra Gupta Mourya, when he went out in hunt, of the women, some are on chariots, some on horses, some even on elephants, and they are equipped with weapons of every kind. In different sculptures (Bharut) women, we find, equipped with weapons. Kautilya in his Arthasastra mentions - "the King on getting up from his bed, shall be received by troops of women armed with bows." Women are sometimes known to have carried on administration.

Formerly the girls went through the Upanayana Ceremony like the boys, but this gradually came to be formal.

Manu prescribes that in the case of Upanayana of girls, recitation of sacred text in prohibited. He lays down that the marriage ceremony was equal to the Upanayana in the case of women (II, 66). Yajnavalkya took further and more logical step of prohibiting the Upanayana Ceremony altogether for girls. This was the signal for the gradual spiritual disfranchisement of women. Minor religious rituals like - Jatakarma, Namakarana, Chudakarana etc. also came to be performed for them without Vedic Mantras.

In contrast to this Buddhism and Jainism offered a more honourable career to women. A large number of them became nuns, and some of them became famous preachers.

The gradual spiritual disfranchisement of women was very much evident in the later vedic period. But formerly it was not so. The women had the honourable right to utter Vedic Mantras and participate in religious sacrifices and rituals.

In the Rigveda (VIII, 33, 17) Indra himself has said - "The mind of women brooks no discipline. Her intellect hath little weight." But there are passages in the Rig Veda, Yajurveda and Atharva Vedas where it is read - "An unmarried young learned daughter should be married to a learned bridegroom. Never think of giving in marriage a daughter of very young age."

"A young daughter who has observed Bramhacharya (i.e. finished her studies) should be married to a bridegroom who like her, is learned." Again, "An Acharya can impart education to his students if he himself has observed Brahmacharya. A young daughter after the observance of Brahmacharya should be married to a young man."

[The Educational system of the Ancient Hindus - S. K. Das, P-223].

Women in early times, enjoyed the right to utter the sacred mantras. In the Aswalayana Srauta Sutra we are told - the wife (of the sacrificer) should recite in a sacrifice this mantra (1.11).

Govila Grhyasutra is quite explicit on the right of women to perform the Agnihotra with Vedic Mantras. "The wife should utter the mantra 'Dhrubaha' and then pray to God for ability to live in her husband's house in safety and steadfastness and then utter her own name as well as that of her husband (1.3).

In Paraskara Grihya Sutra, in Samkhyana Sutra, in Apastamva Srauta Sutra, women are allowed to utter Vedic Mantras. We are to keep in mind that Sutra period is later to Vedic period. So we can safely infer that the right of the women to Vedic mantras was very much accepted as a social and religious norm. We have referred that the position of the women gradually deteriorated. They were defranchised in Vedic affairs. There are reasons why this happened and it is also known that when it did happen. We shall discuss the issue later on.

Jaimini in his Purva Mimamsa says, "Women like men can bless with Vedic Mantras and observe Brahmacharya (VI. I. 24)."

It may be argued that the utternance of Mantras need not necessarily mean the regular study of the sacred texts. In the commentary of the Govila Grihyasutra (1.3) we are told that "The female folk should be taught, for without such studies they cannot perform Agnihotra. In the same Govila Sutra we find (1.6). "The woman should read me (Veda)." In Latayana Sutra (IV. 6) we are told "The wife also sings same Veda".

From Patanjali (2nd Century BC) Mahavasya we read that Brahmin female were accustomed to study Mimamsa Philosophy and also taught it. Such females were named 'Upadhyayi'.

Purva Mimamsa of Jaimini, when read in the light of the comments of Sabara Swami lead to the broad conclusion that in respect of rights to perform one of the Vedic Commands, women are on a level with men. In chapter I of the Jaimini's Mimamsa Darsan, we read of the equal rights of men and women in the performance of sacrifice etc.

According to Madhavacharya, (14th Cent.) a girl of twice-born classes has as much right to be initiated at the age of eight years as boys of the same age and is entitled equally with them to study the Vedas. There was similar initiation of girls in Vedic Age.

Harit, One of the earliest sages, describes that all the four stages of life including that of studentship were open to women and that both the sexes had a right to utter the mantras (vedic texts).

Katyayana Samhita (XIX. 5) says, "If the rite of serving the sacred fire cannot be performed by one, they (the wives) should, either according to seniority or ability, severally or jointly, perform the rite, according to their own light and knowledge of the scriptures."

Daksa Samhita IV. 9, says, "The household of men has the wife for its root, if she follows the Vedas."

It was a general view that girls should be taught Vidya and Dharmaniti. Such women can bring good to the family of her father and that of the husband.

So in Mahanirbanatantra we read, "The daughter also should be properly educated and taken care of."

We know of Lopamudra who was the author of the Rik in the first Mondala I/179/I-2 of the Rigveda, Viswavava composed the Rik in the Rigveda V/28/I-6. Apala composed VIII/91/I-7.

Ghosa, Atrieyi, Paulami and Saswati were authors of the Mantras and rose to the rank of the Rsis.

In the Brhadaranyaka Upanisad there is interesting and significant reference of Gargi holding philosophical discussion with Yajnabalkya in an assembly of the most learned Brahmanas in the lands of Kuru and Panchala. It was convened by the great king Janaka. The questions raised by Gargi were very subtle and deep. Yajnabalkya answered those. Again, we find Maitreyi engaged in discussion with her husband Yajnabalkya on the questions of immortality. It was an abstruse philosophical discussion.

The Upanisads mention several other women as teachers but it is not clear whether they were married.

In the epics (Ramayana and Mahavarata) there are women who were well-versed in dharmaniti and other philosophical issues.

Lilabati, a Brahmin lady was the author of the celebrated subject called Algebra.

From Lalita Vistara we learn that in the time of Lord Buddha (566 BC) girls had a right to study sastras. Goutam Buddha needed maidens well versed in sastras. Girls were not domestic drudge. They had their individuality and free opinions.

It is practically impossible to fix the time when the right of initiation and study of the Vedas were denied to women. It may be traced that in the time of Jaimini (3rd Century, AD) or after him, a school had developed to oppose women to enjoy the rights with men. But Jaimini and Badarayana (contemporary of Jaimini) were not against the equal rights of men and women. Badarayana held the view that any one (man or woman) belonging to three regenerate classes in entitled to perform sacrifices.

When we come to Smritis, we find that the women were thought incompetent to perform sacrifices. Manu is of opinion that the marriage ceremony of woman is the Vedic Sacrament for women and to be equal to initiation, serving the husband is equivalent to residing with the teacher and her household duties are same as the worship of sacred fire (Manu Samhita II, 67). It is supposed that Manu Samhita was composed during 2nd Century B.C. to 2nd Century A.D.). We find Verse no. 18 of Chapter IX of Manu Samhita is very much adament to women regarding their learning of the Sastras. In Narada Smriti in Verse no. 30 of Chapter XIII, there is remark that women have no right to study Sastras. So they have no knowledge of Dharma and Adharma. There are so many instances of Verses of different Smritis, which deny the women to enjoy the right to read sastras.

Mr. Cady Santon in his book - History of Women Suffrage Vol-III P-200 [quoted in S. K. Das's Book P-234] comments that "in almost every nation of the world in the primitive stages of its development, the idea of inferiority of female sex prevailed, woman was not regarded as a person, she was not recognised as a citizen."

It is probably the early foreign invasion of India that may account for this exclusion of women from Vedic studies.

That woman was not a unit but a zero in the Sum of human civilization, was the very notion of the conquering non-Hindus (Mlechchas). When the highly civilised people of Hindusthan came in contact with these conquering non-Hindus i.e. foreign rulers who were less civilized, they might have adopted those rules. It may also so happen that the Hindus put severe restrictions on their women-whose, chastity was a prime factor to them. That may be taken as a defence mechanism of the civilised Hindus caring the chastity of women as first consideration. The foreign invaders were all males and did not come to India with females from their own land. Indian females were their target. Indian males worried about the chastity of their females.

From the time - 2nd century BC to 2nd Century AD approximately, the education of women came to be entirely domestic and vocational. They were being prepared for duties of the household. Men were engaged in social duties, learning, teaching, trades, or were plunged into the delights of Bhakti. They had to be freed from the worries of family life. So the burden was shifted to women. The Satapatha Brahmana and the Buddhist literature and sastras, want women as skilled in weaving and spinning and intelligent enough to do and manage the house-hold affairs.

Vatsyayana (within 2nd Century BC to 2nd Century A.D. not definitely known) in his famous Kama Sutra, enumerates the duties of married wives thus :-

"She should arrange to plant in her garden rows of flower plants such as Kubjaka, Amalaka, Mallika, Jati, Kurundaka, Nabamallika, Tagara, Nandyvartya and other plants. There should also be rows of trees and the grounds should be kept attractive in appearance. She should secure the seeds of various medicinal herbs and vegetables such as Muluka and sow them in time. From the curds that remain after their daily consumption, she should extract its essence (butter) as also oil from Oil-seeds, sugar and jaggary from sugarcane, spinning of thread from out of cotton and weaving cloth with them, the securing of Sikya (a sling for placing vessels suspended from the ceilings) of ropes (for drawing water) of strings (for tieing cattle), of barks, looking after pounding and grinding (of paddy, rice etc), finding some use of tusha, kana, kuti and angara (charcoal), knowledge of wages of servants and their disbursements, the care of cultivation and welfare of cattle, looking after sheeps, cocks, lavakas, parrots, cuckoos, peacocks, monkeys and deer, the recknowing of daily income and expenditure and making up a total of them all - all these are the duties of wife" (Kamasutra BK IV, Chap-I as quoted by S. K. Das P-236). Besides she has to consider annual income and expenditure and also art of cooking. Manu is very much specific regarding the rights and duties of a woman (Chap V, 146-166).

Though the intellectual side of woman received no special care and was left to circumstances, the performance of certain religious rites and ceremonies in which they had to take part, made them well-aware of the mythological stories, folk-lore which had been handed down and accumulated in this country from ancient times. The girls were primarily trained and guided by their mother and after marriage under the control of mother-in-law.

On the whole, during this period literacy and education did not go hand in hand in the case of Hindu women of this country. Many of them were illeterate but all were well-educated. This is a fact which may seem strange to the western mind.

Vatsyayana

From Vatsyayana, we come to learn that certain women such as courtesans, princesses and daughters of noble men, by direct study of Sastras, sharpened their intellect.

Vatsyayana advises that a woman in girl-hood, alone in private, should learn sixty four kinds of sexual knowledge. Such a girl's teacher will be -

(1) A daughter of her nurse who had been brought up with her, and had intercourse with man,

(2) A woman friend who speaks in a frank manner and like wise had intercourse with man

(3) Her mother's sister of her own age,

(4) An elderly woman servant who is trusted and is to the girl like her mother's sister.

(5) A nun who previously had sexual intercourse with man.

(6) Her own elder sister, because of the trust reposed on her by the girl.

Vatsyayana in his Kamasutra ennumerates the 64 Kalas or arts. He comments that a woman gifted with these arts will, by these means live even when her husband is on exile or when she is suffering from some great trouble or has become a widow, even if she is living in a foreign country. (BK I, Chap. III).

Readers may please note that Vatsyayana's scheme of female education was an ideal one including :

(a) Literary accomplishments, kalas - 28, 29, 30, 31, 32, 33, 45, 46, 47, 51, 52, 53, 54, 55, 56, 62.

28 - Prahelika - solving riddles.

29 - Pratimala - reciting slokas, now known as Antakshara competition or Antadi.

30 - Durvachaka Yogah - participating in reciting slokas difficult both in meaning and pronunciation.

31 - Pustaka Vachanan : reading in melodious tones standard works as the Ramayana, Mahabharata.

32 - Natakakhyayika darsanam : Knowledge of drama and stories

33 - Kabya Samasya Puranam : The later part of the Sloka is given, to compose the first part of the given sloka

45 - finding some hidden meaning of some groups of letters, composed to mean various things - Aksara mustika thanam

46 - Mlechitabikalpa : Variety of cypher - languages, unintelligible to all except the initiator.

47 - Desabhasa Vijnanam : knowledge of the languages of different countries.

51 - Dharana matrika - Science of Memory - memory training.

52 - Sapatyam - a feat in which one person recites a known sloka (verse) and another who does not know the sloka, has to repeat it along with the former.

53 - Manasi : a feat in which one has to fill up with the appropriate words or phrases, the blank left in a verse or sentence.

54 - Kavyakriya : Composing Poems.

55 - Abhidhana : knowledge of the lexicon.

56 - Kriyakalpa : Kavya, Alankar and Poetry (poetics and Rhetoric)

62 - Vainayikanam : Knowledge of such arts and sciences by which good manners and obedience are learnt - knowledge of the sciences and arts which educate a person.

(b) Besides these literary accomplishments, Vatsyayana prescribes Kalas Nos. 10, 23 for knowledge of domestic arts.

10 - Sayanarachanam : arrangement of bed according to the taste and condition of the person.

23 - Vichitra Suka - Yusha Bhaksyakriya : Preparation of different kinds of soups, food, vegetables, sweatmeats and other dishes.

(c) Then Knowledge of Culinary arts Kalas nos. - 23, 24.

24 - Preparation of different kinds of drinks including intoxicants

23 - Vichitrasuka

(d) Then knowledge of arts relating to toilet, dress, comforts or luxuries, Kalas nos. - 5, 6, 8, 14, 15, 16, 17, 18, 19, 44, 58.

5 - Visesakachhedyam : Cutting of leaves etc. in the form of certain figures to serve as the mark of forehead.

6 - Tandula Kusumavalivikara : arrangement of coloured ricegrains and flowers of different colours, in various forms as an ornamental exhibit at the time of the worship (of a deity etc.)

8 - Dasana - Vasanangarage : Colouring of the teeth, clothes and body

14 - Stringing flowers into garlands for the purpose of wearing or worshipping.

15 - Sekharapidayoga : Striking flowers in the form of Sekhara or apida (two kinds of head ornaments).

16 - Ways of dressing and decorating oneself with flowers or ornaments.

17 - Karnapatrabhanga : making some kinds of ear-ornaments out of ivory, conch etc.

18 - Gandhayukti : Preparation of perfumatory articles.

19 - Bhusanayojana : making of new ornaments or improving old ones with the insertion of precious stones etc. or the proper way of wearing ornaments.

44 - Dexterity in the process of removing dart from the body in massaging and dressing hairs

58 - Vastragopanam : Covering the private parts of the body with cloth, or weaving a long cloth, in such a way that it may look fit or as if it were a short cloth or wearing a torn cloth in such a way that its damaged parts are not seen by others.

(e) Then knowledge of manual arts (Kalas nos. - 7, 22, 36, 37.

7 - Puspastaranam : Covering the floor of a hall or room with flowers.

22 - Hastalaghava : nimbleness of hand by which one is able to do things easily and quickly.

36 - Taksanam : Carpentry.

37 - Vastuvidya : Engineering specially that part of the science which treats of the ways of constructing dwelling houses, the sites on which they

are to be built, the materials to be used and such other matters as sanitation, connected with the subject.

(f) Then knowledge of recreative arts (Kalas nos. 12, 20, 26, 28, 29, 30, 31, 32, 33, 42, 43, 45, 49, 52, 53, 57, 59, 60, 61.

12 - Udakaghata : strking at other with handfuls of water or by squirting it through some instrument such as syringe.

20 - Indrajalayoga : Producing illusions by playing trickery.

26 - Sutrakrida : Playing with strings of threads cut or burnt are made to appear as unbroken. Or this may be interpreted like this - some plays in which dolls are made to dance and play by means of threads attached to them from behind.

28 - Prahelika : Proposing and solving of riddles.

29 - Pratimala : amusing way of reciting slokas (verses) - Antadi or Antakshari.

30 - Durvachaka Yoga : Participating in reciting slokas difficult both in meaning and pronunciation.

31 - Pustakabachanam : Reading in melodious tones standard works such as the Ramayana and the Mahavarata.

32 - Natakakhyayika : Knowledge of dramas and stories.

33 - Completing a sloka (verse) by composing the other part of the verse or sloka.

42 - Mesa - Kukkuta - lavaka - yuddhavi : training rams, cocks and lavakas (some bird) to fight.

43 - teaching parrots to speak human language and sending messages through them.

45 - Akhsara - mustika - Kathanam : to find out some hidden meaning of some groups of letters ingeniously composed to mean various things, as in our 'shorthand'.

49 - Puspasakatika : making of carts, planquins, horses, elephants etc. out of flowers.

52 - Sapatyam : a feat in which one person reads a known sloka and another who does not know the sloka before, has to repeat it along with the former.

53 - Manasi : another feat in which one is to fill up with appropriate words or phrases, the blank left in a verse or sentence.

54 - Chhali Kayoga : Some processes of deception or fun in which voice and person are disguised so as not to be recognised.

59 - Dyutavisesa : Varieties of gambling.

60 - Akarsa - Krida : A particular type of gambling with dice

61 - Balakridyanakani : Plays for children with balls and dolls.

(g) Then Knowledge of Scientific arts (Kalas Nos. 9, 13, 17, 21, 34, 35, 38, 39, 40, 41, 50).

9 - Manibhumikakarma : in certain parts of the house studding the floor with precious stones etc.

13 - Chitrascha yoga : various kinds of preparations by compounding drugs and other medicinal substances or spell against others (enemies) to disable or deform them.

17 - Karnapatravanga : making some kinds of ear-ornaments out of ivory, counch.

21 - Kanchumarscha-yoga : Some preparations out of drugs to increase verility and strength of the body.

34 - Pattikavetra Vanavikalpa : making of different articles of furniture from canes and reeds.

35 - Taksakarmani : Cutting into required shapes certain materials - wood, metal etc. making from gold, steel, wood, silver or any other substance unnatural forms of male organs for using them as substitutes in sexual intercouse (these are called Apadrabyas).

38 - Rupyaratnapariksha : testing, valuing etc. of precious stones

39 - Dhatuvada : the combination, purification and precipitation of minerals, making valuable metals out of interior kinds, as gold from iron.

40 - Maniragakarajnanam : Knowledge of the process of dying crystals and precious stones and of the location and working of mines.

41 - Vriksayaurveda : Knowledge of medicines of Plants

50 - Yantramatrika : Construction of machines for locomotion, pumping water etc. and of guns and other weapons for war purposes.

(h) Then Knowledge of Music, Kalas nos. 1, 2, 11, 27

1 - Gitam : Singing

2 - Vadyam : Playing on musical instruments.

11 - Udakavadyam : Playing on water so as to produce a musical sound

27 - Vinadamaruka Vadyani : Playing on Vina or Damaruka (a kind of drum).

(i) Then Knowledge of Drama, Kala no. 32

32 - Natakakhyaika darsanam : Knowledge of dramas and stories.

(j) Then Knowledge of Etiquettee, Kala no. 62

62 - Vainayikanam Vidyanam Jnanam : Knowledge of such arts and sciences by which good manners and obedience are learnt or knowledge of the sciences and arts which educate a person.

(k) Then comes the Knowledge of Painting (Kala no. 4)

4 - Alekhyam : Painting

(l) The Knowledge of Physical exericse (Kalas nos. 3, 63, 64)

3 - Nrtyam : dancing

63 - Knowledge of such sciences as will bring victory over opponents

64 - Knowledge of such sciences as are connected with the physical exercise and the development of the body.

Vatsyayana refers to another set of sixty four Kalas (arts) taught by Panchala which he has fully described in BK II dealing with Samproyogikam or sexual intercourse. Vatsyayana says that King's daughter or the daughter of a noble man well skilled in these arts will have her husband under her sway even when he has one thousand wives in his harem.

In Jaina Kalpasutra we find the Arhat Rsabha saying that during his reign he taught among other subjects the sixty-four accomplishments of Ladies. [S. K. Das's Book P-245].

Singing and dancing were regarded as particularly feminine accomplisments and are dubbed 'unmanly' in the later Vedic texts.

In the Ramayana hundred daughters of Rajarsi Kausanava were well versed in dancing and singing and music. The wives of Ravana were highly proficient in dancing and singing.

The Mahabharata refers to dancing Hall of King Virata.

In Malabikagnimitra and Ratnabali there are refereaces of Chitrasala, dancing and Music hall. Paes (1537 AD) gives a vivid description of the dancing Hall of the King of Vijoyanagara.

Draupadi was best educated a woman. She learnt Brahaspatiniti from a Brahman tutor - appointed by her royal father.

In Indian literature there are women characters who were really well-educated. Kalidasa's wife as well as woman characters created by him were educated.

Among the Tantrics there were many learned women. Kalhan in his Rajtarangini refers to women as preceptors in Tantric cult.

Buddha of the 6th Century BC himself was not in favour of women joining Samgha. He refused his aunt three times. But Ananda persuaded Buddha. Women were declared eligible to join Samgha. Buddha pointed out, 'The pure religion would have lasted long, the good law would have stood first for a thousand years, but now [women allowed to join Samgha - as Vikshuni] it will last only 500 years. [Maha parinirvana sutta V 23. quoted by S. K. Das in his book P-251] The Buddhist nunneries became centre of education and culture. Those who were admitted received instruction in Buddhist doctrines. We hear of the intellectual attainments of the Buddhist nuns and some of their literary compositions are preserved in the famous 'Therigatha'.

In the time of Ashoka there were many learned Buddhist women including his daughter Samghamitra, who taught Vinayapitaka, both in Bharat and Ceylone.

From the Arthasastra by Kautilya (4th Century BC), we learn that actresses were taught by teachers, arts such as singing, playing on musical instruments, reading, dancing, acting, writing, painting.

Kautilya's Arthasastra make us known that the female slaves were taught by teachers different arts like singing, dancing, playing, musical instruments, manufacture of scents and garlands. Khujjuttara a maid servant of the queen of the King of Kosambi, mastered the Tripitaka.

On Prostitution

While talking on prostitution, prostitution in Bharat dates from the earliest time as is the case in other parts of the world. Prostitution is mentioned in the Rigveda (S. K. Das, P-256]. While in the Vajasneyee Samhita it seems to be recognised as a profession. In Manu, the prostitute is regarded with disfavour. [IX 259, IV-209, 211, 219, 220, V-90]. The Jatakas also refers to prostitutes knowing different arts. But they seem to have lived a more intellectual life. Amrapali invited Buddha. There are references that qualified prostitutes charged 50 to 100 Kahapanas per night.

Kautilya refers to prostitution. They were noted for their beauty, youth and accomplishments. Kautilya lays down that superintendents of prostitute should employ such women at the King's court on a salary of 1000 Panas per annum.

Vatsyayana in describing the qualities to be possessed by a courtesan says that she must possess a knowledge of sexual science and its attendant arts, and a taste for Arts (sixty-four in number). Vatsyayana in his Kamasutra (BK I, Chap. - III) is very much explicit regarding the education of prostitutues. A prostitute having high standard and knowledge should be ranked as Ganika (a more honourable class among Vesyas).

Kautilya prefers that prostitutes are to be trained by efficient teachers and these teachers should be paid by the state. He also mentions that the teachers of prostitutes should train the sons of Prostitutes to be actors on the stage (Rangopojibi).

Vatsyayana lays down the rules for the education of the daughters of prostitutes.

In the famous Sankrit literature of the old there are characters like Rupanika, Vasantasena, Ragamanrjari, Chandrasena.

Devadasis

It is to be noted with care that allied to the institution of courtesans was the girls maintained in the great temples of Bharata, for the worship of God. They i.e. such girls were named Devadasi.

Kautilya in his Arthasastra refers to Devadasis. Kalhana in his Rajtarangini and Kalidasa in his Meghaduta refer to Devadasis. In Kathasaritsagara, the character Rupanika combined the professions of a prostitute and temple servant. The chinese traveller Chau-Ju-Kwa in his work, Chu-fanchi dealing with chinese and Arab trade during 12th and 13th Centuries, refers to 4000 Buddhist temple buildings (in Gujrat) in which lived over 20 thousand dancing girls who sang twice daily while offering food to the Buddha idol and while offering flowers. Marcopolo (about 1290 A.D.) refers to such dancing girls attached to temples in Tanjore. One of the Tamil inscriptions shows that in 1005 A.D. the chief temple at Tanjore had four hundred dancing women. The whole chola Country was full of temples with Devadasis.

Sri S. K. Das in his book comments that, connection of dancing girls with temple worship was not peculiar to India. Among the ancient Jews harlotry appears to have been connected with religious worship - and this was encouraged. In Egypt, Phonesia, Chaldia, Cannan, Persia, the worship of Isis and other deities consist of the most extravagant social orgies and temples were the centres of vice. The dancing girl is not necessarily bad but there is in her life much temptation to do evil and little stimulous to do right and to live a blameless respectable life. Thus in time, harlotry came to be regarded as inseparably connected with the vocation of dancing girls and an essential feature of temple worship.

It is known from Kautilya's Arthasastra that the institution of both secular and religious prostitution were utilized by the state as secret service agents. According to Kautilya, women of accomplishments should be employed as spies in the houses of kings who are not friendly and inimical. They should be employed in the department of Governments. It is clear that such woman artisans and prostitutes knew the art of reading signs, of cipher-writing and the art of playing musical instruments which helped them to move from place to place.

It is interesting to find that some women had knowledge of Military arts and Sciences. From Rigveda we know that non-Aryans (not so cultured or sophiticated) joined the army in good numbers. Patanjali (2nd Century BC) refers to 'Saktiki' which means a female spear-bearer. In the Ramayana, there is reference that queen Kaikeyi fought against the enemies to save her husband - Dasaratha. In the 64 Kalas of Vatsyayana Kalas nos. 50 and 63 refers to military Art to be learnt by woman. Kautilya says, 'On getting up from bed the king shall be received by the troops of women armed with bows. Rabindrnath depicts Chitranggada (a female character in one of his dramas) as a warrior.

Paes who came to India in 1581 A.D. says, "They also say that each of them (queens of the King of Vijayanagara) has sixty maidens, with these maidens, they say there are 12 thousand maidens for you must know that that there are women who handle sword and shield and others who wrestle and others who blow trumpets and others pipes and other instruments which are different from ours." [S. K. Das, P-262]

It may be concluded that the education of the girls in Ancient Bharata, fitted them for the role they were to play in life as a good house-wife, an expert actress or a trained dancing girl. The frequent prayers for the concord of husband and wife in the Vedic texts are certain proof that feminine subservience cannot be taken for granted. There are lady-hymnists in vedic literature. In the Upanisada, we find, women view with men in intellectual and philosophical issues, the Buddist period also there were ranked nuns who carried the philosophy of Buddha.

Thus the sexes came to regard their functions as complementary and not competitive. In course of time, the education of women emphasised on modesty, regard for family life, care of religion, children and the kitchen and on domestic management and husbanding of resources.

Marriage and Divorce

Among the Grihya Sutras, only the Aswalayana Grihya Sutra and most of the Dharma Sutras, mention eight types or forms of marriage. The Grihya Sutras give detailed rules regarding the proper seasons for marriage, the qualification of the bride and the bridegroom, and the various stages of marriage ceremony. The bride should not be a 'Sapinda' relation of the bridegroom's mother, nor belong to the same gotra as her own. The bridegroom should be a youngman with intelligence, character and good health and should, above all, come from a good family.

On the whole, they forbid marriage relation between agnates and cognates upto a certain limit. A remarkable exception to this was the custom of marrying the maternal uncle's daughter prevalent among the Southerners which though forbidden by Manu (XI 172-173) and most other smritis, is approved by Brihaspati, who also sanctions the marriage of brother's widow prevailing in North-West India. (Anuloma and Pratiloma marriages took place. Anuloma marriage means the male is of higher caste than the female. Pratiloma marriage means the male is of lower caste and the female was the higher caste. The worst pratiloma marriage was a sudra male and a Brahmin female. The off springs were chandalas.)

Eight forms of marriage are mentioned in the Dharma Sutra and repeated by Manu.

1. **Brahma** : Where the father gives his daughter, decked with ornaments and jewels, to a learned man of good conduct invited by him.

2. **Daiva** : Where the father gives his daughter, decked with ornaments, to a priest who duly officiates at a sacrifice, during the course of its performances.

3. **Arsha** : Where the father gives his daughter after receiving from bridegroom a cow and a bull of two pairs.

4. **Prajapatya** : Where the father gives his daughter after addressing the couple with text - May both of you perform together your duties.

5. **Asura** : Where the bridegroom receives a maiden after giving as much wealth, as he can afford, to the Kinsmen and to the bride herself.

6. **Gandharva** : A voluntary union of a maiden and her lover

7. **Rakshasa** : Forcible abduction of a maiden from her home.

8. **Paisacha** : where a man by stealth seduce a girl who is sleeping, intoxicated or disordered in intellect.

The first three, four or six are approved by different authorities. The last one is condemucd by all and the seventh is generally commended only in the case of Kshatriyas.

The condemnation of the last four forms proves that the basic idea of a proper marriage was that the father or guardian of the girl should freely select the bridegroom on account of his qualifications and no party should be influenced by any consideration of wealth which the other may give.

The various stages of the marriage ceremony are as follows ;

1. The wooers formally go to the girls' house.

2. When the bride's father has given his formal consent, the bridegroom performs a sacrifice

3. Early in the morning of the first day of the marrige celebration the bride is bathed.

4. A sacrifice is offered then by the high priest of the bride's family and a dance of four or eight women (not widow) takes place as part of the 'Indrani Karmana'.

5. The bridegroom then goes to the girl's house and makes the gift of a garment, unguent and mirror to the bride who has been bathed as mentioned already.

6. The 'Kanya Pradana' or the formal giving away of the bride now takes place, followeds:

   (a) By the 'Pani grahana - the clasping of the bride's right hand by the bridegroom with his right hand.

   (b) The treading on stone

   (c) The leading of the bride round the fire by the bridegroom.

   (d) The sacrifice of fried grains, the most important ceremony of all,

   (e) The 'Saptapadi' - the couple walking seven steps together as symbolic of their life long concord, Finally the bride is taken to her new house. Marriage is not a contract. It is the inititiation of a life-long journey of the two in weal and woe. The prayers and rites of the ceremony clearly indicate that matrimony was a holy bond and not a contract and that progeny (especially male progeny) was the goal of marriage.

The women, however, held an honourable position in the household. That a life of merriment, song, and dance was not denied.

Some Dharmasutras treat of the widow right in the property of the husband, the possibility of general prevalence of 'Sati system' is ruled out.

The Vasistha Dharmasutra speaks of the marriage of widow under certain circumstances and son of a remarried woman is one of the twelve sons enumerated in the Dharma sutras. So the marriage of a widow was not as strictly prohibited as it appears to have been in later days.

The custom of 'Niyoga' (levirate) or appointment of widow is recognised by the Dharma sutras which give detailed rules laying down the circumstances under which it is permissible. Some of the later Dharma Sutras however, condemned it.

It appears that the Dharma Sutras take a more lenient attitude towards woman than the Smritis of a later age or the customs and practices of the present day. In Boudhayana and Manu Smriti (IX, 81) there is injunction that a barren wife should be abandoned in the eighth year, whose children die after birth, in the tenth year, who bears only daughters, in the eleventh year, but who is quarrelsome without delay. But Apastamba forbids a husband to take a second wife unless the first wife has no male child or neglected her religious obligations. According to Vasistha, a wife should not be abandoned even though she be quarrelsome or tainted by sin, or has left the house, or has suffered criminal force, or has fallen into hands of thieves. Even a wife who has committed adultery, becomes pure and is taken back by her husband after she has done proper penances, Apastamba imposes severe punishment on a husband who unjustly forsakes his wife. On the other hand, a wife who forsakes her husband has only to perform a penance.

Age of Marriage : As regards the age of marriage, the prescriptions of the Grihyasutras differ. The older texts which describe the consumation of marriage as 'Chaturthi Karmana' or the ceremony of the fourth night (just after marriage) evidently imply that the bride is of mature age. The modern Grihyasutras and the Dharmasutras, however lay down the rule that the bride should be 'nagnika' (naked) i.e. one who has not yet had the monthly period or one whose breasts are not yet developed.

The evidence of the Mahavarata is in favour of the marriage of well developed and grown up girls. It means consumation was a part of marriage ceremony.

The Ramayana in one passage (Aranya Kanda) states that Sita was of six and Rama was of thirteen years at the time of marriage. But other and more reliable passages indicate that Sita was fully developed at the time. In the Mahabharata also there are passages (Anusasana Parva) which mention the age of the bride and bridegroom as 10 and 30 or 7 and 20 as the proper age.

There was a tendency in Sutra texts to lower the age of marriage of girls. Manu prescribes, man of 30 to marry a girl of 12 or a man of 24 to marry a girl of 8.

It may be concluded that while child marriage was gradually coming into vogue, the older custom of marriage at a mature age was neither uncommon nor regarded with disapproval. If a father failed to give her daughter in due time and the mature girl remain unmarried, the girl could find out her own husband after waiting for 3 months to 3 years.

Yajnabalkya insisted that a girl should be married before she attains puberty.

It has been suggested by some that the rules of Smritis about early marriage of girls applied only to the Brahmanas and not to other castes.

The lowering of marriagable age of woman was detrimental to general education and culture of women. Extreme emphasis on physical chastity of women and their unquestioned loyalty to respective husbands affected other aspects of their life. The result was gradual deterioration of the position and status of the class.

During the period 600 BC to 320 AD, the final stage of the deterioration did not reach. It may be taken as a transitional period.

One thing must be mentioend in this context that in the literature of this period different pictures of woman are reflected. One view (as reflected in verses) hold that the woman as a class should ever remain in subjugation during girlhood under father, in youth under husband and in old age under sons. In other set of verses we see woman is the glory of the home - the symbol of prosperity and fortune. She is the better half of the husband - friend, philosopher and guide.

It is very difficult to explain Manu in this context. He says that Gods are pleased with those houldholds where women are held in honour and that a husband should be punished by the King, if he casts off his wife who is not guilty of any crime causing loss of caste. (III 55-59, VIII 389). At the same time he lays down that the husband has absolute right on her wife. A wife has to worship her husband etc. (V-147, 154)

During the first half of the period from 600 BC to 320 AD, there were highly educated women holding honourable position in the society and household.

Two classes of women students are mentioned - Brahmabadini and Sudyodwaha. The first group was a life long student of sacred texts and the second group prosecuted studies till marriage.

The Buddhist and Jaina texts also refer to women of Brahmabadini class. They remaiend unmarried. Their songs are preserved in Therigatha.

Besides, the women generally received training in fine arts like music, dancing and painting. Some of them went for military training also as mentioned by Patanjali (2nd Century BC).

Formerly the girls went through Upanayana ceremony like the boys. But this gradually came to be formal. Manu prescribes the Upanayana of girls. But that should be performed without recitation of sacred texts. [II. 66].

In contrast to this, Buddhism and Jainism offered a more honourable career to women. A large number of woman became nuns and famous preachers.

The growing of importance attached to physical chastity explains the gradual discouragement of widow remarriage, divorce, levirate and encouragement of the system of 'Sati'.

Divorce : We learn from Kautilya's Arthasastra that divorce or repudiation was not unknown or uncommon in Bharata. [The period of Kautilya is much debated. In the 2nd volume of History of Culture of the Indian People edited by R. C. Majumdar, there is a long discussion on Kautilya. He may be of 4th Century BC or 300 AD. He was the Minister and Advisor if Chandragupta the emperor (323 BC to 300 BC). The Indian tradition is unanimous that Arthasastra is the work of Kautilya who was known as Vishnugupta and Chanakya. The work - Arthasastra would thus be of 4th Century BC The divergence of opinion between Manu and Kautilya show the antiquity of the former. Manu's period is also debated. But it is somewhere between 200 BC to 200 AD. The Civil and Constittional laws explained by Kautilya are similar to those recorded by Megasthenes (4th Century BC)

According to Kautilya (Arthasastra) if a husband either is of bad character or is long gone to abroad, or has become a traitor to his king, or is likely to endanger the life of his wife, or has fallen from his caste, or has lost verility, he may be abandoned by his wife. (IX 32) Divorce on the ground of ill feeling was also allowed on mutual consent, but not at the will of one party. Kautilya places husband and wife almost on equal footing. This standing was not allowed by Manu - who is supposed to be of later period. Manu gives a long list of 'grounds' on which a husband could supersede his wife and then adds that a wife who, being superseded, departs from her husbands house in anger, must either be confined or cast off in the presence of the family. He also propounds that a wife thus superseded is not free from marital obligations, even if she is sold or repudiated by her husband (IX-46). Even if a wife shows disrespect to her husband for his bad or evil passion, shall be deserted for three months and be deprived of her ornaments and furniture.

These painful injunctions on wife relegates the woman folks to inferiority.

On the other hand Narada says that if a man leaves a wife who is of very good qualities and mother of a male child, the king shall make the husband mindful of his duties by inflicting severe punishment. Narada even propounds that when a faultless maiden is married to a man who has a blemish (unknown before marriage), the wife is permitted to leave him and repair to anothr. But her relatives should be made known and aware.

Regarding 'Niyoga' system (Levirate) Manu supports and lays down rules and regulation in one verse. In another verse he condemns it. Yajnabalkya, Vishnu and Narada permit it within certain limit.

Sati (Immolation on Husband's Pyre)

Mahabharata records a few cases of Sati. Madri burns herself on the funeral pyre of her husband Pandu. The bereaved wives of Krishna immolate themselves in Indraprastha after his death. The epic is silent regarding the fate of the widows of Duryodhana and numerous other Kings who died in this great war. In view of the testimony of Greek writers regarding the prevalance of this practice in Punjab, the possibility has to be conceded that the practice of Sati was confined to the warrior class.

Inspite of the barbarous aspect of the custom, it is interesting to note that sometime it was very much voluntary and that was practised by wives in eager delight. The testimony of the Greek writers : In 316 BC, the leader of an Indian contingent having two wives died in battle in Iran. Both the wives were eager to immolate themselves on his funeral pyre. The Macedonian and Greek generals prevented the elder wife who was with child and gave permission to the younger. [Diodorus XIX 34, quoted in Cambridge History of India Vol-I P-415 and History and Culture of the Indian People Vol-2, P-568].

In modern age, we came to know of this barbarous custom and the fight of Rammohan Roy which culminated in passing of an Act in 1829 prohibiting the custom. It may be annexed that in later age every 'Sati' was not voluntary.

In this connection a reference should be made about a class of courtesans who enjoyed a social status not accorded to them anywhere else in the world, save perhaps in ancient Athens.

The story of Amrapali (Ambapati) is known to many - through Vinaya texts. She was the daughter of a rich man of Vaisali, named Mahama. Many suitors sought her hand. Her father brought the matter to the notice of the Lichchhavi 'Gana' and it was discussed by the Assembly. The Assembly decided that she was not to be married to anybody but was to be enjoyed by the 'Gana'. Amprapali agreed to lead the life of a public woman, but asked for fine privilages which were granted. Amrapali was exceedingly charming and accomplished in all the sixty four Kalas.

King Bimbisara and even Gautama Buddha were acquainted with Amrapali.

Kautilya in Artha Sastra says that a prostitute noted for her beauty, youth and accomplishments was to be appointed superintendent of prostitutes on a salary of 1000 Panas (per annum) ; together with a rival prostitute on half that salary. The prostitutes had to attend courts and were regularly employed in the royal household on a big salary. They held the royal umbrella, golden pitcher and fan and attended upon the King seated on litter, throne or chariot. They were also employed in the store-house, kitchen, bathroom and harem of the King.

Kautilya tells us that those who teach prostitutes, female slaves and actresses, arts such as singing, dancing, acting, writing, painting, playing on the instruments like lyre, pipe, drum, reading the thoughts of others, manufacture of scents and garlands, shampooing and the art of attracting and captivating the mind of others, shall be endowed with maintenance from the state. The courtesans as a class were not held in odium and neither great kings nor renowned religious teachers looked down upon them.

Conclusion : From the discussion on female education made so far, we can infer the position of woman in this period i.e. from 600 BC to 320 AD.

There is no hint to show that women as such occupied a position lower than that of men in Vedic Society. In intellectual life, they occupied the same position as men. Some of the Vedic poets were women. There were woman warriors who faught bravely in wars. There were also woman philosophers. Both Gods and Goddesses occupied the same position and rank in the religions of India. The complete equality between men and women is found in all parts of the Vedic literature, from Samhita to the Upanisads.

The position of women was not so in the later periods. It degenerated so deeply that in the 20th Century AD a slogan - 'empowerment of woman' was raised all over the World - specially in our land. We shall discuss the issue systematically along with the issue of female education.

Women were not denied eduation. Women teachers are called - upadhayi or upadhyaya, Acharya. They themselves were teachers and not wives of teachers. Panini has referred to women students.

The Ramayana tells of women who were Bhikshunis like Shramani Sabari (she was not a sabara), Jatila, Siddha, Tapasi with her Ashrama on the bank of Pampa river.

Women Educaiton in Buddhist System

There is a chapter on women Educaiton of this period. But Women Education in Buddhist system deserves special mention.

The very scheme and philosophy of life proposed by Buddhism would only regard women as objects to be shunned. Buddha himself was very much reluctant to admit women in the system. But the pressure from his foster mother Mahapajapati and his most favourite disciple Ananda, that he consented to admit women as his disciple on their renouncing the world and their house-holders' state.

The rules laid down for regulating their lives focus that they were considered inferior., The nuns were kept under complete subordination to the monks. The Order of nuns could not complete any transaction unless it was confirmed by the chapter of Monks. The probation period of a woman was as long as two years.

A monk specially selected by the brotherhood was to impart instructions and admonition to the nuns twice every month in the presence of another monk.

With all the restrictions based on the estimate of woman's worth, the Order of Nuns opened up avenues of culture and social service to the woman of Buddhist India. Some of them became very distinguished.

Women in Vedic Tradition

Women, it appears, were then considered as equal of men in their eligibility. Education was not denied to women. The Upanisads mention several women as teachers, but it is not clear whether they all were married excepting the wives of Yajnavalka. Brihadaranyaka Upanisad mentions an interesting ritual by which a person prays for the birth to him of a daughter who should be a pandita-a learned lady. The Kausitaki Brahmana tells of a lady proceeding to the north for study and obtaining the title of Saraswati (Vak) by her learning.

Women were admitted to full religious rites and consequently to complete educational facilities. The wife was a regular partcipator in the sacrificial offerings of the husband. [Rig Veda : (i) 122-2, 131-3, (iii) 53 - 4 - 6, (v) 43 - 15, (viii) 31, 5 (x) 86.10 Please Read as Mondal Sukta Rik respectively].

Women sages were called Rishika and Brahmabadini. The Rigveda knows of the following Rishikas - Romosa, Lopamudra, Apala, Kadru, Viswavara, Ghosa, Juhu, Vagambhrini, Paulomi, Jarita, Urvasi, Yami, Indrani, Savitri, Devajani. In Samveda Nodha, Akristavasa, Sikatanivavari, Ganpayana Brahmabadinis were the products of the educational discipline of Brahmacharya for which women were also eligible. In Rigveda there are instances, that young maidens completing their education as Brahmacharianis gain husbands in whom they are merged like rivers in occeans. Yajurveda states that a daughter who has completed her Brahmacharya should be married to one who is learned like her. The Atharvaveda refers to maidens qualifying by their Brahmacharya, the disciplined life of studentship, prepared for married life in the second Asharama.

Education and Upanayana of Women : The vedic tradition of women education continued in this period. The Rigvidic women Rsis, such as, Ghosa, Romasa, Lopamudra, Viswavara were called Brahma - Badinis. She is a Kumary - she does not marry. Harit says, women are of two clauses. (i) Brahma-Badini, (ii) Sadyo-Badini. The former is eligible for Upanayana. Agnyadhana (sacrifica to fire), Veda study and practice of begging within the household. The second class had only to perform Upanayana in some form before she is married.

Yama also says, "In times of yore, girls were eligible for Upanayana, the study of Veda and Savitri vachana.

The Srauta or Grihya sutras mention vedic mantras being uttered by the wife at ceremonies along with her husband. Gobila states that the wife should be educated to be able to take part in sacrifices. Again Adhikarana III of Chapter I of Jaiminis Purva Mimamsa is taken by Sabara Swami to deal with the equal rights of men and women in the performance of sacrifices. Madhavacharya says, "Brahmana boys of eight are to be initiated and taught and the same right also belongs to the girls."

Lastly, we may quote Himadri who says, "Kumaris, married girls, should be taught Vidya and Dharmaniti. An educated Kumari brings good to the families of her father and husband. So she should be married to a manishi (learned) husband as she is a Vidushi (learned woman).

[The references are all quoted from R. K. Mookerjee's book).

Status and Progress of Female Education in different periods of History

320 AD to 740 AD

Female Education : The ban on the vedic study by women and their utterance of vedic mantras, which was imposed by the older smrities, was continued. Harit Smriti divided women into two clases - students of the sacred lore Brahmacharinis and those who married straight way. This development led to reduce the marriage age of women. On the other hand, women of the Upper classes enjoyed such opportunities for education in the fine arts that some of them became accomplished poetesses and authorities on belle - letters. Princess Rajyasri (sister of Harsha Vrdhana), Avanti-Sundari (wife of Raja Sekhara), Kadambini and Mahasweta (Bana's prose romance), Kamandaki (in Bhababhuti's drama), seem to suggest the existence of institutions for girl's training. In the Jaina stories of a later period (10th Century) we are told how princesses were skilled in the art of painting, Music, versification etc,.

740 A.D. to 1000 A.D.

Female education in this period appears to be one of most disappointing.

Long before the present period, the smrities had denied the right or privilage of vedic study to women. By progressively sanctioning early marriage of girls, they further deteriorated the chances of higher education of women. In the contemporary lexicographical works the significant omission or absence of reference to women teachers, proves how backward was the state of higher education among girls. Medhatithi refers to the general ignorance of the Sanskrit language among the women. But we have reasons to believe that women of all classes had some opportunity for liberal education as well as training in the fine arts as was in the preceding Age - some princesses and daughters of high officials, courtezans and concubines had shown their merit in composing verses. The dramas and prose romances of this period also illustrate the contemporary state of learning among women. In the plays of Rajsekhara, we find that court ladies and even the queen's maid were capable of composing excellent Sanskrit and Prakrit verses. Rajsekhara's wife Avanti Sundari was an accomplished woman. In numbers of stories of this Age there are references of the skills of princesses in painting, music and versification.

While considering the education of women in this age, we are to take note of the marriageable age of girls. Medhatithi agrees with the views of the authorities of the preceeding age. Girls, says he, should be given away in marriage when they are 'nagnika' (six or eight years old). He again says that the right time of marriage of a girl is between her eighth year and her attaining puberty. The relative ages of the bridegroom and the bride laid down by Manu, must not be taken in literal sense - is the opinion of Medhatithi. He explains that one should marry - a girl very much younger than himself, such being the practice of cultured men.

The age of marriage of girls being so seriously fixed, it was not at all possible to offer higher education to women. There is to reference of elementary education of women.

1000 A.D. - 1200 A.D.

We have no special reference regarding the education of girls in this period. Independence of women was never admitted. But the interest of wives, even if guilty of adultery, was always looked after. The laws relating to supersession and abandonment of the wife had a strong tendency to emphasise the interest of the wife. Wife's right to maintenance and living in the house of the husband were always secured. A husband wrongfully deserting his good wife should be punished like a thief by the king.

The religions and social inferiority of the women were accepted. Harit classifies women into two classes, namely, those who are students of the sacred lore and those who marry straight away. The former were entitled to the investiture of the sacred thread, offering sticks to the fire, Vedic study and begging within the house hold. There is reference to female teachers - Upadhyaya, Acharya, Upadhyayi.

Inspite of the accepted doctrine that women are inferior relating to religious and social matters, we find some commendable women rulers in this period. Some one or two of them with male names and adminstered Kingdom. This is found in the Deccan and South India. There is an instance in Kashmir, Suryamati, queen of King Ananta commanded influence upon the administration of the state. There are instances in Chalukya dynasty of Kalyana, the queen of Someswara I and the queen of Vikramaditya VI of Chalukya dynasty ran administration. In the latter half of the 13th Century, queen Ballamahadevi of the Alupa dynasty (South Canara distt.) ruled for at least 14 years with the masculine titles of Maharajadhiraja. Queen Rudramba bearing the male name of Rudradeva Maharaja ruled the Kakatiya kingdom for nearly 40 years.

1526 A.D. - 1765 A.D.

Women's education was not completely ignored. But no regular separate schools for girls seems to have existed for imparting education to women folks. The girls usually had their lessons from their parents. Girls in their childhood attended schools along with boys and learnt the Quran (if mahamedan) and one or two other lessons by rote. The rich appointed tutors to teach their daughters at home.

The daughters of Rajput Chiefs and some Bengali Zamindars were usually able to read and write.

Special Care was taken for the education of Mughal Princesses, almost all of whom daily read the Quran and occassionally corresponded with their relatives. Some of them even composed verses. Regular studies of the princesses ended after marriage which took place at an early age. As a result, their education remained unfinished and incomplete. For example, Gulbadan Begum dared writing Humayun-nama abounds with spelling mistakes and clumsy sentences. The poems of Zib-un-Nisa and Zinat-un-Nisa do not rise so high in poetic excellence as those of the contemporary male authors.

There is, however, little doubt about the literacy of the average middle class women who had sufficient knowledge of Hindu, Persian or native provincial language to enable them to study the religious scriptures. [But many consider this generation of education of women to be doubtful]

The knowledge of Sanskrit was wide spread in the South. A Malayalam work - Chandrotsavan gives us an idea about the general reading of educated women in the South and this includes - Sakuntalam, Malavikagnimitram and other Sanskrit dramas.

A well known work of the period entitled - Mahilamriduvani, gives us a list of 35 women who were not minor poets.

Special stress was laid on the education of the widows, some of whom became teachers. [Ref. Article by P. N. Chopra as published in the History and culture of the Indian people (H.C.I.P.) Vol-7, P-703-709].

1835 - 1854 A.D.

By the end of the 18th century a woman's position in the society was almost that of an appendage to the male. The social system denied women education. This denial was reinforced by the spread of a superstition among the majority of the Hindu families that education for a woman was likely to result in her widowhood. Women were denied the freedom of an outdoor life. The only justification for her existenace was that She was previlaged to cater the needs of husband and his family. There was early marriage of women. There was multi-marriage of men. Number of widows under 15 years of age was many.

The process of progressive deterioration of Hindu women in India was to a large extent due to Muslim rule in India. The Muslims married Hindu girls and Hindu Society did not like Muslim association as they considered Muslims as Mlechchas.

During the 1st half of the 19th Century, some members of the aristocrat society guided simply by consideration of management of estates, and the christian Missioneries prompted by their zeal of propagation of Christanity through conversion, took interest in female educaiton. The East India company remained indifferent to it.

A picture of the abjectly low position to which women had been degraded in the early part of the 19th century may also be had from the writings of two pioneers who were most interested in the ameleoration of the condition of women in society. They were Raja Rammohan Roy (1772-1833) and the other was Pandit Iswar Chandra Vidyasagar (1820-1891).

From Adam's Report (1835-38) it is learnt that women education was the least important issue of the society and the rulers.

Adam found only 4 literate women against 21907 men in a total population of 496574. This is regarding Bengal.

Things appear to be no better in Bombay where Elphinstone made an enquiry in 1823. No girl pupil was attending the indigenous schools.

Munro's enquiry in Madras in 1822, revealed that "the women of the Rajabundah and among some other tribes of Hindus, were generally taught. The return of the indigenous schools showed as many as 5480 girls in a total enrolement of 184110.

In Punjab there were special schools for girls in charge of women teachers.

For the rest of India, nothing is known. On the whole, therefore, it may be concluded that excepting an extremely small number of women who received some education in the family or in the school, almost the whole female population of the country was deprived of education.

It appears that it was in August 1818, the movement for the abolition of 'Sati' system (the wife has to sacrifice herself in the funeral pyre of the husband) was taken up by right earnest. Rammohan Roy took a leading Part. A petition was submitted to the Governor, signed by a large number of the most respected inhabitants of Calcutta. After a few years the issue was reopened at the instance of the Judges of Nizamat Adalat. Lord Amherst declined to intervene though he considered 'Sati' as a 'detestable superstition.'

Lord Bentinck passed a Regulation dated 4 December, 1829, prohibiting the practice of 'Sati'. It was declared 'illegal' and punishable by the Criminal Courts.

The company avoided the issue of education of women simply by saying that the prejudice against the education of women which prevailed among the people was so deep rooted in their social and religious life that any attempt to educate women would create a very great commotion and the first attempt of the company should be restricted to the education of men who would themselves, at a later date, undertake the education of their women folk.

Bentinck courageously prohibited Sati system and after him Lord Dalhousi (1848-1856) decided that open patronage of government should be extended to the education of women. It relates to his order dated 11th April, 1850, a portion of which reads:

"It is the opinion of the Governor General in Council that no single change in the habit of the people is likely to lead to more important and beneficial consequences than the introduciton of education for their female children. The general practice is to allow them to grow up in absolute ignorance, but this custom is not required or even sanctioned by their religion and in fact a certain degree of education is now given to the female relatives of those who can afford the expenses of entertaining special instructors at their own houses.

The Governor General in Council requests that the Council of Education may be informed that it is hence forth to consider its functions as comprising the superintendence of native female education, and that wherever any disposition is shown by the natives to establish female schools, it will be its duty to give them all possible encouragement and further their plans in every way that is not inconsistant with the efficiency of the institution already under their management. It is also the wish of the Governor General in Council that intimation to the same effect should be given to the Chief Civil Officers of the Mofussil calling their attention to the growing disposition among the native to establish female schools and directing them to use all means at their disposal for encouraging those institutions and for making it generally knwon that the Government views them with very great approbation." [Selection from Educational Records Vol-II P-59-60]

This view was subsequently confirmed by Wood's Despatch 1854. Just a year back of this Declaration of Lord Dalhousi in April 1850, on 7th May 1849, Calcutta Female School was established by J. E. D. Bethun with the help of Iswar Chandra Vidyasagar who managed this institution after the sudden death of Bethun. Bethun himself was a Law Member of the Governor General's Council and also the President of Council of Education. It was the first school of its kind. To commemorate Bethun's name, it was named Bethun school which subsequently was raised to the status of a college.

Vidyasagar was famous for his Learning and Donating. He was a reformer of all - Religious, Social, Educational practices and so on. His deep sympathy for the women folks was so realised by the Poet Madhusudan that he said, Vidyasagar has the heart and feeling of a Bengali mother. He was then the Principal of Sanskrit College and reorganised it in every way. He was given the charge of female education in the 4 districts of Bengal - Medinipur, Hooghly, Nadia and Burdwan as the special Inspector of Schools (at first as Asst. Inspector). He had set up 35 girls schools in 5 months (Nov. 1857-May 58). He even advanced money from his own pocket. The speed of Vidyasagar, probably irritated the then Director of Public Instruction W. Gordon Young. His relation embittered with Vidyasagar. Out of disgust and for the rarest sense of self-respect Vidyasagar resigned. But continued his eduational efforts and reforms according to his own line of thinking which was practically inconcievable at that period of time and from a man of authority in Sanskrit. He made English a compulsory subject and had the partinence and knowledge to utter that Samkhya and Vedanta were false philosophies. He fought for widow remarriage and won it. He fought against child marriage and multimarriage of Hindu Males. But before he could attain any success, the upsurge of 1857 happened which made the Britishers cautious and afraid of interfering prevailing system.

1854 - 1947 A.D.

Women's education made steady progress though slow, during the period inspite of predicaments discussed above. Though in Primary schools the number of girls was encouraging, in higher classes only middle class and upper middle class could be found. The early marriage of girls was a factor though, the syllabus which was more intellectual and theoretical, did not attract the guardians as these did not help a girl in her father-in-law's house in future. Moreover, during that period of time, a highly educated i.e. matriculate or college girls were not so favourite with the old fashioned father-in-laws and mother-in-laws who were habituated to avoid such girls as their daughter-in-laws. So a girl's father had to face problem to get her daughter married.

As compared with the previous period, the number of girls students increased in every stage. But the total number of girls was very small compared to boys.

In India the ratio of male female was - male 1000, female 935 in 1941 census. The number of women who could read and write was only 1.1 percent and male 11.3 percent in 1911. In 1921 it was female 1.8, male 13.6 percent.

The reservation regarding girls' education in the minds of the people (young and old) began to dilute gradually. So the position was found improved in this period. Let us consider the following figures.

Total No. of girls under Instruction		
1937-38	3012212	
1941-42	3726876	
1946-47	4297785	
	No.of girls colleges General and Professional	No. of girls students
1937-38	41	3810
1941-42	58	6072
1946-47	91	10315

A new feature in women's education developed and that was co-education. Divergent opinions were expressed in favour and against this new feature. The general trend of opinion seems to have been that girls of the age group 13-18 should be educated in separate institutions. Many favoured the idea of separate colleges also.

The Hartog Committee (An auxilliary com. appointed by Simon Commission which was presided over by Sir Philip Hartog) in 1927-28 observed.

"In recent years repeated demands have been made by representative Women's association for the differentiation of the curruculum in girls schools from that adopted in boys' schools. The first All-India Women's conference on Education Reforms, held at Poona in 1927, recommended alternative courses for those who do not want to take up college education - domestic science, fine arts, handicrafts and industries. Similar recommendations were made by other conferences. In Primary Schools separate optional for girls are common. In secondary schools separate alternative courses are less common. Little has been done to provide alternative courses in the universities."

The Radhakrishnan Com. observed : (1948)

Some of the arguments given are a women cannot develop her personality in the man's college : that there is no need for women to undergo the nervous strain of examinations : that women's education should be more in keeping with the temparament and needs of women as wives and mothers: and that over crowding is more serious for women than for men."

On the other hand it was argued that separate college for women would mean unnecessary increase in expenditure and were likely to be, in many cases, poor or inferior duplicates. Further, a healthy association and competition of grils with boys in academic fields would perhaps be beneficial to the development of personality and character of both. As a matter of fact, both the systems, separate college for girls and co-education were in vogue during the period under review. Co-education was almost a necessity in the post-graduate stage and number of girl students in post graduate as well as Degree classes had been steadily on the increase. But co-education being, comparatively speaking, a recent innovation, the system had many defects. At the end of the period under review, as would appear from the following observations made by the Radhakrishnan commission.

"There are truly few co-educational colleges in our country. Rather, there are men's colleges to which women have been admitted as students, which is a very different matter. Quite frequently in co-education colleges nearly all the facilities are for men and women are little more than tolerated. Often sanitary facilities for women are totally inadequate and sometimes wholly lacking. Recreation space and facilities for women similarly are inadequate or lacking."

[Ref. : Radhakrishnan Com. Report P-399].

Question was raised about the common curriculum for men and women. Here again, the opinions sharply differed. The commisison in its report cited several opinions on the issue. The Principal of a college wrote: "Women's present education is entirely irrelevant to the life they have to lead. It is not only a waste but often a definite disability." Another wrote, "The present system of women's education, based as it is on man's needs, does not in any way make them fit for coping with the practical problems of daily life. Their education should give them a practical bias, specially from the point of view of families, for making them good mothers, doctors and nurses." (Radhakrishnan Committee)

On the other hand, among girls gradually growing tendency of being equal to men, or to surpass them was found. But women who were of advanced age, were in favour of a special curriculum suitable for women. We have already cited the observation of the Hartog committee.

It is not easy to reconcile the two objectives that (1) the education of the grils will be similar to that of the boys and (2) the girls should have a separate curriculum. The solution may be this that subjects said to be suitable for girls be included in the curriculum and allow the girls and their families to select the subjects. One important but often unnoticed fact is that in 1928 there were in British India nearly 600 Companies and Flocks with an enrolement of 10 thousands Guides and Blue Birds - it was the result of Girl-Guide Movement in the country.

1947 - 1975 A.D.

In the post-ibndependence period the issue of women education received an impetus, and a good deal of progress was made. The enrolment of girls in 1960-61, was considerably higher than 1949-50.

In 1949-50, enrolment of girls per 100 boys was 33 but in 1960-61 the enrolment of girls per 100 boys increased to 42. The enrolment increased not only in Primary sector, almost in all sectors - Primary, Secondry, University, Professional and Vocational.

But before 1960, Govt. of India appointed a National Committee for Women educatin under the Chairmanship of Smt. Durgabai Deshmukh. The committee was advised to go deep into the difficulties that deterred the progress of female education and to make recommendations regarding the manner in which the education of girls could be brought at par with the boys, specially at the primary and secondary stages.

The Committee recommended among others, the following most important ones:

(1) The education of women should be regarded as a special issue and for some years special fund to be provided.

(2) There should be a National Council for the Education of women at the Centre and similar Council in states, and Union Territories. The main object of these councils will be to educate the public and advise the Govts. the measures to be taken.

(3) There should be a special unit in the Govt. of India to look after the programmes of girls education and in each state Department of education, a special officer should be appointed at the Directorate level. The existing Inspectorate for Girls schools should also be considerably stengthened.

(4) It is necessary to develop a large number of special programmes for bringing about a rapid expansion in the education of girls. The most important of these are the preparation and employment of women teachers and provision for special amenities for girls, such as grant of free books, writing materials, scholarship, clothing or provision for mid-day meals.

The major recommendations have been accepted by the Govt. In 1959 a National Council for the Education was set up under the Chairmanship of Smt. Durgabai Deshmukh. Most of the State Govts. have appointed Asst. Director or Deputy Director incharge of Women education. The strength of Inspectress has increased. Special fund has been allotted.

The Central social welfare Board has adopted a scheme of condensed course for adult women (18-35 age group) who once had to give up education but now had been interested. Through this condensed course such intending women may qualify themselves as teachers, nurses, midwives etc. The training is of two to three years.

Data on Women Education

Enrolment in Institutions

Institution	1921-22	1931-32	1941-42	1946-47
Primary School	10871312	1944070	3123643	2715230
Secondary School	124959	196170	410333	442403
Arts & SC Colleges	1207	2685	11778	16284
Professional Colleges	266	521	1725	2468
Profession Schools	19570	17568	40869	38375

[**Source :** Indian Edu. quoted from S. N. Mukherjee's Education in India Today and Tomorrow P-255].

In 1904 Mrs. Annie Besant established Central Hindu Girls school at Benaras with a view to impart Western Education to girls. In 1916 Lady Hardinge Medical College was established in Delhi. The S. N. D. T.

university (see ante) for women was established. In 1917 there were 12 Arts Colleges, 4 Professional Colleges and 1656 Secondary Schools for girls.

The women's movement in contemporary Europe had an influence. Mrs. Annie Besant and Mrs. Margaret Cousins founded **Women's Indian Association** in 1917. In 1925 the National Council of Women was established. It flourished and got affiliated to Internaitonal Council of Women.

In 1927 was held for the first time, All India Women's conference. this conference agitated issues like equal opportunities of education, education of women and amilioration of women's social position.

The National Movements in India and participation of Women in large numbers, highlighted the issue of Women education.

No. of girls Institutions & enrolment

	1947-48	*1960-61*
Institutions	16951	41674
Enrolment	3550503	14259047

From the data available from Govt. of India - programme for Educational Development 1961-66, it will be evident that there was a rapid progress and girls were enrolled in different institutions.

	1949-50	*1959-60*
1. Research	85	657
2. M.A., M.Sc	1656	7679
3. B.A., B.Sc, Intermediate	23540	76643
4. Prof. Edu.	4055	22246
5. Spl. Edn.	771	6570
6. Vocational Edn.	35760	78097
7. School Edn. different stages	575553	12464688

Droup-out is a serious problem in Indian Educational frame. It causes wastage. But the socio-economic condition compels pupils to drop from school education in every stage. This is more evident in girls cases. If the drop out is the result of poverty, the girls drop out is the result fo social system i.e. to give them in marriage at an early age. This affects the number of women's availability as teachers nurses etc.

A meeting of Education Ministers of India was held (may be in 1961 or 1963, the report was published in Times of India on 15 Nov, 1963). The conference suggested:

1. Construction of quarters for women teachers
2. Hostels for girls in rural areas
3. Free education to girls at least upto secondary stage
4. Improvement of training facilities for women.

and so mamy such suggestions. In case of drop-outs (discontinuance of study) it was learnt that 100 pupils admitted in Class I and only 41 of them reached Class IV. This wastage was more prominent in case of girls.

The initial inspiration of getting admitted to school and having education of the girls, was remarkably encouraging which is evident in the following data :

Enrolment Picture

Year	Class VI-VIII	Class IX - XI
1950-51	5.3 lakhs	1.90 lakhs
1955-56	8.7 lakhs	3.32 lakhs
1960-61	14.7 lakhs	5.27 lakhs

[**Source :** Education in India 1959-60]

Output of Girls in University Examination

	1949-50	1959-60
Intermediate	8252	25091
B.A. and B.Sc	4694	18554
M.A and M.Sc	744	4186
Professional Subjects	1232	6166

[**Source :** Edn. in India 1960-61]

Besides, the S.N.D.T. Women University, The Prayag Mahila Vidyapith, Allahabad, had separate special courses for girls and Degrees it offers are also different. It was established in 1922 and aims at spreading girls education. The examinations held by the Vidyapith are : Pravesika, Vidya-Vinodini, Sugrihini, Vidushi, Saraswati and Bharati. The Arya Kanya Mahavidyalaya at Baroda is a residential one. It lays great stress on physical activities.

It was felt that girls should have a special type of course of study. So, Home Sciences as a subject was adopted in 24 Universities.

During the period under review there were 75 colleges teaching this subject. In 8 colleges, Post-graduate courses in the subject are taught. Those 8 are : Faculty of Home Science, Baroda, Lady Irwin College, New Delhi, St. Thresa Colleges, Ernakulum, Queen Mary's College, Madras, Women's Christian College, Madras, SIET Women's College, Madras,

Sri Avinashilingam Home Science College at Coimbatore and Maharani's College for Women, Bangalore.

Though Women are receiving and have been receiving training in various subjects, their largest enrolment can be found in teachers' training institutions. In the professional field Nursing is practically a monopoly of women. In 1946, two colleges were set up. The Nursing Council was constituted under the Nursing Council Act of 1947. The third and fourth nursing colleges were set up in 1959 and 1961. Now many Nursing Colleges for training have been set up.

A scheme for technical education and vocational training for girls has been drawn up by the Govt. of India under which competent authorities may establish - polytechnics, technical schools and integrated institution for girls.

Women workers are needed in community Development Project. Each Block needs one Mukhya Sevika, two Gram Sevikas, one Health Visitor (lady), four midwives. Centres for their training have been set up. The training period is of few months only.

Lastly, we must be very much clear about the ideals of women education. The old idea is, a women's place is home and hearth and they should be so educated. The modern view is, women are equal with men. So they will cover all aspects and not be confined to home and hearth.

Whatever view is taken, one thing must be kept in mind that women in India, have some traditional ideals to guide and inspire them. Probably, there are a few country in this world which have this heritage. Moreover, in India marriage is not a contract, as it is found else where. Modernity should not mean that one has to give up one's own national cultural heritage and immitate a foreign culture. The Indian women must be Indian and the content of education should be such that they do not fall prey to foreign culture in the name of modernity.'

1975 to 2002 AD

Female Literacy

As per Census 2001, 30 districts in U.P., Bihar and Orissa are identified where the female literacy is below 30 percent. These districts have sizeable population of women from weaker section and the minorities.

In U.P. nearly 100 NGOs were involved in an accelerated programme of female literacy. Approximately, 20 lakhs women are undergoing literacy classes in 1.25 lakhs centres.

In Bihar, the lieracy programme has focused on involvement of women volunteers including a sizeable number from minorities. Roughly 30 lakhs women are undergoing literacy classes in about 2.5 lakh centres in 15 districts.

In Orissa approximately 8 lakhs women are being made literate in 7 low-female literacy districts.

Foreigners who visited India at diffierent times and wrote about India and referred to in this book

1. Megasthanis : 300 BC
2. Fa-Hien : 399 - 414 A.D
3. Hiuen Tsang : 629 - 645 A.D.
4. I-Tsing : 673 - 687 A.D.
5. Al-Biruni : 973 - 1048 A.D.
6. Utbi : Secretary to Mamud of Ghazni
7. Marco-polo : 1290 A.D.
8. Ibn-Batuta : 1304-1384 A.D.
9. Zia-u-din Baruni : 1320 - 1412 during Tughluk Dynasty
10. Badauni : 1540 - 1615 A.D. (Jahangir)
11. Feristha : 1570 - 1612 A.D.
12. Pacs : 1581 A.D.
13. Travernier : 1605 - 1690 A.D.
14. Bermier Time of Shajahan 1620 - 1625
15. Mannuci : Italian - Venice. Physician to emperor - Aurangzeb 1639 - 1717.

Thinkers on Education in modern India

It is believed and said that a man and a nation is know by the educational philosophy and educational system followed.

That Bharatvarsha boasts of good monarchs, strong emperors, brave generals and commanders, highly intellectual and philosophical pandits, scientists, literatures of excellence, traders, sailors, soldiers, workmen and above all a high sense of value that monitored the life of beggar to emperor, are the products of education in Bharatvarsha - an education which was all time free from any political bias or dependence.

Bharatvarsha is and has been a land of thinkers and philosophers. In modern India, there were stalwarts whose philosophy on education and the practice of that philosophy had deep significance. The pity is, modern India and India after independence cared a little of these indigenous thinkers and their philosophy on education. Some of them had established institutions of their own where they followed what they believed and propouned. But their ideas never became a part and parcel of National Education System.

Modern India has an elaborate system of education. But as to 'national system' there is a void as our leaders were not and are not unanimous on what is meant by 'National'.

However, in this chapter of this book, we shall mention only a few of 18th to 20th Century educational thinkers - who had a philosophy and who had followed the prophased philosophy with individual initiative. To mention chronologically, they are :

(1)   Rammohan Roy : 1772/74 - 1833.

(2)   Pandit Iswar Chandra Bandyopadhyaya known as Vidyasagar: 1820 - 1891

(3)   Swami Dayananda Saraswati : 1825 - 1883

(4)   Kesab Chandra Sen : 1838 - 1884

(5)   Dhando Kesab Karve : 1858 - 1962

(6)   Rabindranath Thakur : 1961 - 1941

(7)   Swami Vivekananda : 1863 - 1902

(8)   Mohandas Karamchand Gandhi : 1869 - 1948

(9)   Sri Aurobindo : 1872 - 1950

(10)   Kanaiyalal Maneklal Munsi : 1891 - 1971

(11)   Jiddu Krishna Murthy : 1895 - 1986

Of course there were many who worked strenneounsly to spread education among people. There were many who contributd largely for education of woman folks. We have referred to Gokhle who first tried to introduce compulsory free primary education. There was Madan Mohan Malvya whose contribution to build up Benaras Hindu University is historic.

It is to be noted with great respect that the educational thinkers were always related to social reforms. Education, though by itself a social reformation, yet there were remarkable ones who took up social reformation as a separate cause along with education.

Raja Rammohan Roy, Pandit Iswar Chandra Vidyasagar, Swami Dayananda were educationists and social reformers. They all faught against superstition, caste system, social degeneration and religious bigotry and took it for granted that spread of education only can counter and stop all these evils.

(1) Rammohan Roy (1772/74 - 1833) was a scholar in Sanskrit, Persian, Urdu, Arabic, Bengali and English. He well knew Greek, Latin, Hebru. Thus he was well acquainted with nine languages and mastery over six. He was out and out a religious reformer and social reformer. He could think of Internationalism when the British concept of Nationalism did not develop in India. To him education and education only, could save India from social degeneration, religious bigotry, superstition and idolatory. He wanted English education in India and tried for it. He of his own initiative established an anglo-Hindu school (1822) in Calcutta. As an educationist, he wanted Western Science and literature are to be learnt by Indians. It was the time when history records the big debate between Orientalists and Anglicists. He wanted a blending of Oriental Wisdom and Western Science. He, as a result incurred the wrath of his own country men.

Of his social reforms movement he is known as one who could abolish the inhuman practice of Sati (immolation of wife's life in the funeral pyre of husband) by convincing the British Govt. which enacted a law in 1829 prohibiting sati and declared it to be an offence of Criminal nature.

He fought incessantly against child marriage, polygamy. He fought for women's right to property and education. Liberty of Press was his another important agenda to fight with.

Rammohan believed in Divine worship. Brahma is the cause of everything we find or understand. So, Brahma is to be worshipped and Brahma has no image.

He established Brahma Samaj in Calcutta in 1813 and man or woman of any other belief could join the prayer of Brahmo Samaj.

Though by heart he was an orientalist, he was the first among the Indians of his time, who invited Western education in Indian Education system.

1. He was free from all superstition, casteism and bigotry of any kind. He was a philosopher and rationalist. He cared nothing but reason, rationality and humanism. His deepest faith in Brahmo made him a great soldier to fight against any evil and his fight to establish good in society.

2. Iswar Chandra Vidyasagar (1820-1891) was known as Vidyasagar (Ocean of Learning) for his scholarship in Sanskrit Language, literature, grammar and scriptures. But he was well-versed in English and Hindi. He had a soft heart for the woman-folk and had sympathy for everyone who

used to come to him in distress. So he was popularly known as Dayar Sagar (Ocean of Kindness). He had a strange habit of incurring loan to donate a man in distress.

His self-respect was unimaginable. He gave up a salary of Rs. 500, a post of a principal and a post as an Inspector of Schools for the sake of his self-respect.

He was a man of invincible manliness and indelible humanity. His character was uncompromising. He did not compromise with his British Bosses, not with his best friends, not with his only son and wife and even not with his mother - who was his only Goddess on this earth and she is the one to whom only he bowed. He never compromised in the matter of Principle.

Vidyasagar fought for education social reforms, rights and education of women. For his non-compromising attitude - he was a lone traveller. He himself was an army and did win all the battles he fought.

He was successful in each of his activities excepting a law on prohibiting polygamy and child marriage. The Sipoy war of 1857, cautioned the British and they stopped interfering social reforms of the country. But Vidyasagar was successful to introduce widow marriage law in 1856 as Rammohan was successful in abolishing 'Sati' by an enactment in 1829.

In the field of education he invited Western Philosophy and science in the education syllabus of India. He was the man who declared Vedanta and Sankhya as false philosopies. But he was an authority in Sanskrit literature and Sanskrit scriptures.

For women education he established schools and induced the British Government to establish schools for women education.

3. Swami Dayananda Saraswati (1825 - 1883) known as Maharsi Dayananda. He was a scholar in Sanskri and had mastered the Vedas. He was a Sannyasi. He opposed early marriage of girls and advocated education for girls. He founded an organisation named Arya Samaj to eradicate social evils. Though in 1875 he founded his orgaisation in Bombay, he established many schools for girls in North India.

4. Kesabchandra Sen (1838 - 1884) was better known as a follower of the philosophy propounded by Rammohan and that relates to social and religious reforms. Rammohan's 'Brahma Samaj' found its super expression through Kesab Chandra. He established Brahmo girls' School and society for Theistic Friends. Kesabchandra was an educationist and believed that social reforms greately depended on girls. So his prime interest in the field of education was - girls' school.

5. Dhando Kesav Karve (1858 - 1952). He started a university in Bombay for women for which he received a large donation from Sir Vithaldas Thackersey. The name of the university is Srimati Nathibai Damodar Thackersey (SNDT) University. It is the first of this kind in India.

6. Rabindranath Thakur (Tagore) (1861 - 1941) Chiefly known as a Bengal poet winning Nobel Prize, was a philosopher, patriot and founder of a new system of Education in India. His place of work was Shantiniketan at Birbhum Distt. in West Bengal which turned to a university known as Viswa Bharati University.

Rabindranath was an erudite scholar though never passed any examination from any school, college or university. He could find out the ailment in the sponsored education system and easily concluded that by that prevailing system a child can not grow out as a complete man.

Hence he devised or initiated an education system that could build up a complete man.

Primarily he was sure that English as a medium of instruction to Indian students was not helpful. This causes schism in society, so a child should be instructed through its mother-tongue.

He set up a school at Shantiniketan in 1901 and the school was in close proximity with nature. It was like a boarding school where teachers and students willingly lived in the same campus. It was called Brahmacharyashram or Ashram.

From this Ashram of 1901 was born Viswa Bharati - a university of international character in 1918. His views on Education is revealed in his own words.

"In every nation, education is intimately associated with the life of people. For us modern education is relevant only to turning out clerks, lawyers, doctors, magistrates and policeman. This education has not reached the farmers, oilgrinders, nor the porter. No other educated society has been struck with such disaster. If even a truly Indian University is established, it must from the very beginning implement India's knowledge of economics, agriculture, health, medicine and all other everyday science from the surrounding villages. Then alone the school or university can become the centre of community's way of living. This school must practise agriculture, dairying and weaving using the best modern methods. I have proposed to call this schools - Viswa Bharati."

Rabindranath was interested in fusing Oriental and Western knowledge in our education system. But the universities in India were not doing that.

He was also dissatisfied that Indian Universitites and education of the country were not much interested in our national heritage and he was sorry to find that there was no intention to preserve our national heritage. He was pained to note that the total system of education had no or little connection with the life of the people of the country. He stressed much on mother tongue as medium of instruction.

For better financial condition of the peasants and people of rural area, he established another institution Sreeniketan. This was part of his education system. He also set up a cooperative society to help the peasants that they may take loan for agriculture and handicrafts.

His principles and ideology on education were revealed in his Shantiniketan, Sreeniketan and Biswa Bharati which are unmatched. But the Governments foreign or national - did not learn from this and did not accept as a policy of education.

7. Swami Vivekananda (1863 - 1902) whose original name was Narendra Nath Dutta is world famous for his address in the Parliament of Religions in Chikago (USA) in 1893. He established the idea that Hinduism - so long neglected by the World was the religion which is based on humanity and secularism. This religion does not discriminate but unite all people as they all are part of Divinity. So his theory was, one who serves man serves God - what ever be his method of worship.

Regarding education he declared that there is perfection in every individual, education can only manifest that perfection.

In his ideology the role of the teacher was the most important factor. Any Tom Dick Harry cannot be a teacher. The teacher has to work for the character - building of pupils. To him Religion is not separable from education, as it is a way of life. That Religion is not a method of worship. Religion is the faith in the Supreme power and to serve others is the best form of worship - which student must be taught. In his system of education he emphasised on reconciling modern knowledge with the ancient spiritual thought.

For the sake of sense - control and self-discipline he emphasised on Brahmacharya in student life. He wanted all round development of body and mind. Man making and character building were the objects of his education, as he proposed it. He advocated women education as he believed that an educated mother can rear up a child in proper direction.

He died at an early age and did found any educational institution on his philosophy. But the institutions he founded - Ramkrishna Math and

Ramkrishna Ashram run educational institution said to be founded on the philosophy of education of Swami Vivekananda.

8. Mohandas Karamchand Gandhi (1869 - 1948) was not satisfied with the British education system followed in India. He had his own idea and planning of education which he published in his own newspaper Harijan in 1937. The scheme was known as Basic Education - which has been discussed in Chapter X of this book. His scheme of Basic Education got a good support from the Government in Independent India. But now it is almost a given up system.

9. Sir Aurobindo Ghosh (1872 - 1950) had a definite goal on education and during his life time he started such education centre - Aurobindo Ashram in Pondicherry. Now, this Institution of internaitonal character is named Auroville and it is in Pondichery.

From his childhood he had his education in England. Coming back to India he started as an educationist and turned revolutionary to drive out the British from Indian soil.

His depth of study and knowledge was immeasurable. He studied French, German Greek, Latin, Italian besides English and his mother tongue Bengali. Though qualified otherwise, he did not care to be an ICS British officer in India. He was against the British rule in India. Maharaja Sayaji Rao Gaekoward of Boroda picked him for his University. He became a revolutionary. He left Calcutta for Pondicherry which was not under British domain. Since 1910, his life changed as one of spiritual man.

Education was of utmost importance to him. He was pained to note that institutions only try to develop intellectual faculty of a taught. To him education meant an integrated development of physical, mental, intellectual, psychic and spiritual aspects of a people. The syllabus of education should aim at that integration and the teachers had to work with this aim in view.

He emphasised Brahmacharya to increase heat (Tapas), light (Tejas), electricity (Vidyut and life-force (Orjas). The role of teacher and parents, to him was very significant. They were like gardeners helping young plants to grow. He believed that there is divinity in human beings, which is required to be kindded and broughtout.

The Auroville belongs to humanity where any one is free to live as a citizen of the world. It is the visioin of Aurobindo translated into action.

10. Kanhaiyalal Maneklal Munsi (1891 - 1971) known as K. M. Munsi, established Bharatiya Vidya Bhawan in 1938. It is a centre of promoting

national culture and education. This institution has a publishing house and published among others, The History and culture of Indian People (upto 1947) in eleven volumes of approximately 9000 pages in a period of 26 years under the efficient chief editorship of Dr. Ramesh Chandra Majumdar. This is the best available history of India in all its aspects that has been published yet.

K. M. Munsi has left a lasting legacy in culture and education. He was lawyer, freedom-fighter, creative writer, member of the Indian Constituent Assembly and Governor of Uttar Pradesh.

He was a nationalist out and out. He desired for a national education system which would blend oriental and western knowledge that would create an individual with deep love for humanity and nation of one's birth. But he could do little for his ideology of education.

11. Jiddu Krishnamurthy (1895 - 1986) was a philosopher per se. According to him, the purpose of education was to create a rounded individual - who would be capable of dealing with life as a whole. Education, according to him, must free the mind and spirit so as to make it soar on its own. Like Sri Aurobindo, he was for a 'integral education' system. He said, "Education should encourage self-observation and the experiencing in life as a whole, not to 'me' and 'mine' but to go above and beyond to discover 'real'. The teachers have to help the students to discover his inner resources and develop its strength and find out where his weaknesses were, so that he could develop in those areas. Teaching and education as a whole must be a way of life, more than a strategy for earning one's bread.

Sri Krishnamurthy established eight schools in different parts of the world.

[Indebted to the book - Education in India, P-123, by Padma Ramachandran and Vasantha Ramkumar].

Addition to : Four Thousand-years of Education in Bharatvarsha - A History.

Acknowledgement

1.   The History and Culture of the Indian People (HCIP), Pub. : Bhatiya Vidya Bhavan, Kulapati Munsi Marg, Bombay - 400 007, Volumes I to XI.

2.   The Cultural Heritage of India, Pub. : The Ramkrishna Mission (CHI) Institute of Culture, Calcutta, Vols - I to VIII

3. The Historyof India - As told by its own Historians (HIED) by Sri H. M. Elliot and John Dowson, Pub. : Low Price Publications, A-6, Nimri Commercial Centre, Near Ashok Vihar, Phase-IV, Delhi-110052, Vols 1 to 8.

4. India's contribution to World Thought and Culture, Pub. : Vivekananda Rock Memorial Committee, 2, Pillaiyar Koil Street, Triplicane, Madras-5.

5. Ancient Indian Education Brahamanical and Buddhist by Radhakumud Mookerji (RKM), Pub. : Motilal Banarasi Dass, Bunglow Road, Jawahar Nagar, Delhi-6.

6. The Educational system of the Ancient Hindu - By Santosh Kumar Das, Pub. : Gyan publishing House, 23 Ansari Road, Daryagunj, New Delhi - 110002.

7. Ancient Indian Education, by F. E. Keay, Pub. : World Public Library, P.O. - Box 22687, Honolulu, Hawail 96823

8. A student's History of Education in India (1800-1973) by J. P. Naik and Syed Nurullah, Pub. : Macmillan Publishers, India, Ltd. 2/10, Ansari Road, Daryagunj, New Delhi - 110002.

9. A student's Hisory of Education in India by Syed Nurullah and J. P. Naik, Pub. : Mac Millan and Company.

10. Education in India - Today and Tomorrow by S. N. Mukerji, Pub.: Acharya Book Depot, Baroda (Raopura Road)

11. Ancient Buddhist Universities in Indian Sub-Continent by J. B. Barua, Pub. : Fulton Books Inc. Meadville, PA Prined in the United States of America.

12. Universities in Ancient India by D. G. Apte, Pub. : Faculty of Education and Psychology, Maharaja Sayajirao University, Baroda.

13. India 2004 : Research, Reference and Pub. : Ministry of Information and Broadcasting, Government of India, Patiala House, New Delhi - 110001.

14. Vayu Puran, Bhishnu Puran, Nara Puran and other Purnas, Pub. : Nabapatra Prakasan, Kolkata.

15. Puran Prasanga by Debi Prasad Sengupta, Pub. : Biswakosh Parisad, 60, Patutala Lane, Kolkata - 700 009.

16. The Rigveda Samhita by Ramesh Chandra Dutta, Pub. : Jnan Varati, 156, A. J. C. Bose Road, Kolkata - 700 014.

17. The Upanisadas, Pub. : Haraf

18. Promotion of Learning in India during Muhamadan Rule N. N. Law

19. The Vedas Pub. in Bengali by Haraf Prakasani, Kolkata, A 126 College Street, Kolkata. (b) Rigveda - Ramesh Ch. Dutta (in Bengali)

20. Articles - mentioned in the dfferent parts of the Book, written by most credited authors whose authenticity is respected.

21. Manu Samita

22. Arthasastra by Kautilya

23. Publications on different Commissions appointed by the Govt.

24. Central Govt. Publications on different Projects and Plans

25. Indian Musims - who are they K. S. Lal Voice of India, New Delhi

26. The Wonder that was India - I by A. L. Bashan, Pub. : Rupa and Company, 7/16, Ansari Road, Daryagunj, New Delhi - 110002.

27. The Wonder that was India - 2 by S. A. A. Rizvi, Pub. : Rupa and Company, 7/16, Ansari Road, Daryagunj, New Delhi - 110002.

Index